MEDIEVAL INDIA

Essays in Intellectual Thought and Culture

MEDIEVAL INDIA

Essays in Intellectual Thought and Culture

VOLUME I

Edited by
IQTIDAR HUSAIN SIDDIQUI

MANOHAR
2025

First published 2003
Reprinted 2022, 2023, 2024, 2025

ISBN 978-81-7304-499-1

Published by
Ajay Kumar Jain *for*
Manohar Publishers & Distributors
4753/23 Ansari Road, Daryaganj
New Delhi 110 002

Printed at
Replika Press Pvt. Ltd.

Contents

Preface

This pioneering collection of studies is concerned with the way in which the intellectual life and thought interacted with society and the state system, as well as the manner in which the early medieval Indo-Persian literature enriched the cultural heritage of the country. The volume fulfills the long-felt need of presenting essays on an important but neglected theme of intellectual culture during the Delhi sultanate period that provided a cultural reference point throughout the Mughal period. The reader will find each essay, designed either to focus on intellectual life and thought or the impact of the role played by an intellectual minister or officer on the institutions—political and cultural—connected with the life of people, or to draw attention to the interesting historical information contained in the literary works other than the chronicles. None of the essays is confined to narrow conventional concerns, such as the chronology of important battles or the centralizing efforts of individual sultans through the control of the nobility. The objective is both to promote the study of Medieval Indian Culture and History and encourage interaction between the scholars in India and abroad.

I am grateful to all the contributors for their patience in waiting so long for the publication of their work. My thanks are due to my friend, Ishtiyaq Ahmad Zilli in extending cooperation in the preparation of this volume. Peter Hardy has been kind enough to provide me with guidance from time to time. I am thankful to him for considering my request to contribute his essay on the concept of time as reflected in the writings of Indo-Persian historians. In addition, my thanks are due to William C. Chittick who on my request generously contributed his illuminating essay on Sufi psyche as discussed in the treatise, composed by an Indian follower of Ibn al-Arabi.

22 January 2003 I.H. Siddiqui

Introduction

Islam, in the very first century of its rise in Arabia, was introduced in south India by the Arab traders when they landed up along the coastal regions in connection with their overseas trade.[1] Since foreign trade constituted an important source of income to the state, the Hindu rulers allowed the Muslim traders to setup their establishments in different port cities along the Malabar coast and were also granted full religious freedom. With the passage of time the Muslims grew in number.[2] It is also true that Islamic culture, with all its brilliance and egalitarian ideal does not appear to have attracted any layer of urban people outside the Muslim diaspora. Unlike the Muslim traders, the Arab conquerors of Makran (modern Baluchistan) and Sind and Multan towards the beginning of the eighth century AD, happened to be culture imprinters.[3] The policy of reconciliation adopted by the Arab conquerors towards the Indians prepared the ground for the establishment of symbiotic relationship between Islam and Brahmanism, at least in the urban centres. Besides the foundation of new cities, such as al-Mansura and al-Baiza, old towns also underwent demographic changes on account of the addition of new Muslim settlements. The new settlements had emigrants from Muslim lands. They represented different cultural traditions and urban ethos; their mingling with the local people went a long way in enriching the urban culture. Arabic language and Islamic religion created the atmosphere of openness, and Universalism seems to have had much effect on peoples' outlook in the towns and cities.[4]

As regards the north-western Panjab beyond the territory of Multan, it began to undergo cultural transformation after its annexation by Sultan Mahmud of Ghazna (*d.* AD 1030). Lahore, the administrative headquarters of the Panjab under the Ghaznavid rulers, began to emerge as a centre of Islamic culture; its bazaars began to be thronged with merchants from different countries; and new ideas, crafts and foreign merchandise came along with the merchants. Lahore also attracted scholars, sufi saints and poets from the neighbouring Persian speaking countries. Persian poetry produced by the early poets of Lahore is characterized by the purity of diction and their *diwans* (collections of verses) are now included among the classics of Persian literature of Iran and Central Asia. Of the sufi saints who took abode in Lahore, Shaikh Ali Hujwiri (*d.* AD 1079) composed the celebrated *Kashf-ul-Mahjub*, the first known treatise on sufism written in Persian prose. Its lucid style proved that Persian language, like Arabic, could serve as a vehicle of religious ideas and philosophy.[5] Equally important is the contribution made by Indo-Persian prose-writers in the field of *dastan* (fiction), lexicography[6] and *Malfuz* literature, besides historiography. In these fields the Indian prose-writers were trendsetters.

The flight of the Ghaznavid sultan from Ghazna to Lahore, caused by the Ghuzz Turks' invasion in AD 1153-4, provided the impetus to the progress of Lahore as an urban centre. Subjected by the Ghuzz Turks to alien tyranny, the elite and merchants fled from Ghazna and Khurasan and took refuge in Lahore. The construction of palaces, beautiful villas and laying out of gardens in the Central Asian style enhanced the glory and prestige of Lahore. The arrival of rich merchants, moving in caravans, loaded with commercial commodities, from country to country as far away as China led to the emergence of Lahore as a trade emporium. Like them the scholars among the emigrants also had an internationalist attitude, they travelled to foreign lands for the acqzuisition of knowledge and experience. Their pupils in India followed their example and gained fame abroad for their erudition. Later the residents of Lahore, Multan and the towns around them in the Panjab and Sind regions spread to different parts of India after they had been conquered by Sultan Muizuddin Muhammad bin Sam (*d.* AD 1206) and his lieutenants towards the close of the twelfth century AD. Having urban ethos, they influenced the cultural patterns in north India and right up to Bengal.

Garrisons of Muslim soldiers, planted at strategic places with mosques, *madrasas* (colleges) and *khanqahs* (Arabic *rabats*, constructed for providing facilities to the travellers), served as civilizing institutions. In the *khanqah*, the travellers were provided with food and accommodation free of charge. Its charge was entrusted to a religious scholar known for his honesty. The charge of the fortress-like *khanqah* of Multan was assigned by Sultan Qutbuddin Aibek (reigned: AD 1206-10) to Shaikh Bahauddin Zakariya, the founder of the Suhrawardi Silsilah in India.[7]

The role of the sultans and their nobles in providing patronage to the men of learning and talent is also worth mentioning. Many important socio-economic changes resulted from the patterns of political and cultural behaviour of the great sultans and the nobility under them. Scholars and men of talent were needed to serve as civil officers and cater to the educational needs of the ever-expanding sultanate; the large-hearted patronage extended by the sultans and the nobles attracted them from the neighbouring Muslim countries.

The *madrasas* established by the sultans in large cities promoted Islamic culture and civilization. Besides, seminaries run by individual scholars, the *Madrasa-i-Firuzi* founded by Sultan Nasiruddin Qubacha (*d.* AD 1228) in Uchh, *Madrasa-i-Muizi* and *Madrasa-i-Nasiriya* in Delhi were higher seats of learning. Similarly, the *madrasas* founded by the Khalji rulers of Bihar and Bengal produced graduates to man the civil administration. It may also be recalled that the *madrasa* system did save the Islamic egalitarian ideal from entirely receding, it did find expression in this institution; its doors were thrown open to all. Students from the lower strata of society received education and could thus hope to attain important positions, although their rise in the official hierarchy caused indignation among the elite with foreign background.[8] As a matter of fact, the expansion of the sultanate under the Khaljis and Tughluqs had created the need to recruit officers in large numbers and hence educated persons were employed irrespective of birth. Thus, the monopoly enjoyed by the old aristocratic families in serving on high posts in civil and revenue administration ended.

The conflict of ideas held by the *ulama* (religious divines) and *mashaikh* (sufi saints) about the concepts of love and man's position *vis-a-vis* God's lordship may also be referred to. The *ulama* attached importance to the Koranic term *muhaba* (love) as, in their view, it had spiritual dimension, meaning man's sincere devotion to God. The sufi concept of *Ishq-i-Ilahi* was not acceptable because *ishq* (intense love) was the outcome of carnal desire between two human beings.[9] Unlike the sufis, the *ulama* also held that communion between the Creator and the created was not possible. The *ulama* were also rigid in following only one school of Islamic canon law blindly as the permission to follow different schools simultaneously could weaken as such the grip of religion on the followers.

The Islamic orthodoxy was able to suppress the rationalist thinkers in the thirteenth century. They allowed the teaching of *Ilm-i-Manqul* (traditional sciences). However, with the rise of the Khaljis to power, restrictions were removed from the way of the rationalist thinkers. They were patronized and also made courtiers and counsellors.[10] In short, the standard of education was raised high.

The breakup of the Delhi sultanate in the fifteenth century was paradoxically paralleled by the diffusion of Islamic culture. In place of Delhi, cities of the regional kingdoms (sultanates) and principalities founded by the erstwhile governors of the Delhi sultans emerged as centres of culture. The regional sultans emulated the traditions of the Delhi court in every respect. Delhi, which had become a ghost city after its sack by

Timur in 1398, was put on the road to recovery and progress by Sultan Bahlul Lodi (1451-1488-9). The Lodi period (1451-1526) is important in more sense than one. The old cities such as Lahore and Delhi were restored to their past glory and again began to serve as centres of learning, trade and culture. The process of urbanization was set in motion. A number of towns were founded with Agra as a new metropolis.[11] Furthermore, the revival of library culture helped the progress of intellectual culture during the Lodi period. In short, the Lodi sultans of Delhi and Agra and the regional sultanates of Bengal, Malwa, Gujarat and the Bahmani rulers of the Deccan prepared the cultural and economic foundations of the empires of Sher Shah Sur and the Mughal emperors.

The reign of Emperor Akbar is characterized by the progress made in different fields. The state policies followed by him brought Hindus and Muslims culturally close to each other. The empire was Indianized and full religious freedom was ensured to all; Hindu converts to Islam could re-enter the fold of Hinduism because apostasy had ceased to be a crime punishable with death. Akbar's religious leanings caused resentment among the Muslim orthodoxy and his death in 1605 provided its members with an opportunity to revive Muslim's interest in Islamic sciences. Shaikh Abdul Haque Muhadis of Delhi and Shaikh Ahmad Sirhindi published books and epistles for this purpose. In AD 1594, Mulla Abdul Qadir Badauni published his book, *Najat-ur-Rashid*, the outline of which was prepared by Nizamuddin Ahmad, the *mir bakhshi* (paymaster general) of Akbar for reviving among Muslims respect for Islam and the Prophet.[12]

However, the Mughal rule during the second half of the sixteenth and seventeenth century is an important period for the progress of visual arts, for the buildings built by Akbar in the capital cities of Fatehpur Sikri and Agra, for the founding of Shahjahanabad and beautiful edifices erected by Shah Jahan in Agra, Lahore and Srinagar which throw light on the emperor's aesthetic sense and creative imagination. Lastly, it may be stated that the cultural traditions that developed during the Delhi sultanate period continued to evolve till Emperor Aurangzeb's reign in AD 1707. Aurangzeb's successors failed to arrest the process of rapid decline of their power. After the dissolution of the empire, during the later half of the eighteenth century, the Mughal court continued to provide cultural reference point to the regional rulers, irrespective of the fact whether they were Muslims or non-Muslims. The new rulers founded new cities or beautified old ones which they had selected as seats of their government. They emulated the Mughal emperors in patronizing men of learning, artists and poets in order to raise their prestige. Even the Rohila chiefs who had migrated form their tribal land in the north-western region and had no pretension to aristocratic culture adopted the Mughal way of life. They promoted Islamic culture in the territories under their rule.

The present volume contains essays contributed by eminent scholars from India and abroad. Each essay is designed either to focus on intellectual life or the impact of the ideas and work of the elite on institutions, connected with the state and the life of people. The progress of scientific temper exemplified in some essays did help the development of material culture and visual arts. The essays offer a distinctive contribution to certain aspects of medieval Indian history that are of great current interest.

The first essay by me discusses how Al-Beruni's inquisitiveness and scholarly pursuits led to an interaction on intellectual plane between Hindu and Muslim scholars. I also take into account the importance of Al-Beruni's contribution in the fields of astronomy and mathematical geography. The second essay, also by me, takes up the study of the Indo-Persian poetry of the thirteenth century that has been neglected by the scholars of history. Verses composed by the thirteenth-century Indo-Persian poets not only provides us with insights into intellectual culture but also reflect directly on the social life and conditions in the society. The third essay by Peter Hardy is a pioneering work on the concepts of time as reflected in Indo-Persian historiography of Medieval period. It opens new vistas for further investigation. The next two essays by me extend the discussion of how intellectual ideas and religious thought acted as a catalyst of social change in the sultanate of Delhi till AD 1526. The essay, by Afzal Husain, deals with the role performed by an intellectual bureaucrat, Khwaja Shah Mansur in working out the permanent land revenue settlement for Akbar's empire that went a long way to serve as a model even after the fall of the empire. The essay by late Syed Athar Abbas Rizvi, discusses the historical interest of Abul Fazl's *Munajat* (invocations) that contains references to the reigning Emperor Akbar, casting light on the religious psychology of the author and his royal patron that did influence the Mughal polity and the culture of the empire. Similarly, Ishtiyaq Ahmad Zillis' account of Mulla Abdul Qadir Badauni's *Najat-ur-Rashid* presents an analysis of the contents of the work, pointing out its author's response to the currents and cross-currents of thought in India under Akbar. William C. Chittick introduces Shaikh Abd al-Jalil Ilahabadi's treatise on sufi psychology, concerning wayfaring (*suluk*), the invocations, and the disciplines which take the wayfarer in the direction of the gnostic sciences in the perspective of Ibn al-Arabi's spiritual philosophy of *Wujud* (Being). Zia Uddin Desai's essay brings to light the newly discovered important source that formed the basis of the *Mirat-i-Ahmadi*, compiled by Ali Muhammad Khan, the last diwan of Gujarat under the Mughals and the Marathas during the eighteenth century. This work was compiled by Mithal Lal Kayasth in Persian for providing the diwan detailed information about the life and conditions in the towns and cities, *parganas*, *sarkars* with their area, revenue and tribute collected from each fiscal-cum-administrative unit in the *suba* of Gujarat. It contains the valuable additional information about certain matters that had been left out by Ali Muhammad Khan. The last essay by me, draws attention to the *tazkiras* of Urdu poets and their *diwans* that form the part of our intellectual heritage. It deals particularly with the literary works of Qa'iam Chandpuri whose account of Urdu poets as well as his verses cast interesting light on the intellectual pursuits, culture of the elite as well as the condition of the daily wage-earners in the region of Katehar (modern Rohilkhand) under the Rohila chiefs during the second half of the eighteenth century.

These essays are hopefully designed to suggest an agenda for future research on intellectual life and material culture in the history of South Asia. Lastly, I should thank my friend Ishtiyaq Ahmad Zilli, Professor at the Centre of Advanced Study in History, the Aligarh Muslim University, for playing an important part in the preparation of this volume.

NOTES

1. The gold coins found in Kerala and examined by N.M. Lowick of the British Museum, London, shed light on the Muslim presence there during the first century of Islam. Cf. *Indian Express, The Sunday Standard*, New Delhi, 3 June 1979.
2. Cf. Masudi, tr. into French, C. Barbier de Maynard and Pavet de Courteille (9 vols., Paris), II, p. 856, as cited by Richard Maxwell Eaton, *Sufis of Bijapur*, Princeton, 1978, p. 13.
3. Cf. Iqtidar Husain Siddiqui, 'Money and Social Change in Medieval India', Symposia Paper: 12, *Indian History Congress*, 56th Session, Calcutta, 1995, pp. 2-5.
4. Iqtidar Husain Siddiqui, 'Dynastic History of Sind', *A Comprehensive History of India*, vol. 4, part 1, pp. 322-7.
5. Cf. Amir Khusrau, *Aijaz-i-Khusravi*, vol. 1, Newal Kishore Press, Lucknow, pp. 56-7.
6. Cf. Iqtidar Husain Siddiqui, *Perso-Arabic Sources on the Life and Conditions in the Sultanate of Delhi*, New Delhi, 1992, pp. 90-4.
7. 'Money and Social Change in Medieval India', Symposia Paper: 12, op. cit., pp. 7-8. Also 'The Pir and Murid: A Case Study of the Sufis of Suhrawardi Silsilah in India', *Hamdard Islamic*, vol. XXXI, no. 3, July-September 1998, p. 24.

8. Cf. 'Money and Social Change in Medieval India', Symposia Paper: 12, p. 8.
9. Cf. Iqtidar Husain Siddiqui, 'Sufia-i-Kiram Aur Ishq-i-Majazi Ka Tassawwur', *Fikr-o-Nazar* (Urdu), vol. XXIX, no. 2, Aligarh, 1992, pp. 42-50.
10. Ziya uddin Barani, *Tarikh-i-Firuz Shahi*, Calcutta, 1862, pp. 199, 456-66.
11. Nimatullah Harvi, *Tarikh-i-Khan Jahani*, ed. S. Imam al-Din, vol. I, pp. 195-6; also Iqtidar Husain Siddiqui, 'Life and Culture in the Sultanate of Delhi during the Lodi period', *Islamic Culture*, April 1982, p. 129.
12. Abdul Qadir Badauni, *Najat-ur-Rashid*, ed. S. Moin ul-Haque, Lahore, 1972, pp. 1-2.

Abu Raihan Al-Beruni: His Life and Works

IQTIDAR HUSAIN SIDDIQUI

Abu Raihan Al-Beruni was a man of many talents, a comparative religionist, a mathematician, an astronomer, a geographer, a physician with deep interest in pharmacology, and above all a staunch humanist free from cultural chauvinism. He studied the different religions and the achievements made by their followers in different fields including science, and this is reflected in his *Asar-ul-Baqia* (*Chronology of Ancient Peoples*). His descriptions of Judaism, Christianity, ancient Iranian religions and Brahmanical Hinduism are characterized by objectivity; he seems to have carefully collected authentic information about each religion. He was led to believe that everywhere religious beliefs are subjected to the influence of identical psychological motives; in every religious tradition is perceptible a distinction between the articles of popular faith of the masses and those of the chosen. Consequently, Al-Beruni expounds on various religious teachings without resorting to polemics and preserves as far as possible the authentic expression of the followers of a particular religion. The principle of love, preached by Christianity, such as to give him who has stripped you of your coat your shirt, to offer to him who has beaten your cheek the other cheek, to bless your enemy and pray for him, fascinated him.[1] Likewise, he is all praise for the Hindus who show tolerance towards the followers of different schools of thought within their own tradition. He remarks: 'On the whole there is very little disputing about theological topics among the Hindus; at the utmost they fight with words, but they will never stake their life or their body or their property on religious controversy.' Al-Beruni found that many Hindus had distinguished themselves as scientists and artists.[2] He is also said to have written more than a hundred treatises on religion and science, but posterity has preserved only those works that were thought valuable and worth preserving. In fact, all his extant works are characterized by his investigative curiosity as well as objectivity, in his approach.

It is worth recalling that long before Al-Beruni, Muslim scholars evinced interest in the literature and sciences of different peoples with whom they came in contact through military conquest or as merchants engaged in overseas and overland trade. This had led to the rise of cultural movements in different parts of the Islamic world. The centres of learning and culture greatly benefited from this interaction between Muslims and civilized non-Muslims. Muslim scholars adopted and assimilated knowledge from other countries and then made valuable contributions through their own researches in different sciences. They are singular for their achievements in history, mathematics, astronomy and medical science. The aim of this essay is first to discuss briefly the life of Al-Beruni and then argue for the importance of his research and discoveries in astronomy and mathematical geography.

Al-Beruni's real name was Abu Raihan Muhammad bin Ahmad Al-Beruni. The surname Al-Beruni indicates that his birth place was situated somewhere in the suburb of the city of Khwarazm, the metropolis of the territory known as Khwarazm. The residents of its suburb were known as Beruni, i.e. people who resided outside the metropolis.[3] The ruling dynasty of Khwarazm at that time was known as the Al-i-Iraq dynasty and its last ruler, the patron of Al-Beruni was Abu Abdallah Muhammad Khwarazm Shah. The murder of the latter in AD 995, put an end to his dynasty's rule. Al-Beruni being twenty-three years old at this time had benefited from his association with scholars and scientists of eminence attached to the royal court. Mention may be made here of Abu Nasr bin 'Ali, the cousin of the reigning Khwarazm Shah because he is said to have stimulated Al-Beruni's interest in mathematics and astronomy. In his *Asar-ul-Baqia*,[4] Al-Beruni calls him his patron and teacher.

Nothing is known about Al-Beruni's family background. Perhaps the reason was that none of his family members was ever able to rise to prominence before him. Al-Beruni's own fame rested on his learning. The number of treatises he wrote on different popular sciences must have brought him fame, even during his early life and before the fall of the dynasty of Al-i-Iraq. For soon after the fall of his patron he was invited by Shamsul-Ma'ali, the ruler of Jurjan and Tabristan, to join his court. It was in Jurjan that Al-Beruni brought to completion his famous *Asar-ul-Baqia*, dedicated to Shamsul-Ma'ali. In this work mention is made by Al-Beruni of his *Kitab-ul Tajrid ul-Shu'at ul-Anwar*. A study of the *Asar-ul-Baqia* shows that besides astronomy, its author was interested in mathematics, geography, history and medicine. In short, his erudition helped him become a status symbol for the court of his royal patron. He was now relieved of financial problems and able to devote himself to the pursuit of learning.

Al-Beruni's knowledge of astronomy in particular, and other sciences in general, as displayed in *Asar-ul-Baqia* must have made him a distinguished scholar of his age. Not only does he describe in this work the achievements of ancient peoples in different sciences but he also makes incisive comments on past discoveries. His own research carried him forward so much that he began to question accepted truths about the universe. He suggests 'the possibility of the centrality of the sun in a solar system, with the earth both revolving around it and turning on its own axis, but, for various reasons, this did not then seem the most likely hypothesis'.[5] Al-Beruni also appears to have been interested in improving astrolabes. For example, he explains a flattened astrolabe, which served as a stellar chart, on which the pole of ecliptic circles of longitude were represented as equidistant concentric circles and the circles of latitude by equidistant radii'.[6] It was also in Jurjan that Al-Beruni successfully worked out the circumference of the earth by determining the distance between two altitudes.[7] He completed his treatise *Tajrid ul-Shu'at* also in Jurjan.[8]

Although he enjoyed the royal favour at the court of Shamsul-Ma'ali, Al-Beruni did not feel at home in Jurjan because of his patron's oppressive rule.[9] He disliked the climate of Jurjan too: on account of excessive rain, the place abounded in mosquitoes.[10] He left Jurjan and returned to his own country, Khwarazm, as soon as he was invited by its ruler, Ali bin Mamun. This ruler was not only a patron of men of learning but was also benevolent.[10] He and his wazir, Abul Husain bin Ahmad bin Ahmad al-Suhaili had gathered a fairly large sprinkling of scholar scientists, including Abu Ali Sina. Al-Beruni stayed in Khwarazm till its conquest by Sultan Mahmud of Ghazna in AD 1017.

Impressed by the excellent qualities of the king, Al-Beruni compiled a history of his country, entitled *Masamir ul-Khwarazm*. This study is not extant but was utilized by Baihaqi for the preparation of the *Tarikh-i-Al-i-Subuktigin*, particularly on the fall of Mamuni dynasty of Khwarazm.[11] Provided with all facilities, Al-Beruni established an observatory where he observed the movements of planets. He mentions his observations and research there from the year AD 999 to 1016 in his *Qanun-i-Masudi*. In 1017, however, Al-Beruni was arrested by Sultan Mahmud and brought to Ghazna along with the princes and other dignitaries of Khwarazm. As he was a distinguished intellectual, particularly famous for his knowledge of astronomy, he was set free and allowed to proceed to India, where he probably stayed for thirteen years.[12]

In India, Al-Beruni travelled in Panjab, Sind and other places, made friends with Hindu scholars and learnt Sanskrit. He acquired first-hand knowledge about Indian sciences and culture through a study of Sanskrit literature and interaction with people. He states that as long as he was ignorant of their language, he behaved like a disciple before them. When he had learnt their language and could communicate easily, he argued with them on astronomical problems and mathematics so much that they were astonished by his knowledge. In astonishment they would enquire whom he had met in India and where he had gained knowledge. In certain respects Al-Beruni was able to prove that he had an edge on them in his knowledge of astronomy and mathematics. As his resources were limited in India during Sultan Mahmud's reign, he saved money as much as he could and spent it on acquiring Sanskrit manuscripts. He had to travel to distant places and endure hardship, all on account of his insatiable thirst for knowledge.

Al-Beruni was thus able to have access to important Indian works dealing with astronomy and astrology. He translated several Sanskrit treatises on astronomy and mathematics. Unfortunately, not all his translation is extant. One of the treatises, entitled *Gharat ul-Zijat*, a translation into Arabic of the *Karna Tilak* on astronomy and astrology, is available in the Pir Muhammad Shah Library in Ahmadabad. It is a rare and extremely important manuscript because the original *Karna Tilak* is not traceable. It records observations of solar and lunar eclipses. It was completed before Al-Beruni started his famous *Kitab ul-Hind fi-Tahqiq Milal Hind* (*India*). The reason as to why Al-Beruni took up the translation, in his words, is:

> In India I came across a *Karna* book which was very concise and was written (in Sanskrit) by Vijay Nandi, son of Jaya Nandi, one of the commentators of the city of Varanasi. The Hindus have high regard for it from the religious point of view and the author has named it as *Karna Tilak*. Some of my friends, who are fond of knowledge, have expressed their desire to get it converted into Arabic. So I hastened to do this work in order to spread knowledge among those who deserve it. I am translating it in such a way that its reasonings are expressed clearly, and with this in view I have not added anything from my own side except the examples which are meant to make the understanding of the subject easy. And it is God, who, through his kindness, helps in achieving the object.[13]

It was really not one-way traffic. Al-Beruni also acquainted the Indian scholars with Ptolemy's Majesty and the invention of astrolabe (*San'at al-usturlab*) as well as the techniques of using it.

Al-Beruni seems to have returned to Ghazna during the last years of Sultan Mahmud's reign. There he sat to write the *Qanun-i-Masudi*. Upon the death of Sultan Mahmud in 1030 he dedicated it to his son and successor, Sultan Masud (AD 1030-40). The new Sultan was a great patron of men of talent and learning. Soon after the presentation of the *Qanun-i-Masudi*, a work of high standard on astronomy, Al-Beruni became a prized member of the Sultan's court. Conscious of the high quality of his work, Al-Beruni writes:

> As I found the Sultan interested in promoting learning and I remained pre-occupied with the study and research in mathematics since my early life and was a known adept in this science, I decided to compose a work *Ilmul Hayat* (astronomy). This science has gained popularity on account of the interest evinced by the Sultan in its study. I have adorned it with the best of jewels (i.e. researches). It is marked by improvement on my early works and, therefore, I have dedicated it to his (Sultan's) illustrious name. The book of (standard) serves as a greater memorial than any monument. In its preparation I have not only utilized the discoveries made by my predecessors but also pointed out errors committed by them and corrected them on the basis of my own research. I have put forward my argument regarding correction for the convenience of the reader and posterity.[14]

In this *Qanun-i-Masudi* Al-Beruni has used the formula of interpolation for valuing the various intermediary angles of trigonometry functions from his tables which were calculated for every increase of fifteen minutes. He gave geometrical proof of the interpolation formula.[15] During the same reign, Al-Beruni also wrote his *Lavazim ul-Harketain* at the instance of sultan Masud.[16] In short, Al-Beruni was a special recipient of Sultan Masud's favour. He stayed at his court and basked in its aura.

Upon the death of Sultan Masud in 1040, the Ghaznavid empire suffered chaos and anarchy. Prince Maudud, the son of Masud and the governor of Balkh defeated the rebels and restored order soon afterwards. Like his father, he also showed favour to Al-Beruni. In return, Al-Beruni dedicated to him the *Kitab al-Jamahir fi Marifah ul Jawahir*, on precious stones and minerals. Thus even in old age Al-Beruni was preoccupied with science and research. His contemporaries like Baihaqi testify to the fact that he never rested even for a few days; day in and day out he worked on scientific problems.[17]

Besides astronomy, another field in which Al-Beruni made an original contribution was mathematical geography. His work on geography, *Tahdid ul-Nihayat al-Amakin li-Tashih Masafat al-Amakin*, in AD 1025 is outstanding. Early Arab geographers, particularly al-Batany and al-Khwarazmi had written on the geography and culture of Africa, South-Eastern Asia and northern Asia, and they had followed Greek models.[18] Unlike them, however, Al-Beruni freed the science of geography from Greek and Jewish Biblical influences. The reason for his success was the establishment of the vast empires by Mahmud in Central Asia and Iran, and the Qarakhanid empire of Samarqand. He could acquire information on different countries on account of the establishment of peace and order and the trade relations between these empires and other civilized countries of Europe, Africa and Asia. He could obtain substantial data on eastern Asia from travellers through eastern Turkestan and the sea route south of Asia. Yet, concerning eastern Europe, he could consult only Bulgarian or Khwarazmian merchants. The ambassadors from China to the Ghaznavid court who came either by way of sea or via India, also supplied data to him about eastern Asia, the south pole, and the Oceans.[19]

Indeed, Al-Beruni is the first among Muslim geographers to mention the names of the river Angara and of the population of Baykal region in eastern Siberia, as also to give accounts of the Scandinavian Warangians, the metal work of northern Europe, and the Ice-Sea north-east of Europe. Likewise, he seems to have collected very useful data on south Africa, Mozambique and other transequatorial countries where, according to his sources, 'during our summer winter prevails'. For such a well-informed scholar, the wall of Gog Magog, which earlier geographers had sought northward of the Caspian Sea or in the neighbourhood of Tianshan, was only the western portion of the wall of China.

Compared to the Greek and early Arab geographers Al-Beruni made great strides in the field of geography. It is also true that in the tradition of his earlier Muslim predecessors, Al-Beruni assigned value also to civic and cultural life of the population of a country. It may also be stressed that in his work the determination of geographical latitudes and longitudes of places is so exact, and the data for the lines of March are so explicit, that a map of Iran and Transoxiana compiled from them would show no very great mistakes as compared with our present-day maps. Moreover, he takes into consideration the alterations caused by environmental changes while determining afresh the latitudes and longitudes and would not blame the ancient geographers for their errors. Similarly, his description of the water ways and countries in this work provides us with interesting information about oversea trade between India, China and the Persian-Gulf countries.[20]

A passage from his *Nihayat al-Amakin*, translated by Ahmad Zeki Validi, shows that Al-Beruni was conscious of the importance of his work. He says:

> My object therefore is to establish the geographic longitude of a certain city on the earth-globe, that is to say, Ghazna. Hitherto I have been able to determine only the degree of latitude of this city, as for what concerns the longitude, I was not able to establish that properly owing to adverse circumstances. But if I were to plead

these obstacles as an excuse for such negligence and were to show myself as therefore blameless, I should have portrayed myself as a denier of God's open and secret favour as well as of the benefits of the dispenser of kindness (i.e. Sultan Mahmud of Ghazna), whose hand has brought me into full prosperity.

And I say: most of the data of geography (of Ptolemy) concerning the longitude and latitude of points on the earth have really been adopted only on the ground of summaries which had come from far off districts. In the practical use of such data Ptolemy himself must have hit on the right way; but others have only imitated him and it is possible that the latter, moreover, have diverged from the right way. Anyhow, the ground on which these data rest is mere report; indeed those lands were very difficult of access in the past owing to the national divisions, for national division is the greatest obstacle to travel in countries. We see, for example, some people who think as do the Jews to come nearer to God through treacherous attacks on folk of other nationalities. Or they take foreigners as slaves, as do the Romans, and that is the lesser evil. Or travellers, because they are foreigners, are turned back, held in every kind of suspicion and they are just brought to a very unpleasant dangerous plight.

But now the circumstances are different, Islam has already penetrated from the eastern countries of the East to the West; its spread Westward to Spain (Andalus), Eastward to the borderland of China and to the middle of India, Southward to Abyssinia and the country of Zanj (i.e. South Africa), northward to the countries of the Turks and Slavs. Thus different peoples (*al-umum al-Mukhtalifah*) are brought together in mutual understanding (*ulfat*), which only God's own art can bring to pass. To obtain information concerning places of the earth has now become comparably easier and safer (than it was before). Now we find a crowd of places, which in the (Ptolemic) 'Geography' are indicated as being to the east of other places, actually situated to the West of the others named, and *vice versa*. The reasons (of such errors) are either confusion of the data as to the distance on which the longitude and latitude were estimated, or that the populations have changed their former places.[21]

Al-Beruni's other work also casts interesting light on his interest in geography. He eagerly made use of the opportunities made available by the expansion of the Islamic power in Asia and Africa. For example, in his work, *Kitab al-Jamahir fi-marifah-ul-Jawahir* he writes about water ways and trade between different countries. He says on the authority of a merchant of the seas:

It used to be our custom that we carried goods for poor people as we expected a blessing through it. One day we went at Ubula and had got ready our ships for the voyage to China when an old man came up to us and said: I have a request to make with which I have approached others, but they have disappointed me about it; so I have come to you, trusting that you will not do the same. I said: what is it? He replied. I shall not tell you till you have given a firm undertaking. So I did. Then he brought a bale of lead weighing about ten maunds and said: My wish is that you order it to be carried till you reach such and such a deep sea and then command it thrown over board. I said: I shall not do that. He replied: And what about your undertaking? So he urged upon me till I accepted the bale and entered it into the ledger under his name together with his address in al-Basrah. Now, when we came to that deep sea, God Almighty on account of the storms made us forget ourselves, not to mention that lead. Then we reached our destination and sold the goods which we had brought, when a man came and asked us whether we had any lead, I replied: we brought none, then the steward reminded me of that bale and I said: I had to act contrary to my undertaking, then why shall I not sell it? So the man bought it for 130 *dinars* and I purchased for the owner some of the valuable goods of China. Then we went away (and having reached home), the old man did not come to me. I, therefore, went up to his house and made inquiries about him and was told that he had died. I asked: Has he left no heirs? They said: He had a nephew in one of the seaports and his house is in trust in the hands of a trustee appointed by the Qazi. Then I was perplexed and returned to Ubula and sold those wares for seven hundred dinars. I was there one day when a man came up to me and said to me. Are you so and so? I said: Yes. He said: Did you make a voyage to China and sell there a bale of lead last year? I replied: Yes. He said: I was the purchaser and when I cut it open to make use of it, I found it to be hollow and inside twelve thousand dinars. Now I have come with them to you. Take them. Then I said to him, you have made matters worse; the money does not belong to me. Then I told him the story. He smiled in amazement and asked: Did you know the old man? I replied: No! Except what I have told you. Then he said: He was my uncle. He had no other heir beside me. He used to ill-treat me to such an extent that I was forced to flee from al-Basrah seventeen years ago. He intended to turn his property away from me, but God decreed otherwise in spite of him, as you see. So I gave him the seven hundred dinars and he took possession of the house of his uncle and lived in the utmost comfort.[22]

It is, however, a pity that this rich material available in Al-Beruni's works for practical sciences, above all for economic and cultural history of Islamic peoples, remains almost unutilized. Except for the *Kitab ul-Hind*, *Asarul-Baqia* and *Qanun-i-Masudi*, his work remains unpublished.

NOTES

1. Cf. E. Sachau, *Al-Berunis' India*, Eng. tr., London, 1910, p. 161.
2. Ibid. (Introduction), p. xix.
3. Cf. Abdul Karim, *Kitab-ul-Ansab* (Gibb Memorial Fund), p. 98.
4. Al-Beruni, *Asar-ul-Baqia* (Arabic text), pp. 37-8; also Eng. tr. by Edward Sachau, *Chronology of Ancient Peoples*, London, 1879.
5. Cf. G.M. Wickens, *Astronomy, Introduction to Islamic Civilization*, ed. R.M. Sovoyo, Cambridge, 1976, p. 116.

6. Cf. *Islamic Culture*, Hyderabad, vol. XIX, January 1945, rpt., New York, 1971, pp. 49-50.
7. Cf. Hasan Barani, *Alberuni: His Life and Works* (Urdu), Muslim University Press, Aligarh, 1927, p. 53.
8. Loc. cit.
9. Cf. Al-Berunis' *qasida* in praise of Abul Fath Basti in *Ishad ul-Arib*, vol. VI, p. 312.
10. *Asarul-Baqia* (Arabic text), p. 247.
11. Cf. Baihaqi, *Tarikh*, Calcutta edn., p. 311.
12. Muhammad Fazlallah Qureshi, *Al-Beruni*, Urdu Da'rat-e-Ma'arif, Lahore, 1971, p. 263.
13. Syed Samad Husain Rizvi, A unique and unknown book of Al-Beruni: *Ghurat-ul-Zijat or Karna Tilak, Islamic Culture*, vol. XXXVII, no. 2, April 1963, pp. 112-30 for details.
14. Cf. *Muqadimah to Qanun-i-Masudi* (Arabic text incorporated in Hasan Barani's Al-Beruni (Urdu), op. cit., pp. 225-34.
15. Sir Ziyauddin, *Islamic Culture*, Hyderabad, vol. III, Jan. 1929, p. 203.
16. Yaqut, *Al-Muajam-ul-Ubada*, pp. 310-11.
17. Ibid., pp. 308-9.
18. Cf. E. Honigmann, *Die Siegen Khmata*, Heidelberg, 1927, pp. 112ff.
19. Yaqut, *Dictionary of Learned Men*, ed. Margolioth, vol. VI, p. 310.
20. Cf.F. Krenskow, 'The Old Western Account of Chinese Porcelain', *Islamic Culture*, Hyderabad, July 1938, pp. 468-9.
21. Validi Tughan, Tahdid-ul Nihayat al-Amakin, *Neue Nachrichten*, pp. 100-12; idem, 'Islam and the Science of Geography', *Islamic Culture*, vol. VIII, Oct. 1934, pp. 517-18.
22. 'The Old Western Account of Chinese Porcelain', op. cit., *Islamic Culture*, July 1938, pp. 470-1; Iqtidar Husain Siddiqui, *Perso-Arabic Sources on the Life and Conditions in the Sultanate of Delhi*, New Delhi, 1992, pp. xiii-xiv.

The Intellectual and Historical Dimensions of the Indo-Persian Poetry of the Thirteenth Century AD

IQTIDAR HUSAIN SIDDIQUI

The foundation of an independent sultanate in north India in the beginning of thirteenth century attracted, apart from soldiers, also scholars, poets and men of arts from foreign countries. Every town and city was studded with institutions of learning (*madrasas*) to cater to the intellectual, religious and cultural needs of the new settlers. Since most of the immigrants hailed from Persian-speaking Khurasan and Central Asia and, with the exception of *ulama* (religious divines), could not understand Arabic, the sultans and the members of ruling elite patronized Persian poets. The verses composed by the latter appealed to their aesthetic sense. The large-hearted patronage extended by the rulers to these poets enabled them to make a substantial contribution to early Persian literature. The poets in India left behind *diwans* (collections of poems) that inspired future generations of the poets in India and outside.

Poetry is doubtless the greatest form of literary expression. It provides insights into the changing concepts of love and beauty, categories of religious and social thought and urban culture of the people in question. In fact, no intellectual history of any nation or people is complete without a reference to its poetry. Besides, poems written on special occasions such as the coronation of a king, or the return of an army to the capital in triumph, the celebration of a certain festival, or the reception of the foreign emissaries in the metropolis take us back in time, providing glimpses of life and culture. In contrast, the histories and chronicles compiled by medieval writers abound in details of political events, such as battles fought, conquests made and court intrigues; they seldom focus on events of cultural importance. The available evidence in our sources shows that the early Indo-Persian poets, being learned scholars, occupied important positions in the civil administration of the sultanate and were engaged in imparting instructions to the scholars in various popular sciences also.

The aim of this study is first to discuss briefly the favourable atmosphere created by state patronage for the progress of Persian literary culture, and then present an analysis of its intellectual dimension, showing how it led to the rise of humanist trends and the cultivation of aesthetic taste amongst the intelligentsia.

In reconstructing the history of the origin and growth of Persian literature in India, we have to begin with the establishment of the Ghaznavid rule in the eleventh century. Ghaznavid sultans chose Lahore as the provincial headquarters of their dominion in India. This helped it grow from a village into a metropolitan city. Among the men employed by the Ghaznavid sultans to man the civil administration were poets who founded in Lahore that tradition of written poetry that went a long way to inspire future scholars. India-born poets Abul Faraj Runi and Masud S'ad Salman of the Ghaznavid period are recognized as the leading poets of early Persian literature of the world. 'They were writers of good and chaste Persian . . . their style is plain and simple and in all their verses they have shown to their best advantage their power, their resources, their fertility and their fine artistic instincts.'[1]

Born and brought up in Lahore, the poets had attachment to the land as they composed beautiful poems in praise of its climate, fauna and flora, and the seasons, particularly the rainy season. Welcoming the monsoon, Masud S'ad Salman calls it the spring of India that provides relief from the extreme heat of the summer and brings fresh life to vegetation. It imparts sweetness to mankind:[2]

به شکال ای بهار هندوستان
ای نجات از بلائی تابستان
دادی از تیرمه بشارتها
باز رستیم از آن حرارتها
هر سو از ابر لشکر داری
در امارت مگر سرداری
سبزها را طراوتی دادی
عمر ها را حلاوتی دادی

Significantly, we find the beginning of the use of Hindustani words and phrases in Salman's Persian poems. In a *qasida* depicting the scene the siege of Agra by the Ghaznavid governor of Lahore, he says:[3]

چو رعد از ابر بغرید کوس محمودی

بر آمد از پس دیوار حصن مارا مار

In the second line the phrase *mara mar* (strike) shows his familiarity with the spoken idiom of the Panjab.

The occupation by the Turks of Ghazna city and the flight of Sultan Khusrau Shah to Lahore with his entourage in AD 1152-3 added to (Lahore's) grandeur as a centre of culture. The early thirteenth-century immigrants from foreign lands found it a magnificent city. It was the prestige and glory that Lahore enjoyed as the capital of the last Ghaznavid Sultans that led Sultan Muizuddin Muhammad bin Sam to make it his winter capital.[4] It was a city of beautiful palaces, gardens and bazars. Its merchants carried on trade with foreign countries.[5] Like the merchants, scholars and poets also resided in Lahore in a large number since the time of Khusrau Malik. On the fall of the latter in 1186, the poets transferred their allegiance to Sultan Muizuddin Muhammad bin Sam. Thus the overthrow of the Ghaznavid ruler did not entail a break with the cultural tradition of Lahore. It suffered neither culturally nor materially. C.E. Bosworth states:

> It is, indeed, Awfi who provides us with valuable information about what was obviously a numerous and talented circle of poets at Khusrau Malik's court and who quotes numerous examples of their verse, which in all cases seems to have survived only here in the *tadh kirat ash-Shuara* literature and not as independent diwans of the individual authors.[6]

The foundation by Sultan Qutbuddin Aibek of an independent sultanate after his master's assassination in AD 1206 attracted a large number of *ulama* and poets to India. The Sultan went out of his way to provide them with financial assistance and the comforts of life.[7] Everyone of these poets had a *diwan* to his credit, but none seems to have survived. We have access only to the verses quoted by Awfi in his *Lubab-ul-Albab* which enable us to assess the literary significance of their contribution to the literary tradition set by the Ghaznavid poets of Lahore. Mention may be made here of a few poets.

There was Jamal uddin Muhammad bin Nazz, who is called by Awfi as the chief of the poets and scholars. Though his *diwan* is not extant, his specimen verses contained in the *Lubab-ul-Albab* bear testimony to his creative imagination. He calls Sultan Qutbuddin Aibek the great conqueror of the world to whose authority the rulers acquiesced voluntarily:[8]

خداوندا شهی گیتی ستان
که شاهان جهانش بندگانند
گهی آثار او در هند بیند
گهی فرمان او در روم خوانند

The World-Conquering Lord,
To whose authority the rulers of the earth have acquiesced.
At times, his achievements are witnessed in India,
Sometimes, his mandates are proclaimed in Rum (i.e. Anatolia).

Maulana Bahauddin Aushi was an outstanding poet who came from Aush and associated with the court of Sultan Qutbuddin Aibek. Both Awfi and Minhaj-i-Siraj Juzjani speak highly of his accomplishments. A man of facile pen, he wrote in verse and prose both. He was also an orator, and delivered sermons on religion and morality. His sophistication, learning and wit impressed Qutbuddin Aibek so much that he was made a close associate. The Maulana was also impressed by the towering personality of his royal patron and composed *qasidas* in his praise. Awfi has quoted a *qita* (distich) from one of his *qasidas* in praise of Sultan Qutbuddin Aibek, highlighting the latter's chivalry and large hearted generosity:[9]

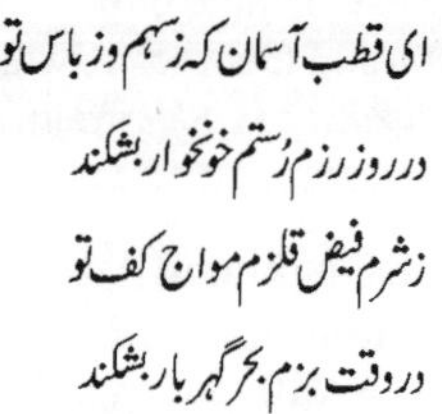

Oh: the Pole-star of heaven, from fear of thy bravery the blood-thirsty Rustam (warrior) falls down.
From the shame caused by the waves from thy palm's generosity, the pearl-scattering sea became subdued at the time of festivity.

Minhaj-i-Siraj also quotes his following *raba'i* (quatrain), in praise of Qutbuddin Aibek:[10]

ای بخشش تو لک بجهان آورده
کانرا کف تو کار بجان آورده
از رشک کف تو خون گرفته دلِ کان
بس لعل بهانه درمیان آورده

> Truly, the bestowal of laks thou in the world didst bring: Thy hand brought the mine's affair to a desparate state. The blood-filled mine's heart, through envy of thy hand, therefore, produced the ruby as a pretext (within it).

Upon the accidental death of Qutbuddin Aibek in 1206, the political situation in India changed and Maulana Aushi returned to Aush. The Sultan's death was followed by a civil war for the throne. Malik Nasir uddin Qubacha, the slave general of Sultan Muizuddin Muhammad bin Sam and the son-in-law of Qutbuddin Aibek, assumed the title of Sultan in Uchh and then seized Multan, Sind and Lahore. Ismail, the *Malik-i-dad*[11] of Delhi, invited Iltutmish, the *sipahsalar* of Badaun, to Delhi and declared him Sultan Shamsuddin Iltutmish. In Bihar and Bengal Husam Uddin 'Iwaz Khalji assumed the title of Sultan Ghiyathuddin 'Iwaz (Khalji) and consolidated his power there. As for the nobles posted around Delhi and Awadh, they also became independent and opposed Iltutmish. Of these rulers, Awfi and Minhaj i-Siraj describe Sultan Nasiruddin Qubacha as the most benevolent. He extended patronage to scholars who came from Khurasan, Central Asia, Ghur and Ghazna after their lands had been overrun and conquered by Chingiz Khan. The number of refugees was great but the Sultan bestowed on them all costly presents and liberally provided for all of them.[12] These refugees were settled in different towns and cities of his dominion, with the result that, besides Lahore, Multan and Uchh also emerged as centres of learning and began to play an important role in the spread of intellectual culture around. According to Ali Bin Hamid Kufi, Uchh, the capital of the Sultan (Nasiruddin Qubacha), was called *Hazrat*[13] and had become a heaven for scholars and poets. They composed excellent works and dedicated them either to the Sultan or his wazir, Husain 'Ashari, entitled 'Ainul-Mulk.[14] There was a fairly large sprinkling of poets in Uchh. They enjoyed the patronage of the Sultan and his *wazir*. A certain scholar, Majduddin, associated with the Sultan's court, compiled an anthology-cum-*tadhkira* of the poets of Uchh but it is not extant. His contemporary, Awfi, who joined Sultan Nasiruddin Qubacha's court later, took notice of only four poets left out by Majduddin. Of the names only two are legible as the manuscript is in poor condition. Lachhmi Narain Shafiq, a later anthologist, mentions Fazli Multani as one of the missing names on the basis of another manuscript copy that was accessible to him. The two poets whose names are found intact in the *Lubab-ul-Albab* are Shams-uddin Muhammad Balkhi and Ziya Sijzi. The following are the couplets from a *qasida* composed by Fazli Multani in praise of Sultan Nasiruddin Qubacha.[15]

ناصرِ دین خسروِ دنیا قباچه شاه شرق
ای ماه چتر تو بر گردون مینا آمده
حُلیهٔ خطبه ز القاب تو زینت یافته
چهره سکه ز انساب تو زیبا آمده

(Sultan) Nasir-i-Din, The Lord of the World (is) Qubacha, the King of the East,
Oh Moon! Thy parasol has covered the heaven.
The form of (thy) *Khutba* has gained beauty with thy titles, the face of thy coin has gained elegance from thy genealogy.

As for Shamsuddin Muhammad Balkhi and Ziya Sijzi, Awfi has quoted their *qasidas* in praise of the wazir, Ainul-Mulk 'Ashari. Shamsuddin Balkhi is mentioned as *al-katib*, *Saiyid ul-Nudama* (chief of the courtiers) and *Tajul-Fuzala* (crown of the intellectuals) implying that besides being a calligraphist, he was held in high esteem for his erudition. In poetry he stood unrivalled and was the Anwari of his age. The following couplet in praise of the wazir may be quoted here:[16]

صاحب جمشید رتبت فخر دنیا عین الملک
آنکه ملک از رای او تمکین و امکان یافته

Ziyauddin Sijzi is also called *Fakhr-ul-Shaura* (pride of the poets) by Awfi. His *qasida* quoted in the *Lubab-ul-Albab* is also in praise of the Wazir Ain al-Mulk al-Ashari:[17]

رتبت صدر وزارت جاودان جاه تو باد
کز ترقی جاه تو پیرایه عز و بقاست

In short, Sultan Nasiruddin Qubacha was greatly interested in the progress of learning and literature. He established schools and colleges in his realm and appointed learned teachers in them. In 1227 he entrusted the charge of the *Madrasa-i-Firozi*, the main college in his capital of Uchh, to Minhaj-i-Siraj on his arrival from Khurasan. The latter was a learned theologian, poet and historian and deserved consideration for his close association with the ruling house of Ghur.[18] On Qubacha's fall in 1228, all the poets and scholars, and also Wazir Ain al-Mulk al-Ashari, joined Sultan Iltutmish's service and moved to Delhi.

POETS ASSOCIATED WITH THE COURT OF DELHI UNDER SULTAN SHAMS UDDIN ILTUTMISH AND HIS SUCCESSORS

Sultan Shamsuddin Iltutmish also extended munificent patronage to the scholars and poets who were entrusted with administrative posts and with the popularization of the Sultan through their poetry. In emulating the traditions of the grand wazirs in the past, Nizam ul-Mulk Junadi, who held the joint charge of the offices of *wazir* and *sadr* (chief justice and the minister-in-charge of making land-grants) seems to have patronized a large number of scholars and poets.[19] The scholars were employed in different departments and were granted land in the area around Delhi. They rendered important services to the state as the biographical details available in the contemporary sources reveal. They imparted instruction to students, guided young poets, and served even in the army as warriors. In fact, the beautiful *qasidas* of these men in praise of various aristocrats inspired the later generation of poets and were regarded worthy of preservation by the *tadhkira* writers and anthologists from the fourteenth century onward. It may also be recalled that a few *diwans* of the thirteenth century discovered recently and the specimen verses quoted by the later medieval writers show that the literary output was rich in both quantity and quality. It comprised poems in different genres, the *qasida* that was generally panegyric but could also be satirical, didactic or philosophical; *qit'a* or distich, a piece included in the *qasida* or *ghazal* (love poem) or was a poem complete in itself; the *ruba'i* (quatrain) in which the entire subject-matter could be expressed (in four lines) and the *mathnavi*, a long narrative about romance, moral or metaphysical philosophy, or a historical theme. The *ghazal*, the theme of which is generally love, humane or divine, was yet to gain popularity. The age of Sa'di of Shiraz and Amir Khusrau of Delhi had yet not dawned.[20] Love themes were generally attempted by the poets in the *tashbib* (exordium), an essential part of the *qasida*. We may now briefly discuss the poets who flourished during the period under review.

Majd ul-Mulk Bahauddin al-Jamji was a remarkable man on several counts. Not only a learned man and poet of distinction, he had also gained a reputation for his military leadership and resourcefulness. The detailed account furnished by Awfi about his attainments in India provides us with interesting insights into the problems connected with the expansion of Muslim arms under Iltutmish.

Majd ul-Mulk Bahauddin al-Jamji came to India during the reign of Qutbuddin Aibek and soon gained the Sultan's favour for his family's association with the Glurid court in Ghazna and Firuzkuh. Sultan Qutbuddin Aibek consulted him on state matters. Once the Sultan elevated two persons to the ministerial posts at the centre, a Hindu chief called the Rana of Banaras and Abu Bakr Mubashir. The Rana of Banaras was entrusted with the charge of the *diwan-i-sahib-i-barid*[21] (the intelligence bureau) while Mubashir got the post of *hajib* (chamberlain). Bahauddin al-Jamji composed offhand a quatrain, expressing his displeasure at their elevation, but to no effect.

In Delhi, al-Jamji was also known for his generosity. At times he would distribute all he possessed. Once an emigrant poet, Hamid Qahanduzi, came to him with a quatrain composed in his praise, expecting to get money in reward. But al-Jamji had already given away his treasure and sat drunk. Hamid Qahunduzi recited his quatrain:

ای قاعده تو زر بخشیدن
چه زر؟ بگنجها گهر بخشیدن
روزی صدره چو آب گردو خورشید
از شرم کف دست تو در بخشیدن

It is your habit to distribute money,
What's about money? You give away treasure of pearls.
Once the moon revolved out of shame into a hundred
kinds of waterways, owing to your open handedness.

Since al-Jamji had no money, he also composed offhand the following quatrain; telling him that if he had come earlier he would have received a good amount for each line.

زین پیش ز ما بود اگر بخشیدن
هر بیتی را خانهٔ زر بخشیدن
اکنون چو دِل و خزینه برگشت و تهی
ما ـیم و زبان و کیر خر بخشیدن

After the accidental death of Sultan Qutbuddin Aibek, al-Jamji does not seem to have submitted to Sultan Iltutmish. He was accused of having the *khutba* read in his name and carrying a sceptre in his hand. He was arrested and about 20 lakh *tankas* (silver coins) were seized from him and declared forfeit to the state exchequer. He languished in prison till

1215, when Iltutmish defeated Sultan Tajuddin Yildoz in the third battle of Tarain. Thereupon al-Jamji composed a quatrain congratulating the Sultan on his victory and requesting him to grant him freedom as a thanksgiving to God:

چون ملک تو شد یکی بصد بخش مرا
امید تو حق نکرد درد بخش مرا
هر چند شفاعتم کسی می نکند
شکرانه این فتح بخود بخش مرا

In response the Sultan ordered his release. He was also favoured with a robe of honour and required to stay at the royal court. In AD 1220, he was posted in Awadh as the *sipahsalar* (commander) of the army of Hindustan (i.e. the eastern region). The crown prince, Nasiruddin Mahmud Shah (*d.* 1230) was placed in his care. Al-Jamji had the *khutba* read in the name of the crown prince, declaring him the Sultan of the East.[22]

Driven by Mongol expansion in Central Asia, Siraji Khurasani also sought refuge in India. His *diwan*[23] contains *qasidas* in praise of Iltutmish, the royal princes, and the leading nobles of the realm. His *qasidas* yield historical information about the achievements of the princes and nobles in the military and the cultural field. The intellectual atmosphere generated by state patronage to men of talent and learning is also reflected therein. The characteristic features of his verses are an originality of style and freshness of thought, the use of novel and beautiful similes and metaphors, imagination, and wit. His contribution to Persian poetry is certainly of a high order. In some verses references are made to certain scientific instruments, devices and ideas, which indicate that they found their way into India along with immigrants in the beginning of the thirteenth century. For instance, in one *qasida* in praise of Prince Nasiruddin Mahmud we find a reference to the astrolabe, an astronomical instrument used in western and Central Asia to observe the movements of stars and planets, and also to measure time. He says:[24]

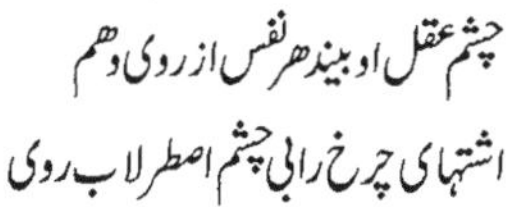

Although Siraji composed poems in different forms, he was essentially a poet of *qasida*. The talent possessed by a poet in *qasida* writing brought him name; in fact, his status among poets was determined by it. Like his famous predecessors, Siraji generally devotes the *tashbib* of the *qasida* to love themes; herein the young and charmful youth, rosy cheeks, slanted but piercing eyes of the Turk or Chinese girl, her ripening breasts are all explained with beautiful similes and metaphors. A few verses may be quoted:

عاشق سرمست باروی جوانی میشود
چشم اوچون برنگارنار پستانی میرسد
حور فردوس برین رادل تصور میکند
دیده چون برساقی سیمین زنخدان میرسد
ای تنگ چشم، ترک سمن ساق، ماه روی
ازچشم من نهان چه کنی سال وماه روی
درخاک هندروی تو چشم من بدید
کردم زآب چشم چورود بیاه روی

Nasiri is reported to have migrated from vilayat[25] to India in the reign of Sultan Iltutmish. In Delhi, he stayed with Shaikh Qutbuddin Bakhtiyar Kaki, the celebrated sufi and the chief *murid* (disciple) of Shaikh Muinuddin Sijzi, the founder of Chishti sufi *silsilah* in India. Mention made by Minhaj-i-Siraj Juzjani of Nasiri suggests that he was a famous poet who could act as a soldier also. In narrating an attack by the Ismailis of Qaramitah sect on the Jama mosque at the time of congregational prayer, Minhaj-i-Siraj Juzjani refers to Nasiri, the poet as one of the saviours of Muslims:

> The Qaramittahs collected together at Delhi from different parts of India, such as Gujarat, the vilayat of Sind and the area around Delhi, lying along the banks of the Jamuna and the Ganges. They pledged themselves to be faithful to each other and conspired. . . . When they attacked the Muslims, and outcry arose, the warriors of the city, such as *Nasiruddin Ai-yitim Balarami and Amir Nasiri*, the poet, and other armed men from different directions rode fully equipped with arms.[26]

Shaikh Nizamuddin (Auliya) and Fakhruddin Mubarak Shah Qawwas[27] also testified to his greatness and the popularity of his verses during their own time. He is reported to have composed after his arrival in India a *qasida* in praise of the reigning Sultan Iltutmish, and requested his host, Shaikh Qutbuddin Bakhtiyar Kaki, to pray for its acceptance (by the Sultan).

The Shaikh offered the prayer and then Nasiri proceeded to the royal palace. Having been granted audience, he recited the *qasida*, the opening lines of which are:[28]

ای فتنہ از نہیب تو زنہار خواستہ
تیغ تو مال و فیل ز کفار خواستہ

Because of thy power, sedition seeks shelter;
Thy sword receives wealth and elephants from the infidels.

According to Shaikh Nizamuddin (*d.* 1325) the Sultan was flattered by this couplet and quickly committed it to memory and repeated it. The later historian, Mulla Abdul Qadir Badauni would have us believe that the Sultan ordered the couplets of the *qasida* to be counted. It contained fifty-three couplets, and Nasiri was given 1,000 silver *tankas* for each.[29] Maulana Fakhruddin Qawwas quotes in his *Farhang-i-Qawwas* (lexicon) the following beautiful couplet:[30]

گرد قمر کلالہ ھا زیر کلال لالہ ھا
خوردہ زمی پیالہ ھا مست سوار میرود

It is a pity that his *diwan* has been lost and only specimen verses are found in medieval manuscripts, although he enjoyed popularity in his lifetime and his memory was cherished by posterity.

Tajuddin Reza was popularly known as Khwaja Taj Reza and held by the elite of Delhi in high esteem for his learning, culture and excellent poetry.[31] Another early fourteenth-century writer, Fakhruddin Mubarak Shah Qawwas, mentions him as Taj Dabir alias Reza. He also quotes his verses to explain the meanings of certain words.[32] Reza started his career under Sultan Iltutmish and seems to have survived his reign for long. In the year 1228, when the emissaries came from the Abbasid Caliph al-Mustansir Billah of Baghdad to Delhi with robes of honour and the diploma of authority for Iltutmish, his sons and the grandees, he recited a *qasida* commemorating the occasion. The Sultan is reported to have hosted a grand feast to which the residents of Delhi were invited, and then the caliphs' emissaries were accorded a reception.[33] In all round jubilation, the Sultan, the princes of the blood and his nobles put on the robes. The poets recited their *qasidas* to celebrate the event. Taj Reza also recited his *qasida*, a fine specimen of eloquence and noteworthy for its combination of beauty of language and melody:[34]

مژده عالم راز عالم آفرین آورده اند
زانکه شه راازخلیفه آفرین آورده اند
شادی عامست درشهر اینکه بهر شهریار
خلعت خاص امیر المومنین آورده اند

They have brought glad news from the creator of the world to the World.
(Because) they have brought blessing from the Caliph to the King.
There is feast in the city for all because the special robe from the Lord of the faithfuls has been brought for the King.

In AD 1232, when Iltutmish conquered Gwalior, Taj Reza was with him and composed the quatrain (*rubai*) which was then inscribed on a slab and fixed on its gate:[35]

هر قلعه که سلطان سلاطین بگرفت
از عون خداوند نصرت دین بگرفت
آن قلعه کالیور وآن حصن حصین
در ستمایه سنه ثلثین بگرفت

Every fort which the king of Kings conquered,
He conquered by the help of God and the aid of faith.
The fortress of Gwalior and that strong fortification.
He took in the year six hundred and thirty (*Hijra*).

The following *qasida* seems to have been composed by Taj Reza in praise of the Sultan's Wazir, Nizam ul-Mulk Junaidi, patron of scholars and poets:[36]

ای صاحبی که چون اثر رحمت حذای
باران جود تو بزمین وزمن رسد

Oh Lord: Owing to the effect of divine mercy,
The rain of thy generosity reaches the earth and the world.

On the accession of Sultan Ruknuddin Firuz Shah to his father's throne in 1236, Taj Reza recited this qasida:[37]

مبارک باد ملک جاودانی
ملک را خاصه در عهد جوانی
یمین الدوله رکن الدین که آمد
درش از یمن چون رکن ایمانی

All hail to the everlasting Kingdom,
Above all to the King, in his heyday of youth,
Yamin u'd-Daulat Rukn Uddin
whose door became like the pillar of the Prophet's faith
from its auspiciousness.

Fakhruddin Mubarak Shah Ghaznavi has quoted these verses:

معلوم رای تست که جافی برای من
پیوسته پیش تعبیه در انگبین کنند
از فصل گل چو موسم سوریست باغ را
قمری نگر که شیوهٔ او باز شیولست

As for Taj Reza's death, it seems to have taken place in old age during the reign of Sultan Nasiruddin Mahmud (1246-65). This is indicated by the couplet composed by him on the appointment of Shams Dabir as the *Mustaufi-i-Mumalik* (auditor general of the sultanate) suggests:[38]

صدرا کنون به کام دل دوستان شدی
مستوفی ممالک هندوستان شدی

In short, creative imagination and craftsmanship enabled Taj Reza to make his mark. Assessing the importance of his contribution to Persian poetry, Iqbal Husain observes: 'Subtlety of music and power to condense a lot of thought in a few words with dramatic and picturesque effect characterizes Tajuddins' poems. They are extremely simple and have a natural flow.'[39]

Amir Ruhani was also a refugee from Bukhara, escaping the Mongol onslaught in his homeland. As a man of learning, he received patronage from Sultan Iltutmish and settled in Delhi. In 1227, when the Sultan returned to Delhi in triumph from his expedition against the fort of Mandor (Siwalik hills), Amir Ruhani recited a long and beautiful *qasida*, lauding the achievements of his royal patron in different fields. Especially worth mentioning is the allusion to the help rendered by the Sultan to refugees from Central Asia and other lands, subjected by the Mongols to alien tyranny. The early fifteenth- and sixteenth-century historians Muhammad Bihamad Khani and Mulla Abdul Qadir Badauni have quoted a few couplets of his *qasidas* in their respective histories:[40]

خبر باهل سما برد جبرئیل امین
ز فتح نامۂ سلطان عهد شمس الدین
که ای ملایکه قدس آسمانها را
بدین بشارت بندید کله آدین
که از بلاد ملاحده شهنشه اسلام
کشاد بار دیگر قلعه سپهر آئین
شه مجاهد غازی که دست و تیغش را
روان حیدر کرار میکند تحسین

The faithful Gabriel carried the tidings to the dwellers in heaven, from the account of victories achieved by the ruler of the age, Shamsuddin, Saying—Oh ye holy angels raise upon the heavens, hearing this good tidings, the canopy of adornment. That form the land of heretics the Emperor of Islam has conquered a second time the sky high fort (of Mondor); The King, the holy warrior and Ghazi, whose hand and sword the soul of Haider-i-Karar (Ali, the fourth caliph) praises, (people come) from the East and the West for the protection of faith, they sought refuge under you from the tyranny of the pagans of China. (i.e. Chingis Khan)

Badauni also quotes a few more couplets from another charming *qasida* in praise of the *wazir's* (Nizam-ul-Mulk Junaidi) love for learning:[41]

چون شرق و غرب جهان در پناه دولت و دین
پناه زان بتو جست از جفاء کافر چین
قصه خویش از زبان قلم
کرده ام یاد در بیان قلم
خواجه منصور بن سعید کز اوست

تیز بازار امتحان قلم
آن بزرگی دارد از بفضلش
بار انصاف کاروان قلم

From the tongue of the pen my own story I tell in the words of the pen
Tis from Khwaja Mansur bin Said thrives the market of test of the pen.
That great one whose words load the burden of truth on the van of the pen.

Mahmud Khattat seems to have been residing in Delhi since the time of Sultan Qutbuddin Aibek, because he composed and recited his *qasida* in praise of Iltutmish on his enthronement in 1211. Neither the early anthologists nor the later *tadhkira* writers provide us any information about his career in the service of the Sultan. Muhammad Bihamad Khani mentions him as *Malik al-Kalam* (chief of poetry). A few couplets from this *qasida* recited by Mahmud Khattat at the time of the accession of Iltutmish may be quoted:[42]

جهان را باد سال و ماه ازین
بتاج و تخت سلطان السلاطین
خداوند جهانداران عالم
سلیمان فر احمد آئین

The world got embellishment from the month and the year of the Sultan of Sultans.
The Lord of the inhabitants of the world (has) Solomon's Splendour and Ahmad's (i.e. Prophet's) laws.

Other *qasida* verses are available in the fourteenth-century anthology, *Munis-ul-Ahrar*. These are composed in praise of the Wazir Nizam-ul-Mulk Junaidi.[43]

ای رشک خورشید و قمر
ای سرو بستان جمال
ای پرتو نور لقا
ای حسن رویت برکمال

Tajuddin Bukhari was one of the leading scholars whom the Sultan and the nobles held in high esteem. The Sultan is reported to have assigned him the responsibility of tutoring the princes and his slaves in popular science. Zia uddin Barani tells us that once Sultan Ghiyasuddin Balban (1266-87) told his nobles,

> We two brothers studied the '*Adab-ul-Salatin*[44] under the guidance of Khwaja Tajuddin Bukhari, one of the courtiers of Sultan Shams Uddin (Iltutmish). I finished reading it from beginning to end under his supervision. We were presented before the Sultan after the work had been thoroughly examined and studied. Sultan Shamsuddin rewarded Khwaja Tajuddin Bukhari who by now had grown very old, with two villages besides one lakh *jital*.[45]

His *qasidas* are available in the *Munis-ul-Ahrar* and later *tadhkiras*. One of the *qasidas* composed in praise of the Wazir Nizam ul-Mulk Junaidi narrates his generous nature and philanthropic spirit:[46]

آصف ثانی محمد کوز رغبت بی سوال
لعل ومروارید وزر وسیم بخشند بیشمار
گوہر آل جنید آن کامران سیم وزر
لعل ومروارید جستہ از کف اوز نہار

The *qasida* of Maulana Burhanuddin Bazaz found in the *Munisul-Ahrar* suggests that he arrived in India in his youth and joined Sultan Iltutmish's court. His inclusion by Zia uddin Barani among the leading *ulama* of the reign of Balban reveals that he survived in India for long.[47] The *qasida* composed by him in praise of Iltutmish, commemorating the arrival of the caliph's emissaries from Baghdad in 1228-9, is an example of the repetition of rhymes, a popular technique in those days. This *qasida* is important as it reveals that Burhanuddin was invited, as a poet of distinction along with other poets to recite his *qasida* on this memorable occasion.[48] We also find herein the clue to his authoritative knowledge of the *tafsir* (exegesis of the Koran) and *hadith* (the sayings of the Prophet):

زآنکہ در تفسیر قرآن ھست فوضم بیشتر
زین قبل باشد مرادر صفت اخبار بار

The following couplet resolves the controversy about how the name of the Sultan of Delhi is to be spelt Iltutmish and not Iltimish or Iletmish:

بوالمظفر التمش کو بحکم از تیر تیر
بگوراند در فوالش می بباید تیر تیر

And in this couplet mention has been made of the robe, sent by the caliph to the Sultan:[49]

باد اندر بزم تو صد طرفه بعد او پیش
چون امیر المومنیت تحفه بغداد داد

Very little is known about Hakim Tatari's life and career in India. He may have come as a refugee like so many others during the reign of Sultan Iltutmish. We do not know whether or not he joined state service or the royal court at the death of Iltutmish (before the accession of Firuz Shah) in 1236. The *qasida*, contained in the *Munis-ul-Ahrar*, is in praise of Sultan Ruknuddin Firuz Shah (deposed and killed in 1236):[50]

هست گوئی عارض ترک زیبا آفتاب
گر بود ممکن که دارد برج دیبا آفتاب
شاه رکن الدین که دولت را مهیا دارد او
همچو باغ نو بهاری را مهیا آفتاب

One of those few poets to whose memory posterity paid homage on account of his inventions of new styles in *qasida* writing was Shihab-uddin Mihmara. Although they quoted his verses at length in their anthologies and *tadhkiras*, none of the early writers bothered to provide biographical details about him. Mention made by Amir Khusrau and other writers of Shihab Mihmara only shows that he lies buried in Badaun. We cannot assume on the basis of their statement that he was born in India. Probably he too was a foreigner by birth and an Indian by adoption. He seems to have started his career during the last years of Iltutmish, because the *qasida* quoted by later writers is in praise of Firuz Shah, his son. Thus he was in Delhi in 1236, enjoying a reputation as a poet of eminence. It was owing to his fame and popularity that he could have access to the royal court and express his desire for land in Badaun, a town of his choice. He got it, and may have moved to Badaun in his old age. Amir Khusrau, his junior contemporary, had sought guidance from him during his early career and says:[51]

در بداون مهمره سرمست برخیزد درخواب
بشنود گر نغمه مرغان دهلی زین نوا

In Badaon Mihmara rises intoxicated from sleep
If he listens to this sound of the melody of the birds of Delhi.

In his *Mathnavi Hasht Bihisht* also, Khusrau praises Shihabuddin Mihmara as a mentor who suggested improvements [illegible] Khusrau says his copper was turned into gold when [illegible] mined each line carefully and made alterations:[52]

نوردل چون بعالم افگنده
سایه برکار من هم افگنده
من بدو عرض کرده نامه خویش
او باصلاح رانده خامه خویش
دید هر نکته را رقم برقم
رنج بر خود نهاده منت هم
شمع من یافته ضیاء از وی
مس من گشت کیمیا از وی

According to Badauni, Amid Lowiki Sunami, another thirteenth-century Persian poet, was his disciple. Explaining the reason for non-availability of the *diwans* of leading early poets such as Mihmara, Badauni says:

Since the speech (*kalam*) of the early poets after the appearance of the cavalcade of the Prince of Poets (Amir Khusrau) has become like the stars at the time of the rising of the banner of the glorious sun . . . men speak and write less concerning them, nay more they do not possess them. . . . I have thought it incumbent upon me to include a few odes from that eminent author as a benediction and blessing, in the composition of mine, and to leave a memorial for his friends . . . and to display upon the dais of evidence the excellences of that doughty knight of the arena of eloquence, and more especially to fulfil the demands of fellowship.[53]

As for the new trend introduced by Shihab Mihmara in *qasida*-writing in India, he talked about the importance of moral values and spirituality in human life. His verses in praise of God and the Prophet show that he was inclined towards Sufism and wanted to prevent people from turning wholly materialistic in worldly affairs:[54]

الغم بلوح ہستی هیچ درنشانی
بقائی غیر قایم ز وجود خویش خانی
صفت الف ندارم که الف کسری ندارد
همه نقش من کسر آمد ز صحیفه امانی
دم بلبل است وگل خوش من بیخبر چو سوسن
چون الف زبان ندارم چه کنم بده زبانی
نه چو آبم از طراوت نه چوں آتشم ز رفعت
نه چو بادم از لطافت نه چو خاکم از گرانی
دل وعقل سرکشیده ز گزند گور خانه
برسینه برنهاده پرند گور خانی

I am *alif* in the table of existence and of no value as sign. My existence depends upon the duration of the existence of others, my own existence is transitory.
I have not the attributes of *alif* for *alif* has no crookedness.
All my writing has become crooked on the page of desire.
There is the song of the nightingale, the rose is happy;
while I am careless like the lily.
I am not like water in freshness, nor like fire in sublimity,
Nor like the wind in sweetness, nor like the earth in heaviness.
Your heart and intellect are careless of the tortures of the grave, you have dressed yourself in Gurkhani Silk.[55]

In the following verses from a *qasida* the companions of the Prophet who had succeeded him as his caliphs are praised:[56]

بنوید دوست جانش شده مست بر امیدش
پسر ابوقحافه زده قحف دوستگانی
ربطی بنا فگنده سخنش قضائی حق را
شده از پی سیاست عمرش بعدل بانی
قدم سیوم درین راه ز پیش نهاده مردی
که نزد غرور راهش بمتاع این جهانی
شده رکن چارمینش علی آنکه بد که لیکن

زشعاع ذولفقارش رُخ مهر زعفرانی
زمن آنکه این قصیده طلبنده جانش
چون قصیده ام مزین جواهر معانی

By the good tiding of his friend, his heart became intoxicated with the hope of a meeting.
The Son of Abu Qahaf (the first Caliph) has drunk from the cup of his friendship.
His speeches have founded a fortress for the decrees of God. Umar by his justice became the binder of it, by right government.
One (Osman, the Caliph) third in order has placed the footstep in this way, whose path to the enjoyment of this world was not obstructed by pride.
His fourth pillar was Ali who at the time of battle made the face of the sun pale from the glitter of his sword.
He who demanded from this *qasida*, may his life like my *qasida* be ornamented with the jewels of meaning (i.e. the Sultan's life).

In the following *qasida* composed in praise of Firuz Shah, Shihab Mihmara requests his royal patron to grant him maintenance-land in Badaun territory:[57]

پیل بخشا در بداون بایدم ویرانه
گر چه جای گرگ وکرگ وشیر باشدین دیار
همچو شیر و پیل و گرگ وکرگ در گرمابها
دشمنان بیجان شده بر آخرِ سنگین قطار

O! the elephant-bestower, I desire a place in the wilderness of Badaon,
Even though this region is the abode of the wolf, the rhinoceros and the lion.
May your enemies be left without life like the lions, elephants, wolves and rhinoceros at the end of the story line in the bath.[58]

It is worth noting that the *qasidas* and verses of Shihab Mahmira quoted by medieval writers in their *tadhkiras* and anthologies as specimens of thirteenth-century poetry are marked by freshness and ingenuity. Iqbal Husain rightly remarks, 'Shihab's greatness, unlike that of the other court poets, is curiously original. As the writer of artificial *qasidas*, he is to be remembered for his great originality and skill. His *qasidas* served as models for [Amir] Khusrau.'[59]

Saiyid Izz Uddin Alawi and Amid Lowiki Sunami were two thirteenth-century poets associated with the court of Multan, the governors of which had declared their independence from Delhi during the reigns of the immediate successors of Sultan Iltutmish. Emulating the traditions of their predecessors, the rulers of Multan extended patronage to scholars and poets. The poets were employed and rewarded because they sang the praises of their patrons; their *qasidas* and verses shed lustre on their courts and raised their prestige.

Both Saiyid Izz Uddin Alawi and Amid Lowiki Sunami were associated with the court of Sultan Nasiruddin Muhammad in Multan.[60] The *qasidas*, composed by Izz Uddin Alawi in praise of his royal patron are available in the *Munis-ul-Ahrar*, Saif Jam Harevi's *Majmu'a-i-Lataif-o-Safina-i-Zaraif* and *Khulasat ul Ash'ar*. The royal patron is mentioned therein as Sultan Muhammad bin Izz Uddin Balban. He also composed verses in praise of *wazir*, Tajuddin Muhammad bin Muhammad Junaidi in Multan. Nazir Ahmad may be given credit for the discovery of *Munis-ul-Ahrar*, containing his verses but fails to escape pitfalls in identifying Sultan Muhammad of Multan, although he correctly identifies the *wazir* and the father of the ruler. He states that Izz Uddin Balban could have been one of the Maliks of Iltutmish called Kishlu Khan Balban, once loyal to the throne, turned rebel.[61]

He rebelled against Nasiruddin Mahmud many times. He even joined hands with Malik Shamsuddin Kurt and Hulugu Khan against the Sultan of Delhi and went to Khurasan and Baghdad, returning to India in 658/1260. Thereafter he is heard no more in the *Tabaqat-i-Nasiri*. The *Tabaqat-i-Nasiri* was brought to completion in AD 1260 and the histories compiled by Isami and Ziya uddin Barani that contain relevant information about Muhammad bin Balban Kishlu Khan did not attract Nazir Ahmad's attention. According to Isami and Barani, Muhammad succeeded his father, assuming the royal title of Sultan Nasiruddin Muhammad Shah.[62] Our poet, Saiyid Izz Uddin Alawi, praising his munificent generosity and chivalry, says:

ای بجق خسرو سکندر فن
در دریای عز دین بلبن
شه نصیر دول محمد راد
از کف جود تو زمین گلشن
ویا شهی که ز کوست بچرخ صدا
شگفت گلبن فتح تو در صبا غزا

In the following ornamental *qasida* a religious divine, scholar and preacher is praised for doing justice to people as *qazi* of the kingdom of Multan:[63]

آمد آن مکرم ملک آیات
آمد آن منعم فلک رایات
بوتراب اُمم جلال ملک
آفتاب کرم جمال قضات

As regards Amid Lowiki Sunami, he was born in Sunam (modern Panjab in India, which had developed as a centre of learning and culture during the thirteenth century. His full name was Faiz Ullah while he adopted Amid as a pseudonym. 'Fakhr ul-Mulk' was his official title. He seems to have moved from Sunam to Multan in search of a job, some time after the death of Sultan Iltutmish. His first royal patron seems to have been the King of Multan, Sultan Tajuddin Abu Bakr, the son and successor of Malik Aiyaz, a slave Turk general of Iltutmish who had assumed independence in AD 1241. The other royal patron is the same Sultan Nasiruddin Muhammad bin Izz Uddin Balban Kishlu Khan who had been also the patron of Izz Uddin Alawi. Fortunately, a large number of his *qasidas* and other poems have been discovered, collected and published in the form of a *diwan*.[64] Besides *qasidas*, Amid composed *ghazals* and satires that soon assumed the importance of a literary tradition in the history of Persian literature in India. Amid's *ghazals* are on single themes and characterized by simplicity of diction and a natural flow that makes the poetry smooth and musical.[66] The following couplets of a *ghazal*, describing the beauty and coquettish remarks of the beloved, may be quoted:[65]

روی تو پیرایه صحن چمن
موی تو سرمایه مشک ختن
طره طراز تو عاشق فریب
غمزه خونخوار تو لشکر شکن

Thy face is the ornament of the terrace of the garden,
while thy hair is the sum of the musk of Khutan.
Thy tricky forelock plays treachery to the lover,
While thy blood-thirsty wink smashes the army.

As for the patrons whom Amid praises, some have not been correctly identified by the editor of his *diwan*. For example, the Sultan of Multan and Sind, Nasiruddin Muhammad bin Izzuddin Balban Kishlu Khan has been confused with Sultan Ghiyasuddin Balban's son Muhammad Khan, known as *Khan-i-Shahid*. Like his colleague Saiyid Izz Uddin Alawi, Amid also names his royal patron, Sultan Nasir ul-Haque Muhammad bin Balban or *Shah-i-Jahan*.[66]

The *hasbiya* (prison poem) provides us with insight into prison conditions, coins, rates of interest, etc. The moneylenders charged 20 per cent interest per month. We may quote a few lines in translation:

> No one has seen half a *dang* (token copper coin) weight of gold in my possession. And even if he has, I would not willingly undergo imprisonment for the sake of it. Gold has no value in my sight, how could I pledge it like a usurer so as to get twelve for every ten.[67]

The following lines by the same poet reveal that Amid held the post of *Mushrif-i-Mumalik* (accountant general) and was imprisoned on a charge of embezzlement.

> The fate has turned against (me), if not why have I been thrown into prison, although (the department) of *Ishraf* was managed by me honestly.[68]

Besides, Amid's *qasida* in praise of another historical personage, mentioned as Jalal ud-Daula Mughis Uddin Shah also calls for re-identification of the latter. Nazir Ahmad identifies him with Tughril, the governor of Bengal who had rebelled against Sultan Ghiyasuddin Balban and was defeated in consequence in 1281. But this identifications is incorrect because Amid does not seem to have survived till the period of Tughrils' rebellion; nor did he leave Multan for Bengal. It is also probable that he did not survive during the reign of Balban as there is no *qasida* to the Sultan or his cousin Sher Khan Sunqar. The latter held the territories of Multan and Uchh in his charge during the early year of Balban's reign. In fact, Jalal ud-Daula Mughis Uddin Shah seems to have been none other than Jalal Uddin, son of Sultan Iltutmish who had seized Lahore and Jullundhar territories with Mongol support and acknowledged the suzerainty of the Mongol emperor. Like Nasiruddin Muhammad of Multan, he also assumed the title of Sultan. As there was a friendship between him and the ruler of Multan and both were vassals of the Mongol emperor, Amid composed a *qasida* in his praise also. The medieval Persian poets wrote *qasidas* in praise of rulers friendly to their royal patrons, sent them to the latter and acquired robes of honour and cash as rewards.[69]

We also find mention of some poets of distinction who enjoyed immense prestige as men of learning and the art of poetry during the reign of Balban. Balban himself was tight-fisted, but his sons and nobles were patrons of poets. Of the leading poets of his reign, mention may be made of *Malik ul-Kalam* (master of poetry) Imam Qazi Asiruddin, Shamsuddin Dabir and Khwaja Shams-i-Moin.

Malik-ul-Kalam Imam Qazi Asiruddin is mentioned by Muhammad Bihamad Khani as the leading poet of the reign of Sultan Nasiruddin Mahmud, but survived into the time of Balban also. Amir Khusrau tells us in the *Dibacha* (Introduction) of his *diwan*, *Ghurat ul-Kalam*, that he and Sham Dabir were associated with Prince Bughra Khan, the younger son of Sultan Balban. Describing the visit of Bughra Khan to the place of Malik Alauddin (son of) of Kishl Khan along with Qazi Asir and Shams Dabir, Amir Khusrau says:

> The presence of these two scholars was like the conjunction of the two auspicious planets or the combination of the sun and the moon, and I, who am mercury, felt flattered to be in that company . . . as the poets recited their verses, the cloud of their generosity rained so heavily that it moistened all that is on the surface of the earth. Wonderful gold-scattering! The eyes of the beholders became yellow at the sight of the dinars and the skirts of their robes were torn with the weight of gold they held, like the rose, in a hundred shreds. My sweet verses suited so well the taste of Bughra Khan that, out of that generosity which is characteristic of kings and princes, he ordered a dish full of silver *tankahs* to be brought to me as a present from himself, and with this generous gift he made me a grateful slave of his.[70]

Only Muhammad Bihamad Khani quotes his verses, composed in praise of Sultan Nasiruddin Mahmud who was reduced by his regent to a figurehead. Contrary to the fact the Sultan is portrayed as a powerful ruler:[71]

ای چراغ دوده افراسیاب

ناصر الدنیا شه مالک رقاب

شاه محمود بن سلطان کو گرفت

ملک چون خنجر برون کرد از قراب

آنچه دید از بخت بیدار تو ملک

بخت بدخواهت نمی بیند بخواب

منت ایزد را که سلطان جهاں

برسر تخت بہی شد کامیاب

بارگاہ بادشاہی ترا

مہر تابد بر فلک زرین طناب

Shamsuddin Dabir was a resident of Samana (Haryana), distinguished for his erudition. Gifted with eloquence, he was able to gain popularity in the elite circles of Delhi. In the beginning he was associated with Shaikh Fariduddin Ganj-i-Shakr, the leading Chishti saint, the following statement, contained in the *Malfuzat* (collection of utterances) of Shaikh Nizamuddin Chishti, casts light on the love and affection that Shaikh Fariduddin Ganj-i-Shakr had for Shams Dabir:

> The Sufis (Chishti saints in particular) do not allow the poets to sing their praises in their presence, but the Shaikh ul-Islam (i.e. Ganj-i-Shakr) permitted Shams Dabir out of love and regard to recite the *qasida*, composed in his praise. Having listened to it, the Shaikh asked the poet: 'What do you want'? Thereupon, Shams Dabir offered fifty *jitals* (copper coins) to the Shaikh. His offering was accepted and immediately distributed among the immates of the *khanqah* (hospice). Four *jitals* went to Shaikh Nizamuddin as his share.

Shaikh Fariuddin is also reported to have taught Shams Dabir the *Liwaih* (a treatise on sufism), composed by Shaikh Hamiduddin Nagauri (Suhrawardi). But he should not be identified with Shams-ul-Mulk, the teacher of Shaikh Nizamuddin, the spiritual successor of Shaikh Fariduddin. Shaikh Nizamuddin Auliya studied the *Muqamat-i-Hariri* (the collection of the traditions of the Prophet) under his supervision.[72]

Taj Reza, a senior poet had composed the famous couplet in praise of his friend, Shams-ul-Mulk and not Shams Dabir:[73]

صدرا کنوں بکام دِل دوستان شدی

مستوفی ممالک هندوستان شدی

As already mentioned, he was a client of Bughra Khan, the governor of the territorial unit of Samana and Sunam. Later, Amir Khusrau also joined Bughra Khan's service in Samana and then got into close touch with Shams Dabir. Impressed by his diction, Amir Khusrau composed a *qasida*:[74]

ای دبیری که به پروانه نوک قلمت

تیغ خورشید زرنگار برون آوردند

گره کلک ترا اهل سخن بکشادن

زان همه لولوی شهسوار برون آوردند

نامه مشک زخلق تو بکهسار خزید

موگرفتند زکهسار برون آوردند

On Bughra Khan's appointment as the governor of Bihar and Bengal, Shams Dabir proceeded to Lakhnauti along with his patron prince. In Bengal he is reported to have put down the instructions (*wassaya*) dictated by Sultan Balban to Bughra Khan regarding the governance of the region and its relation with the centre (Delhi). It is sad that the *diwan* of Shamsuddin Dabir has not survived the ravages of time, though in Badauni's words he was one of those 'who sounded the drum of poetry and attained the rank of *Malik-ul-Kalam* (Lord of eloquence)'.[75] Fortunately, we find some of his verses in the *Muntakhab ut-Tawarikh* of Badauni and the later *Tadhkiras*. A few verses may be quoted from a *qasida*, composed in praise of Sultan Nasiruddin Mahmud:[76]

پخته دارم دل ز اندیشه رویت که چراست

رنگ تو پخته همیں نقره پیشانی خام

شاه محمود شه آن سلطان کز فر پدر

زیک یک ارزوش نیست زسلطانی جام

خسروا شمس دبیر ست قوی پخته سخن

نیست چون دفتریان سوخته دیوانی خام

I keep my heart exercised thinking of thy face, and wondering why thy colour is so ripe and thy forehead like virgin silver.

The King Mahmud Shah, that Sultan from whose father's glory the cauldron of one single desire, by reason of his empire, is not left unfilled.

Oh King: Shamsuddin is thy secretary (*dabir*), strong and well-proved in speech he is not like the worthless scribes an inexperienced scribbler.

Mention should also be made of Shams-i-Moin who distinguished himself both as a poet and prose-writer. He enjoyed the patronage of the Naib-i-Mumalikat (regent) Malik Qutbuddin Hasan Ghuri (assassinated in AD 1254) and served him as his *Nadim-i-Khass* (boon associate). According to Ziya uddin Barani, Shams-i-Moin was one of the celebrities of the age. He is said to have compiled volumes on the life and achievements of his patron Malik Qutbuddin Hasan Ghuri. He was alive in the time of Sultan Balban also.

When Malik Alauddin, popularly known Malik Chhaju, son of Sultan's younger brother Kishli Khan, was elevated to his fathers' post of *barbak* and given the golden staff and the *iqta* of Baran, Shams-i-Moin got a fabulous reward from him for a poem of praise. The poet is reported to have approached the court singers and made them commit his poem to memory and recite it at the *nauroz* celebration. Malik Chhaju gave the singers 10,000 *tankahs*,[77] while the poet got a full stable of horses. Barani also quotes the following couplet from his poem:

شہ علاء الدین اُلغ قتلغ، معظم باربک
پور کشلی خان معظم خسرو روی زمین

Shah Alauddin, Ulugh Qutlugh, the exalted Barbak,
the son of the exalted Kishli Khan, is the lord of the earth.

To conclude, poetry produced in India during the thirteenth century supplements contemporary chronicles. The verses contained in the anthologies and histories as well as the surviving few *diwans* of the early Indo-Persian poets not only tell us about the roles of the nobles and Sultans but also extend our understanding of the life and culture in the Delhi sultanate. We also find information on the scientific instruments and ideas that had found their way into India. It will be no exaggeration to say that we are provided by poets with better insights into the concepts of love, beauty, religion, moral and cultural values of the elite of the early sultanate period than by the chronicles. The *qasidas* as well as other medieval literary works await historical scrutiny.

NOTES

1. Iqbal Husain published his *Early Persian Poets of India* in 1937. It is a pioneering effort highlighting the importance of the Persian poets of Lahore under the Ghaznavid rulers. As for poets who flourished under the early Sultans of Delhi, only Tajuddin Reza, Shihabuddin Mihmara and 'Amid Sunami have been dealt with. No mention is made of so many other poets who were able to make their mark as outstanding literary figures. Cf. Iqbal Husain, *Early Persian Poets of India*, Patna, 1937, p. 4.
2. Masud S'ad Salman, *Diwan*, Tehran, AD 1860, p. 241.
3. Ibid., 89.

4. Minhaj-i-Siraj Juzjani, *Tahaqai-i-Nasiri*, vol. I, ed. Abdul Nai Habibi, Kabul, 1963, p. 405.
5. Hasan Nizami, *Taj-ul-Mathir*, Ms., British Library, London, no. Add. 7623, ff. 128a-b; also *Tabaqat-i-Nasiri*, op. cit., vol. II, Kabul, 1964, pp. 163-4, for merchants.
6. Clifford Edmund Bosworth, *The Later Ghaznavids: Splendour and Decay*, Edinburgh (Univ. Press), 1977, pp. 127-8.
7. Cf. Sadiduddin Muhammad Awfi, my translation, *Perso-Arabic Sources on the Life and Conditions in the Sultanate of Delhi*, New Delhi, 1992, pp. 5, 6, 7.
8. Sadiduddin Muhammad Awfi, *Lubab-ul-Albab*, ed. E.G. Browne, Muhammad Qazvini and Said Nafisi, Tehran, 1341 Shamsi, p. 205.
9. Ibid., i/188-9.
10. *Tabaqat-i-Nasiri*, i/416.
11. The *Amir-i-dad* was next to the *sipahsalar* (military governor) in order of seniority. He supervised the distribution of booty and decided cases relating to armymen and the state.
12. *Lubab-ul-Albab*, p. 418; *Tabaqat-i-Nasiri*, i/419-21.
13. Capitals in Khurasan and Central Asia were called *Hazrat* out of respect. Minhaj also refers to Uchh as *Hazrat*. *Tabaqat-i-Nasiri*, i/418.
14. *Fathnama Bilad-i-Sind* or *Chachnama*, ed. N.B. Baloch, Islamabad, 1983, pp. 4-5; also *Lubab-ul-Albab*, pp. 418-20.
15. *Lubab-ul-Albab*, pp. 420-2.
16. Ibid., p. 426.
17. Loc. cit.
18. *Tabaqat-i-Nasiri*, i/369-370, 420.
19. Cf. Iqtidar Husain Siddiqui, *Perso-Arabic Sources on the Life and Conditions in the Sultanate of Delhi*, 1992, pp. 30, 34-5, hereafter cited as *Perso-Arabic Sources*.
20. No doubt, there had been some early poets both in India and foreign countries who composed *ghazals* but they could not make *ghazal* a popular branch of Persian poetry. As a matter of fact, in those days the success of a great poet rested on his ability to compose a *qasida* or a *mathnavi*. Abul Faraj Runi of Lahore, Anwari and Mujir of Khurasan wrote, besides *qasidas*, *ghazals* but their fame rested on their forceful *qasidas*.
21. Cf. Iqtidar Husain Siddiqui, *Diwan-i-Sahib-i-Barid, Islamic Heritage in South Asian Subcontinent*, Jaipur, 1999, vol. I, pp. 96-109.
22. The *Khutba* drafted by al-Jamji in the name of the Prince is a very important document in that we find that Nasiruddin Mahmud was granted the title of sultan by his father while he was still a minor. Moreover, he was declared by al-Jamji as the legal heir to Sultan Qutbuddin Aibek, the founder of the sultanate because of his being the grandson of the latter. His mother is reported to have been the daughter of Sultan Qutbuddin Aibek whom Iltutmish married in Delhi after his accession to the throne. Cf. *Perso-Arabic Sources*, p. 6; Minhaj also mentions the eldest son of Sultan Nasiruddin Qubacha born of the daughter

of Sultan Qutbuddin Aibek with his royal title, suggesting that the crown prince could be called the Sultan during this period.

Tabaqat-i-Nasiri, i/418. The Khalji inscription of Bengal corroborates both Awfi and Minhaj-i-Siraj Juzani because it mentions the crown prince and son of Sultan Ghiyasuddin Iwaz Khalji as a sultan, although his father was alive. Cf. *Epigraphia Indica: Arabic and Persian Supplement*, ed. Z.A. Desai, 1975, New Delhi, 1983, an *Early Thirteenth Century Inscription from West Bengal*, ed. Z.A. Desai, pp. 6-12; also Abdul Karim, disagreeing with Z.A. Desai, says that Ali Shir was not an independent Sultan but called the Sultan as heir apparent as mentioned in the inscription. Cf. *Corpus of the Arabic and Persian Inscriptions of Bengal,* Dhaka, 1992, pp. 18-27.

23. Siraji is one of a few poets whose *diwans* have been preserved. In 1972, Nazir Ahmad published a critical edition with introduction and notes in English. *Diwan-i-Siraj Khurasani*, Aligarh Muslim University, Aligarh, 1972.
24. *Diwan-i-Siraji Khurasani*, op. cit., couplet, 19, p. 304.
25. The term vilayat was used by Indo-Persian writers for Transoxiana and Khurasan, the latter region now included in modern Afghanistan. Cf. Iqtidar Husain Siddiqui, 'Evolution of the vilayet, the Shiqq and the Sarkar during the Sultanate Period', *Medieval India Quarterly*, vol. V, nos. 1-4, Aligarh, 1963, pp. 10-15.
26. *Tabaqat-i-Nasiri*, i/461; Eng. tr. Major H.G. Raverty, vol. I (rpt., New Delhi, 1970), p. 647.
27. Fakhruddin Mubarak Shah Qawwas was one of the leading scholars of the court of Alauddin Khalji. Cf. Zia uddin Barani, *Tarikh-i-Firuz Shahi*, Calcutta, 1862, p. 353.
28. Hasan Sijzi, *Fawaid ul-Fuad*, Lucknow, p. 213.
29. *Muntakhab-ut-Tawarikh*, Calcutta, 1868, vol. I, p. 65.
30. *Farhang-i-Qawwas*, ed. Nazir Ahmad, Reza Library, Rampur, 1999, p. 112.
31. Mention made by Shaikh Nizam Uddin Auliya of Taj Reza as Khwaja Taj Reza shows that he was remembered with respect by sufis after his death. Hasan Sijzi, *Fawaid ul-Fuad*, p. 68.
32. *Farhang-i-Qawwas*, ed. Nazir Ahmad, Reza Library, Rampur, 1999, pp. 54-5.
33. *Tabaqat-i-Nasiri*, i/447, for details about the event.
34. *Farhang-i-Qawwas*, p. 297, also Iqbal Husain, *The Early Persian Poets of India*, Patna University, Patna, 1937, p. 154.
35. Muhammad Bihamad Khani, *Tarikh-i-Muhammadi*, Ms., British Library, London, Or 137, ff. 345 a-b, also Abdul Qadir Badauni, *Muntakhab-ut-Tawarikh*, Calcutta, vol. I, p. 97; *Farhang-i-Qawwas*, p. 55; *Muntakhab-ut-Tawarikh*, Eng. tr. Ranking, vol. I, p. 97.
36. *Farhang-i-Qawwas*, p. 148.
37. *Farhang-i-Qawwas*, pp. 54-5, 148.
38. Shaikh Nizamuddin Auliya quoted this couplet in the presence of the visitors

to his *khanqah*. His statement also reveals that Shams Dabir became jobless and faced adverse circumstances. Shaikh Fariduddin Gaj-i-Shakar prayed for his employment and then he joined Balban's son Bughra Khan as his *dabir* (secretary). *Fawaid ul-Fuad*, pp. 68, 127-8.

39. *The Early Persian Poets of India*, op. cit., pp. 159-60.
40. *Tarikh-i-Muhammadi*, op. cit., ff. 344b-345a.
41. *Muntakhab-ut-Tawarikh*, vol. 1, p. 66.
42. *Tarikh-i-Muhammadi*, ff. 343b-344a.
43. The *Munis-ul-Ahrar* is a fourteenth-century anthology, containing *qasidas* and other poems composed by Persian poets of Iran, Central Asia and India. The verses have been quoted at length to show how poets of talent could skilfully make use of figures of speech and historical flourishes. The rare manuscript copy of this work is available in the Habib Ganj collection of the Maulana Azad Library, Aligarh Muslim University, Aligarh. Its folios have not been marked. Cf. Ahmad bin Muhammad Kulati, *Munis-ul-Ahrar*, Ms., p. 1176; Nazir Ahmed, 'Some Little Known Indo-Persian Poets of the Thirteenth Century', *Studies in Indian Culture*; *Ghulam Yazdani Commemoration Volume*, ed. H.K. Sherwani, Hyderabad, 1966, p. 167.
44. It was a celebrated work related to the art of governance.
45. *Tarikh-i-Firuz Shahi*, p. 145.
46. *Munis-ul-Ahrar*, Ms., pp. 1136, 1137-8 (folios have not been marked); *Tarikh-i-Muhammadi*, op. cit., ff. 343b-344a. *Khulasat-ul-Ash'ar*, f. 289b.
47. *Tarikh-i-Firuz Shahi*, p. 111.
48. *Munis-ul-Ahrar*, p. 1080.
49. Ibid., p. 913.
50. Ibid., A 913; *Khulasat ul-Ash'ar*, 330a.
51. *Muqadimma to the Ghurrat ul-Kalam, in Kuliyat*, Ms., British Library, London, nos. 21, 104, f. 176b.
52. *The Early Persian Poets of India*, op. cit., pp. 163, 164-5.
53. Abdul Qadir Badauni was born in Rajasthan but adopted Badaun for his permanent settlement where he was granted land by Emperor Akbar. Perhaps, the same was the case with Shihab Mihmara. Cf. *Muntakhab-ut-Tawarikh*, vol. I, pp. 70-1; Eng. tr. Ranking, vol. I, pp. 99-100.
54. Ibid., pp. 100, 101.
55. Gurkhani Silk was imported from China. It was called after the name of the Qarakhitai ruler, Gur Khan.
56. *Muntakhab-ut-Tawarikh*, vol. I, p. 75; Eng. tr. Ranking, vol. I, p. 106.
57. Cf. *The Early Persian Poets of India*, pp. 186-9.
58. Baths in the royal palaces had their inside walls decorated with frescoes of animals and flowers during medieval times.
59. Cf. Nazir Ahmad, 'Some Little Known Indo-Persian Poets of the Thirteenth Century', *Ghulam Yazdani Commemoration Volume*, ed. H.K. Sherwani, Hyderabad, 1966, p. 163; also *The Early Persian Poets of India*, pp. 192-3.

60. Cf. *Perso-Arabic Sources*, op. cit., pp. 68-9, for details about Sultan Muhammad bin Izz Uddin Balban of Multan.
61. 'Some Little Known Indo-Persian Poets of the Thirteenth Century', op. cit., p. 165.
62. *Perso-Arabic Sources*, pp. 68-9.
63. Cf. *Munis-ul-Ahrar*, pp. 1112-13, 1166-70.
64. Amid's *qasidas* and other poems are found incorporated in different *tazkiras* and anthologies, compiled during medieval times. This indicates how valuable his contribution to poetry was considered. The anthology *Munis-ul-Ahrar*, compiled by Ahmad bin Muhammad Kulabi Isfahani, *Majmu 'a-i Lataif-o Safina*, by Saif Jam Harevi (Ms., British Library, London, Or. 4110) and the fifteenth century *Tarikh-i Muhammadi* of Muhammad Bihamad Khani (Ms. British Library, London, Or. 137) are the earliest works that contain a good number of his poems. Nazir Ahmad has collected all the verses and published the critically edited text with notes and introduction both in English and Persian. However, some of the patrons praised by Amid have not been identified as I could point out. Cf. *Diwan-i Amid Lowiki*, Lahore, 1984; *Perso-Arabic Sources*, pp. 67-9, for the identification of historical personages.
65. Cf. *Diwan-i Amid Lowiki*, op. cit., pp. 37-40.
66. Ibid., p. 98, for the royal title of the Sultan in *qasida*.
67. Ibid., lines 15 16, 17 18, p. 100.
68. Ranking's translation of the couplet is incorrect because he misread the term *Ishraf* as *Ishraq* and confuses it with Shihabuddin al-Maqtul's doctrine of *Ishraq* (Illumination). Cf. *Muntakhab-ut-Tawarikh*, vol. I, Eng. tr., p. 81.
69. Rashiduddin Fazlullah, *Jami 'ul Tawarikh*, published by Karl Jahn under the title, Rashiduddin's *History of India*, The Hague, 1965, p. 72; also Iqtidar Husain Siddiqui, 'Politics and Conditions in the Territories under the Occupation of Central Asian Rulers in North-Western India', *Central Asiatic Journal*, Wiesbaden, vol. XXVII, nos. 3-4, pp. 88-90, n. 3; also *Perso-Arabic Sources*, p. 70.
70. Cf. Ghurat ul-Kalam, cited by Wahid Mirza, *The life and Works of Amir Khusrau*, Delhi, rpt., 1974, pp. 39-40.
71. *Tarikh-i-Muhammadi*, ff. 538 a-b.
72. Hasan Sijzi, *Fawaid ul-Fuad*, Lucknow, pp. 68, 127-8.
73. *Fawaid ul-Fuad*, op. cit., pp. 213-14.
74. Cf. *The Life and Works of Amir Khusrau*, op. cit., pp. 38, 39, 111.
75. *Muntakhab-ut-Tawarikh*, vol. I, Eng. tr., p. 134.
76. Ibid., pp. 136-7.
77. Wahid Mirza says that each of the musician got 10,000 *tankahs*. But Barani's statement is: He gave the *matriban* (singers) 10,000 *tankahs*. Cf. *The Life and Works of Amir Khusrau*, p. 36; *Tarikh-i-Firuz Shahi*, pp. 113-14.

Pre-Modern Concepts of Time in Indo-Muslim Historical Writing

PETER HARDY

Muslim experiences of life in South Asia had, by the middle of the eighteenth century, diverged significantly from those in western Asia and Iran, where certain notions of time, so profoundly and magisterially stated by Louis Massignon,[1] had, by the end of the twelfth century (when the Muslim conquest of central north India began) come into being. In South Asia, Muslims could dominate, or create, great city centres; physically damage 'Hindu' centres of worship and learning; and apply or divert revenues to the support of the teacher and maintainers of the religion and culture of Islam, but the countryside remained profoundly 'Hindu' in sentiment. Popular non-Muslim religious traditions such as the *bhakti*, the *sant* and the *sikh* may even have been invigorated by the presence of Muslims. In the political sphere, although Muslims established two large-scale empires, the sultanate of Delhi and the Mughal imperium and half a dozen regional kingdoms over large areas of South Asia, they ruled through rather than over armed Hindu chiefs. In the sixteenth century, Abu'l Fazl included an account of 'Hindu culture' in his 'gazetteer' of the empire, the *A'in-i Akbari*. About the same time the great religious epics formative of Hindu civilization, the *Mahabharata* and the *Ramayana*, were, with Akbar's encouragement, rendered into Persian.

An investigator into medieval Indo-Muslim ideas of time might with reason, therefore, anticipate that some elements new to the classical formative period of an inclusive imperious Islamic culture might be discovered. The Indo-Muslim historiography available is bulky.[2] It ranges from universal histories through regional dynastic histories to accounts of one decade of a single reign. Historians write in periods when Muslim political power in India is on the rise, is at a zenith and is in decline. They write in periods when Muslim immigrants to South Asia, and Muslim numbers in South Asia, were relatively few and small and in periods when (as in Mughal times) they obtrude easily upon the attention of foreign travellers. For the purposes of this paper it has been possible, across a period of about five centuries (AD 1200 to 1750), only to sample some materials: poetical epics, versified narratives and biographies have been excluded. But a sufficiently wide range of histories has been consulted to be able to state whether anticipations of some novelties in Muslim notions of time and in Indo-Muslim pre-modern historical writing, have been gratified.

With their use of such expressions as *dar an zaman*, *dar in zaman* (in that time, in this time), *dar in asna*, *dar in wala* (in the meantime, during all this time, or business) *dar azmina mazi* (in past times), Indo-Muslim historians are clearly thinking in the dimension of before and after, and, with their use of various calendars—the *hijra* calendar, the Persian solar year calendar and, in Mughal times, a regnal year calendar, in a dimension with precise calibrations. In their use of such expressions as *'ahd* (age, epoch), *ruzgar* (age), *dawr* (period), *muddat* (period), *hangam* (time, season) or *az waqa'i' in aiyam* (from the events of these days) it is ambiguous whether the historians conceive time as a river or flow of events, or as a sequence of instants. Contexts which stress the importance of a birth or a royal installation occurring at a precise moment would suggest the latter. However, events and human deeds are so described as to convey the historians' assumption that any event, to be meaningful from a practical and empirical standpoint, needs more than one instant in which to occur.

The setting of events in the relation of before and after, and at calibrated intervals—the minute, the hour, the day, the week, the year—is seen by all historians as a setting creating by God. Indo-Muslim histories in Persian mostly begin with a grateful acknowledgement of the Divine Grace and Bounty in bringing the inanimate and the animate world into existence, for creating man and for sending His Messengers and specifically Muhammad the Prophet, to guide man towards the fulfilment of his destiny, which is to return to God in obedience to His Commandments. Man is, so to speak, boxed in by God's creative power. The sequence of events in the created world cannot, unless God so wills it, open out the possibilities or stretch the circumscriptions of human existence, or change the given forms of inanimate and animate species.

Mankind, moreover, does not resemble an agitated ant-heap. Looking back over the past, historians saw on-going structures in men's collective lives. The world's peoples have a common inheritance from an original stock, expressing itself in a unitary sequence of significant personages. Minhaj-i-Siraj Juzjani in his *Tabaqat-i Nasiri* (*c*. 1260) sees all rulers as descended from Adam.[3] Kaimars, progenitor of the (pre-Islamic period) rulers of Iran, is stated to be a son of Adam. Writing in the second decade of the seventeenth century, Khwaja Ni'mat ullah depicts the Afghans as from Adam through Saul, Jacob and Abraham.[4] Time as events is also given shape and direction through the deeds of those whom God has singled out as prophets and scholars, and those whom God has singled out as protectors and enforcers of His guidance (when it takes the form of law), namely caliphs and kings. Indo-Muslim histories as widely separate in time and focus as the *Tabaqat-i Nasiri*, 'Abd al-Baqi's *Ma'asir-i Rahimi* (1630s), Firishta's *Gulshan-i Ibrahimi* (early seventeenth-century), Muhammad Khan's *Mirat-i Ahmadi* (1756-67, centred on events in Gujarat) all see time as organized around rulers performing God-created functions. Some historians assimilate formally non-Muslim rulers of Iran and Central Asia into this pattern. In the fourteenth century the historian Ziya al-din Barani[5] looks to such Iranian folk heroes as Jamshid for advice on kings' good practice, and Abu'l Fazl traces Akbar's descent back to Adam through a succession of Turkish and Mongol rulers. The treatment of the 'careers' of these intended agents and protectors of an Islamic dispensation tends to be organized according to a rigid chronological framework, that is by generation subdivided by region (as by Minhaj-i-Siraj Juzjani), by *hijra* year, or by regnal year. The nearest to a treatment by theme is that of Ziya al-din Barani where events are arranged within each sultan's reign in such a manner as to convey each ruler's qualifications as a true Islamic ruler.

Many Indo-Muslim historians treat events in sequence as signs and symbols of a reality more abiding, and of a meaning more dire, than that which they have in their purely temporal context. Events are seen as warnings and portents which must be read correctly if man is not to suffer in both this world and the next. 'Abd-Allah, author of the early seventeenth-century *Ta'rikh-i Da'udi*, informs his readers that a knowledge of history is not (merely) for obtaining information about the situations (*ahwal*) of earlier sultans, it is a science for increasing awareness and for providing warnings for the pure in heart (*ahl-i safa*).[6] Two other historians writing in the Mughal period, Ahmad Yadgar (in his *Ta'rikh-i Shahi*[7]) and Shaikh Ilahdad Faizi Sirhindi,[8] convey that God informs his servants, through the medium of tradition and report, of the good and bad of past events so that they may take heed (*'ibrat*). Abu'l Fazl tends to find in events a moral or an inner significance which the ignorant and unheeding will miss without his, Abu'l Fazl's, instruction.[9] One of the most systematic expositions of the didactic force of events in time properly understood is to be found in Barani's *Ta'rikh-i Firuz Shahi*.[10] His account of the reign of 'Ala al-din Khalji of Delhi (1296-1316) illustrates Barani's belief that events are signs and symbols. Worldly men believed the political and military success of that sultan to be attributable to his own talents, but godly men with eyes to see knew that his success should be attributed to the spiritual efficacies of Nizam al-din Auliya of Delhi.[11]

Although medieval Indo-Muslim historians assume that temporal events will end inevitably in the Day of Account, at an Hour which God alone will determine, they do not conceive that the course of events will move smoothly, and in one direction only, towards that consummation. There is no steady progress in human history, indeed the quality of later human behaviour will never equal that which characterize the period of the Prophet Muhammad and his Companions. The uniquely best period for mankind was when the words and deeds of the Prophet and of his Companions formed instantly (with the Koran) man's knowledge and understanding of Divine Commandment. Many historians indirectly reveal their assumption that this is so by praising Muhammad and his Companions in the exordia to their histories; Ziya al-din Barani states his position clearly in his *Fatawa-i Jahandari*, a work on the *adab* (proper behaviour) of rulers, rather than a *ta'rikh*, when he puts into the mouth of Mahmud of Ghazna the statement that, by reason of the unbelief and innovations that prevail in the later times of kingly rule in Islam, it is impossible to rule according to the *sunna*, the model practice of the Prophet and of the Muslim community in the time of the first four 'rightly-guided' caliphs (632-61).[12] Within the sphere of leadership of the Muslim community after the Prophet's death, Abdul Hamid Lahori in his *Badshah Nama* of Shah Jahan's reign (1628-58) depicts decline running from the end of the rule of the early caliphs (AD 661) and covering the period of the sultans[13]—but there is a dramatic improvement with the accession of Shah Jahan. Many historians depict the coming to power of the ruler of their own time and place as a moment of the renewal of truth, justice and good behaviour. Even Ziya al-din Barani depicts a remarkable change in the course of events with the acceptance of Firuz Shah (1351-88) as Delhi Sultan. An account of this reign as a golden age is given by Shams al-din Siraj 'Afif, writing after the sack of Delhi by Timur in 1398.[14] Some historians of Aurangzib's reign treat his becoming *padshah* after a struggle with his brothers as the outcome of a divine decision to reverse an age of decay by a renewed dispensation of justice.[15] Sometimes the account of the installation of a new ruler and of the sequence of events in his period is so structured as to suggest that a revival of the application of divine law occurs at the beginning of the reign, only to weaken and to need another revival at the beginning of the next reign.[16] Historians writing after the death of Aurangzeb and the war of succession of 1712, see their time as ones of moral decay, confusion, faction presided over by a palsied ruling house unable to assert its authority.[17]

The historian who most suggests that events in time occur in a rightly-directed sequence is Akbar's historiographer, Abu'l Fazl: for him history has culminated in an age when a perfect man illumined by Divine Light, namely Akbar, is conducting the world's affairs. But the manner in which he treats rebellion against Akbar suggests that it is only through the God-created presence of Akbar that the true and the right have the edge over error and wrong.[18]

The precise sequences of instants that are described as 'time' are treated as of utmost consequence by many historians. In histories written in the Mughal period, great attention is paid to the right relationship of the terrestrial instant to the extra-terrestrial instant judged relevant the most significant relationship is often depicted as astrological. Computations to discover the most auspicious moment, the one when the heavenly bodies are in that affiliation or configuration that will ensure good fortune, success and prosperity to beings in the sub-lunar world are often referred to. Muslim historians did not question that God had provided signs for mankind in the heavens or that He moves the stars and the planets in ways integrally linked to movements and events on earth. Abu'l Fazl provides an instructive account of how, when Akbar was about to be born, the attendant astrologer was very disturbed that, as his mother's labour was going, Akbar was going to be born at a most inauspicious moment. The inauspicious moment passed, however, when Akbar's mother was startled out of labour by the ugly appearance of a mid-wife; when the right moment, chosen by God, arrived, Akbar was born.[19] Other histories bear witness to the importance attached to selecting the right moment for royal installation ceremonies or (a thirteenth-century example) for entering a city.[21] Sometimes, a special horror is seen to attach to the juxtaposition of two events. Thus it was a sign of the awfulness of the murder of the Delhi Sultan, Jalaluddin Khalji, that it occurred about the time of *iftar*.[22] A special virtue was on the other hand, attributed to Firuz Shah for wanting to wear royal dress over his mourning dress for Muhammad b. Tughluq, after reluctantly accepting the throne.[23]

Time as measured by the calendar is not something to be wasted. As personages with responsibility for maintaining peace, order and religion, sultan should be seen to organize their days and nights to the best effect. Humayun is depicted as so arranging his activities within weekly periods that each day is associated with particular categories of worthy and serious persons, and with specific functions.[24] Time spent by rulers offering supererogatory prayers at night is time well spent; as is time spent listening to the reading of improving literature.[25] Time spent in frivolity and self-indulgence, especially if one is a ruler, will be time that brings nemesis.[26]

But however sober, orderly or responsible men may be in their actions, they should not put their trust in those actions. Sequences of actions are deceptive and treacherous; they do not last. It is human presumption and folly to believe that what has happened in the past will give any assurance as to the future. The fifteenth-century *Ta'rikh-i Mubarak Shahi* in effect personifies time and the heavens, and rhetorically declares, 'It is evident to those with certain knowledge and cool experience that the shameless heavens and conspiring time bring forth in playful fancy all manner of tricks . . . and display them before the eyes of the vain and short-sighted.'[27] The author refers to the killing of Jalaluddin Khalji by 'Alauddin Khalji: 'Have you seen what the tyrannical sphere and its stars have done? Do not mention the heavens, nor their revolutions nor time. How it has cast the sun of the kingdom into the dust—let dust be on the brilliant sun of the celestial sphere.'

Other historians, writing about historical periods wherein there is a general consensus that they were periods of decline in Muslim dynastic authority, tend to express their dismay at the turn of events by sombre musing on the untrustworthiness of time. Khafi Khan, author of the *Muntakhab al-Lubab* (finished about 1730-1), who writes about a revolution in the government of the kingdom (*inqilab-i sultanat-i mulk*), reflects that God has favoured man with eyes, ears and intelligence to observe the transience of human good fortune in this fleeting life. One may spend one's time in the enjoyment of power and success amid the distress of one's contemporaries, but in the end, will receive due punishment.[28] Another historians of this period, Kamwar Khan, expresses surprise at the 'trickery' (*nirangi*) of divine decree; surprise at what can appear in the twinkling of an eye from the world of the unseen (*al-ghayb*), at what blood of rulers 'off beam' (*kaj-kallah*) has been shed, and how whole lineages have been levelled with the dust.[29] The use of such expressions as *ruzgar-i na-paydar* (the fickle and transitory age), *zaman-i sitamgar* (the cruel and oppressive age), *zamana-i kaj-raftar* (the time that is going away) is common. (This kind of language in our historians may be merely their idiom of conveying the familiar and general dismay of humankind that human intentions and actions rarely turn out according to hopes and expectations.)

Some medieval historians depict events 'in the dimension of before and after' as occurring at different levels of being. The believed significance of events in the celestial sphere, the regard paid to astrological calculation has already been referred to. There are also frequent allusions to the unseen world, the '*alam-i ghayb*, and its relations to the terrestrial world. The events of the early sixteenth century in northern India, when first the Central Asian Mughals led by Babur established a regime, were expelled in 1540 by Sher Shah, but afterwards make a come-back in 1555-6, greatly exercised historians, especially those who write later, in Akbar and Jahangir's time, when early Mughal failures might seem to need some explaining or explaining away. Perhaps the classic reference to the dimension of the '*alam al-ghayb* is that in 'Abbas Sarwani's *Ta'rikh-i Sher Shah* where he describes Humayun's defeat by Sher Shah at the battle of Qanauj in 1540. God had wished that His creatures should rest and prosper under the new rule by Sher Shah and his Sur successors, but also that Humayun should after some years return to power in India. Hence, for Humayun's own survival and protection, God enabled Humayun to see that men from the world of the unseen (*mardan-i ghayb*) were fighting against his forces and turning his cavalry horses away from the battlefield. When Humayun saw these men from another world in action, he submitted to God's command (*amr*) and abandoned the battlefield to the *mardan-i ghayb*.[30] Ahmad Yadgar's *Ta'rikh-i Shahi*, completed in Jahangir's time, suggests in effect that there were two worlds of events in being: at the mundane level, the Surs were in charge, but in the '*alam-i ghayb* the restoration of Humayun is foretokened.[31] Sher Shah was mortally wounded at the siege of Kalinjar in 1545; he himself had earlier received an intimation from the *ghayb* not to undertake an assault on the fortress, but, as the pen of divine decree had already written that he would, the intimation was to no avail.[32] At this point there appears to be a 'hierarchy of being' of which Sher Shah's death is a sign: first, divine decree or *qaza*, second, an inspiration from the *ghayb* (*mulham-i ghayb*), and third, the explosion which mortally burnt Sher Shah. The *ghayb* appears in other contexts too. Badauni, a historian of Akbar's time, describes an unsuccessful attempt on the young Akbar's life in 1564 as an admonition from the unseen world (*tanbihat-i ghaybi*)[33]—it is suggested that Akbar had had designs on the wives of some of his entourage. In the middle of the eighteenth century, an account of Nawab Alivardi Khan of Bengal attributes the rise of members of his family to prominence to angelic assistance from the *ghayb*.[34]

Some historians included sequences of magical events in their histories. Such sequences are noticeable in a history of the Lodi and Sur sultanates of Delhi, the *Ta'rikh-Da'udi*. Magic capacities are attributed to Sultan Sikandar Lodi (1489-1517), in whose reign also there lived a magician capable of creating a fruit garden in Jodhpur in the twinkling of an eye.[35]

In my reading I have come across just one sequence of events entirely located in the world of dreams. Ni'mat ullah in the *Ta'rikh-i Khan Jahan Lodi* says that before the defeat in 1540 of Humayun by Sher Shah at Qanauj, Sher Shah dreamt that he and Humayun were summoned before the Prophet 'seated on the throne of the Holy Law' to be told that God had bestowed Humayun's kingdom on Sher Shah. The crown and diadem were removed from Humayun's head and placed on Sher Shah's.[36] To repeat terrestrial time, is depicted as a sequence, or rather, many sequences of actions and events, placed in the relationships of before and after and of simultaneity, with the actions' and events' distance from the observers' 'now', calibrated by various calendrical systems (for Muslim historians of course, principally the lunar system calculated from the first day of the lunar year in which the Prophet Muhammad's migration (*hijra*) from Mecca to Medina took place, reckoned to coincide with 16 July 622).

But are there contexts in which the historians place an 'event' or 'events' (*waqi'a, waqi'at, saniha, sawanih*)? All historians use verbs of action in sentences that convey that an event embraces many actions in sequence: sultans and their officers attack, besiege, march, hold conversations or give orders or flee in specific directions. These events are held in some narrative unity by being, so to speak, 'attached' to a person holding a ruling position for some time. This, the most common framework, can however be encapsulated within a lengthier sequence of events—the establishment of Islam in India, the onslaught of the Mongols on the territories of Islam, the Maratha incursions into Mughal Gujarat, for example.[37] Minhaj al-Siraj, writing in India about 1260 treats the Mongol invasions of the Muslim world as an apocalyptic event; he retails a *hadis* from the Prophet that the day of resurrection will not occur until his *umma* (community) has been slaughtered.[38] In my view, the medieval Indo-Muslim history that offers the most systematic thematic representation of history is Ziya al-din Barani's *Ta'rikh-i Firuz Shahi.* He specifically states that in his account of the reign of Muhammad b. Tughluq, he has not 'concerned himself with the arrangement in order of every victory, of the beginning and end of every event (*sarguzashti*—also 'story' or 'narration') or every revolt'.[39] His treatment of the reign of 'Ala uddın Khalji groups events as often undated narratives of success, punctuated with warnings to readers that they should not draw wrong conclusions about the causes and the consequences of this worldly accomplishment. The Mughal historian most critical of his contemporaries at a time when Mughal power was being effectively established, namely Badauni, keeps broadly to a grouping of events by year, but his treatment of the discussions on religious questions in Akbar's Ibadat Khana at Fathpur Sikri is not so structured. Badauni indeed offers a 'situational preparation' for these discussions by referring to the background of Akbar's political and military successes by the time the discussions began. (Badauni also passes a general judgement on the outcome of these events in the Ibadat Khana: 'after five or six years no trace of Islam remained and circumstances became topsy-turvy'.)[40]

Some historians offer general comparisons between identified sequences of events widely separated in time. 'Afif contrasts the period of 'Ala uddin Khalji with that of Firuz Shah. In the former period, the sultan did not grant the income from villages directly to his soldiers because he feared their building up of local followings. But Firuz Shah, being among the *awliya* (friends) of God, was able to disregard such thoughts and confer villages freely upon the soldiery without fear of consequences.[41] Mubarak ullah Wajih, writing in 1714, conveys that he is going to write about a number of general historical phenomena, the like of which there has not been for the last thousand years: a revolution in the state of the world, the conflict of ruling personages, the death of so many royal princes and the destruction of many old prestigious noble houses.[42] In the literature, conventional panegyric abounds: never before the rule of Sultan 'X' has the currency of the Muslim holy law been so unfettered, or the property of the people so well protected, or the price of corn so low. But however conventional such asservations may appear, they do constitute historical generalizations and judgements which imply that, as a human being with human curiosity, the writer cannot visualize a temporal instant to be a meaningful whole in itself.

This leads us to the question whether our historians attach concepts of duration to their concepts of time. In his 'Time in Islamic Thought',[43] Louis Massignon remarks that

> for the Musulman theologian time is not a continuous 'duration' but a constellation, a 'galaxy' of instants. . . . For Islam, which is occasionalist, and apprehends the divine causality only in its actual 'efficacy', there exists only the instant, . . . the 'twinkling of an eye', . . . the laconic announcement of a judicial decision of God, conferring upon our nascent act His decree (*hukm*), which will be proclaimed on the day when the cry of Justice . . . is heard.

Massignon further states that

> the only perfect, self-sufficient instant is the Hour (*Sa'a*), the hour of the Last Judgment, the final summation of the decrees of all the responsibilities incurred . . . all the other days are imperfect, insufficient to themselves; for the decree that

they proclaim is fulfilled only after a delay (*imhal*), at the end of a certain period. . . . It is actually through this idea of a 'period' that the notion of 'duration' was introduced obliquely into Islamic thought; here 'duration' is the silent interval between the two divine instants, the announcement and the sanction (i.e. the penalty or reward). . . . In the Koran the second 'instant', that of the sanction, is called the term (*ajal*) or more precisely the marked term (*ajal musamma*).

Massignon asserted that the variable period between the announcement (i.e. God's *qaza* or decision in eternity) and the penalty or reward is an interval which 'the responsible man must use for expiation in order to conjure the sanction (which remains inevitable)'. One passage in an Indo-Muslim medieval history has been encountered which is in line with Massignon's assertion: Muhammad Saqi Musta'idd Khan in his *Ma'asir-i 'Alamgiri* (completed in 1710-11), describes how a Mughal officer, Khanzad Khan—given the epithet of 'one who brings divine decree, *qaza* to pass'—is deputed to bring to heel a Hindu chief in the Deccan, one Padiya Nayak. Even though the latter does not believe in the Day of Judgement, when he sees the forces of Khanzad Khan plundering his territories he decides to submit, because, Musta'idd Khan writes, he sees the destruction as a token of divine judgement or decree (*hukm*) and of the day of resurrection (*hashr*).[44]

Now, the usages of the historians studied certainly suggest that, for most of them most of the time, there are entities having a duration beyond the instant. In his account of conversations with Muhammad b. Tughluq, Barani describes the sultan as saying that his kingdom is 'ill' (*mariz*) and as asking what earlier rulers have said about the sicknesses of realms (*amraz-i mulki*). (The text of the *Fatawa-i Jahandari* shows that this is Barani's own language too.)[45] The *Ma'asir-i Jahangiri* describes the world as having a different constitution (*nihad*) after the accession of Jahangir;[46] the '*Amal-i Salih* also refers to the age (*ruzgar*) having a temperament or constitution (*mizaj*).[47] But caution is perhaps needed before concluding that the use of such metaphors proves that the historians do *not* hold to an occasionalist ontology. The metaphors of 'sickness' and of 'constitution' may be just that—metaphors. When 'Abbas Sarwani eulogizes[48] the security of person and property under Sher Shah, he does so by listing the particular good deeds that were done or the particular bad deeds that were not done. Although he writes of the prosperity of the country (*ma'muri-i mamlikat*) and of the peace of mind of the cultivators and soldiery, he could be referring to a state of things and a state of mind from moment to moment, that is without duration.

In the absence of systematic exposes by historians of their personal ontological ideas, any conclusion that they were not, as historians, occasionalists, must be drawn from circumstantial and negative evidence. We do not find disorderly listings of events placed in mere sequence—e.g. that a sultan's son killed his father in Delhi, then that the inhabitants of fishing village in the Ganges delta were all drowned in a flood, and then that a husband in Gujarat killed a revenue collector for attempting to seduce his wife, and so on. In the main, medieval Muslim historians place events that express the exercise of power in varied spheres that often overlap—spheres of religious belief and practice, of military and political conflict and of the transfer of resources in a command economy. Such events are carefully grouped, and so suggest the persistence of human relationships and social groupings over a period. The activities of rulers, of their officers, and of rebels are grouped under general concepts with a political and/or geographical connotation. Rulers are referred to as enjoying 'the crown and throne of the sultanate of the country of Delhi' (*taj o takht-i sultanat-i mamlikat-i dehli*). The *Mirat-i Sikandari* describes the activities of the *salatin-i Gujrat*. Firishta, perhaps in his geographical range the most comprehensive historian of medieval India, refers to the independent Muslim rulers south of the Vindhyas generically as 'sultans of the Dekkan'. He refers to particular lines of rulers exercising authority at particular centres either metonymically as, for example, *salatin-i shahr-i ahmadnagar* or eponymically after the title of the founder of an independent line of regionally-centred rulers. But although historians frequently use the term *mulk*—'kingdom', 'power', 'dominion'—to refer to an entity with the duration of worldly authority and the habit of obedience or acquiescence to that authority, the authority appears to be one of persons rather than institutions. Barani[49] blames Malik Kafur, who tried to seize power after the death of 'Ala al-din Khalji, for thinking that that sultan's appointees would automatically transfer their loyalty from the deceased sultan to him, and that continuity and power would be achieved if he but continued implementing 'Ala al-din's regulations.

Medieval Indo-Muslim historians narrate in a manner which presents earlier sequential events as the intelligible antecedents, or conditions, of later events. For example, 'Abbas Sarwani describes Sher Shah, in the period before he expelled Humayun from north India, as switching his allegiance to patrons among the Afghan chiefs, following his (Sher Shah's) dismissal by his father from a fiscal charge which he had managed with success. Sarwani represents Sher Shah as saying, 'These are times of defection and misfortune. Every Afghan who has a following pretends to power and to the seizing of a kingdom.'[50] Abu'l Fazl's account of the rebellions facing Akbar in his eastern territories in 1580-1, includes his interpretation of the 'causes' (*asbab*). The sense of antecedent conditions is often so strong that it, I believe, influences historians' choice of vocabulary. I have argued elsewhere[51] that where acts of resistence against a Muslim ruler in medieval India occur, whether the historians excoriate them with the epithets of rebellion or whether they use epithets expressive of (mere) disturbance or misguided hostility will be related to their awareness of whether a token act of prior submission or allegiance to the ruler had been made.

Yet, I repeat, such modes of representation of the past, apparently entailing a secondary efficacy for earlier events in a sequence, do not prove the historians concerned to have abandoned, rejected or ignored an occasionalist philosophy of time, that is, one which treats time as 'a galaxy of instants' (Massignon's phrase), each of which is the occasion of a divine fiat, related to the next instant only in being willed by the same solely-competent God. For the Islamic occasionalist,[52] being is an array of dimensionless atoms, each totally indeterminate, a point without extension, but with an array or set of accidents, attributes arbitrarily assigned to it by God, which also drop out of existence from moment to moment. Duration is an accident created by God from instant to instant—in effect an appearance that allows man to form (or, rather, God to form for him) an appropriate set of expectations through which he may find his way through life without anomie, personal or collective. For occasionalism, atoms do not really move but are recreated in successive loci at successive instants; to contend otherwise would involve holding that the atom had moved through time and therefore that it had endured. But if time and space are thus quantified into discrete instant and loci, there can be no secondary causation within the being of the instants and loci, for that would accord them substantive continuity. Change in the world for the occassionalist is an appearance brought about by God's allowing some atoms to drop into nothingness, and by His creating new accidents for the recreated atoms. Change is the divine addition or subtraction of atoms and accidents from the succession of galaxies of instants that, as they occur, constitute Creation.

The human perception of antecedent conditions of events and actions, the human grouping of events into a narrative given meaning and direction through general concepts such as 'rulership', 'authority', 'rebellion', 'obedience or disobedience to divine commandment', can be made consistent with occasionalism. I cannot improve on Muhsin Mahdi's exposition in his *Ibn Khaldun's Philosophy of History*:[53]

all objects exist as the result of continuous creation by God in every instant of their existence, and all perception and reasoning consist of separate accidents directly created by God in the substance (*sic*) that is the knower. These accidents were conceived as extrinsic both to the knower and the known: and as discontinuous, customary correlatives of things. Because they are not inherent in the knower or the known and because they do not reflect the nature of things or of the mind, the guarantee of their validity must rest; (1) objectively, on the repeated and uniform creation of the objective correlatives of the act of reasoning by God, and (2) subjectively, on His creation of the same accidents in the mind of the knower when apprehending or reasoning about the same objects. Therefore according to the dialectical theologians knowledge is concerned with the *ad extra* creation and relations of objects, and, consequently it is deprived of all ontological significance. For the enquiry into the nature of things, they substituted the enquiry into the customary relations between objects that are directly created by God in every instance of their existence and the customary relations that are created in the mind when reflecting upon objects.

This could be the position of the Indo-Muslim historians examined. Our historians see divine power acting in history at particular time instants and in sequences of instants. Humayun ordered that a man be trampled to death by an elephant, but that the elephant did not kill him was God's will.[54] After the defeat of Hemu at the battle of Panipat in 1556, God injected merciful sentiments into the minds of Mughal officers so that the people of Delhi were spared the plunder of their city.[55] It was divine decree that Sultan Qutb al-din Aibak fell from his horse and was fatally injured.[56] Sometimes His will is seen as bringing lengthy sequences of events to pass; it was His will and pleasure (*mashi'a*) that Dara Shikoh be defeated in the Mughal succession struggle in 1657-8.[57] God empties the sultanate of Gujarat of justice, so that Akbar may invade and fill it with his justice.

There are, however, some would-be explanatory passages that appear to rest on assumptions that some entities have a 'nature' at earlier moments which portends certain kinds of actions and events at later moments. For example, Barani proclaims that a Hindu convert to Islam, Khusrau Khan (who seized the Delhi sultanate in 1320), had nothing but treachery and rascality in his inner being (*batin*) and acted accordingly.[59] 'Afif describes a functionary God ordained to be *diwan-i Wizarat* in Firuz Tughluq's reign, as having an essence (*zat*), a 'self' from which all attributes of misfortune would be brought forth.[60] 'Afif portrays Firuz Shah as a royal *sufi* whose actions express his *manaqib* (virtues). Abu'l Fazl writes, in his account of events in 985/1577-8, of those who do not have a good destiny by reason of their *fitrat* or original endowment; Abu'l Fazl often describes those with whom Akbar, or his agents, come into collision as having a *bad-gauhar* (a bad 'essence').[61] The mid-eighteenth-century *Ta'rikh-i*

Bangala-i Mahabat-jangi, describes the Nawab of Bengal, Siraj al-Daula, having the 'self' (*zat*) of a coward and poltroon; he is frightened at his own deeds and flees from the battlefield.[62] The principal losing contender in the 1657-8 Mughal succession struggle, Dara Shikoh, has a *zalalat-nihad*, a nature instinct with error.[63] Even if God is conceived as creating a man's nature and his actions in harness from moment to moment, at the very least there is some spatio-temporal contiguity, and from moment-to-moment entities (people) may be expected to act according to this nature, unless there is some specific ground for them not doing so. Nature is a proximate cause not because of logical or inherent necessity, but because that is the way God has arranged His creation. This notion of proximate divine agency was presupposed in medieval India by a historian who described an inverse correlation between divine fiat and created capacities. Mubarak ullah Wajih states that God, having decreed that the career of the Mughal *amir al-umara*, Zu'lfiqar Khan, will come to a certain (disastrous) conclusion, changed everything in his (psychological) nature, temperament, reason and intelligence, so that he began to act vengefully.[64] (This passage also, of course, implies the continuity of an identified human being, Zu'lfiqar Khan; it is his attributes that have been changed by God.) God is the real agent but He acts mediately through characteristics in a human being which He has created at one remove, so to speak, from His decision on that person's worldly end. Time appears to be a continuity between divinely-created characteristics or capacities, and human action.

These notions of mediate divine agency exercised through immanent natures which are features of divine creation, appear to be already within Islamic tradition, by the early thirteenth century. Recent studies of al-Ghazali (1058-1111),[65] (show that both in his works avowedly directed to an examination of the doctrines of the Muslim *faylasuf* and in his other works, al-Ghazali's thought is not to be identified with that of the occasionalists. Though he holds that God has willed everything existing in the perishable corporeal and everlasting spiritual world, and that everything happens in accordance with His decree (*qaza*) His determination (*qadar*), judgement (*hukm*) and will (*mashi'a*), His purposes or ends are brought about by instruments and devices, all part of Divine planning (*tadbir*), a planning which provides for the manner in which entities relate to each other, in conditions which God creates. Al-Ghazali's philosophy of the human individual[66] ascribes to him durable characteristics but not a created unchangeable moral constitution. the soul, created as an immaterial substance (*jawhar*), descends to this world in order to acquire fitness for paradise. Its original disposition (*fitrat*) or nature (*tabi'*) is to seek good and avoid evil, but as it lives in association with a human body, it develops animality and bestiality, with concomitant desire and anger. Man lives on earth in order to attain happiness by a self-discipline which achieves the predominance of the other two faculties of the soul in the world, namely knowledge and justice. Man can improve his moral character by constant practice of good actions and by association with the virtuous, both, however, with the assistance of divine grace. Al-Ghazali's ethical philosophy thus appears to presuppose a soul, human dispositions and faculties which have a duration beyond the instant.

But for all that, I remain unsure that the use by Indo-Muslim historians of the terms *zat*, *gauhar*, *jauhar*, and *nihad* establishes that they are *not* occasionalists in their metaphysical commitments. They could be using such terms routinely to refer to a substratum, momentarily existing, of accidents or attributes, rather than to an entity possessing duration. Or else they could be referring to the momentary aggregation of atoms which together compose a body at an instant, an aggregation brought into existence by the power of God exercised from instant to instant, but an aggregation that will fall out of existence should God not exercise His power of re-creation.

But, whatever the basic philosophy of time-galaxy of instants or duration—Indo-Muslim historians do not write as though the subjective human experience of time should be man's overriding interest and concern. What matters is an objective sequence of events involving human actions which will be assessed for their conformity with divine guidance and commandment on the Day of Account. Medieval Indo-Muslim historians all thought they should preface their accounts of events with acknowledgment of God's existence and bounty in creation—a convention perhaps, but the prefaces show that what happens, has an extra terrestrial setting, that man's theatre of action has been designed and built for him. Time is, ultimately, God's time.

But acknowledgment of God's existence and creative power does not necessarily preclude the setting down of an account of the human experience of events in 'the dimension of before and after'. Babur's 'Memoirs'[67] written under the superscript 'in the name of God, the Merciful, the Compassionate' show Babur to be a believing Muslim. The memoirs contain many accounts of Babur's experience of events and his reactions to them. There are some passages in other histories where historians give their own eyewitness accounts of events, including what a sultan or his officers are supposed to have said.

But it cannot be said that historians set out to discover and to represent human experience. There is a formalism, flatness and stereotyped character in their narrations, in subject-matter and vocabulary, whether they are writing in the thirteenth or in the eighteenth centuries. It is perhaps at this point that theological assumptions do have an explanatory role: human experience is not seen as finally potent, human memories of the past and expectations of the future which find expression in plans of action merely foster an illusion of human creative agency that God will surely dash. History may indeed be the story of the unintended consequences of human intentions and actions (and warnings of the treachery of time may be an idiom for acknowledging this). For Muslim historians to depict time as human awareness and management of situation and change could be to lead men away from their true end, submission to Divine Commandment, and towards the distraction of the meretricious and insubstantial. Man is not created to luxuriate in his own ideas and sensations. Notions of time may be tied to sense perception, but their ontological foundation is not that of sense perception. They rest on the believed fact that God's determination of man deeds from all eternity is not existentiated in this world all at once but in the sequence He decrees. Notions of time are not conceived to exist by reason of some human sensory awareness of change in the world in which man lives. There does appear to be a contrast between the notion of time as an observed sequence of galaxies of instants in the human and in the non-human world, and time as a mode of human perception, the moving experiential perspective of past-present-future. Crudely put, the contrast is between directing attention towards an objective order, the order of divine concern for man, the best of creation because he is the only servant of God with capacity for awareness of servanthood, and directing attention to a subjective order, man's consciousness of himself in relationship to his sensory environment.

But a contrast is not necessarily an antinomy. Divine Providence can be conceived as actively immanent in human consciousness and experience and, therefore, as the proper object of a Muslim historian's attention. Perhaps Ibn Khaldun's science of human culture, his elucidation of persistent secondary causes in history, should be viewed as an exploration of God's way in the world of human nature He has created. We do not have such an elucidation in medieval Indo-Muslim historical writing.

Nor is there evidence of any influence of non-Muslim notions of time native South Asia. One of the earliest examples of medieval Indo-Muslim historiography, the *Chach Nama* (*c*. 1216-17), draws on both Muslim and non-Muslim traditions. Its author, 'Ali b. Hamid b. Abu Bakr al-Kufi, gives an account of rulers in Sind before the Arab conquest in 711. But he transmutes his non-Muslim material into an Islamic idiom. The passage of time is described as a *tadawul-i ruzgar* or a *tadawaul-i zaman*, an alternation of time (*tadawaul*) from the Arabic root *d-w-l* found in Koran III, 140 and LIX, 7). God is referred to as a creator God (*afaridigar-i 'alam*); non-Muslims killed by other non-Muslims in war are described as *kafirs*, unbelievers, who go to (the Muslim) hell, *duzakh*; non-Muslim hierophants are called *'ulama* and *hukama*.[68] Whatever the effect in the countryside of breathing the air of popular Hindu mythology, the Akbar-encouraged translations of Hindu epics into Persian seem not to have touched the writings of Muslim historians. Yet Hindu historians such as Sujan Ray Bhandari and Bhimsen (late seventeenth century), wrote in a Muslim historical style. So the question raised at the beginning of this paper receives a negative answer.

It is easy, but no great help, to suggest that nothing in Muslim history in India before the end of the eighteenth century jolted the Muslim intelligentsia out of traditional patterns of thought. Aware as were the historians of the loss of Mughal authority, they believed the solution to lie in a renewal of true Islamic belief and practice (rather than, say, a search for structural or economic explanations).[69] However, one contemporarian historian was so jolted by Mughal failure as to suggest, not that God might wish to end His time for His creatures, but that men should consider ending their time for themselves. Muhammad Qasim in his *Ahwal al-Khawaqin*, finished in 1738-9, wrote, 'The king is sitting within the four walls (of his palace). If the kings follow the manners of women and act on what the effeminate say, then it is the more necessary that the Muslims take the path to Mecca and Medina, and, if they do not have travelling expenses, it is better that they should commit suicide by taking poison.'[70]

NOTES

1. Louis Massignon, 'Time in Islamic Thought', in *Man and Time: Papers from the Eranos Yearbook*, London, 1958, pp. 108-14.
2. See C.A. Storey, *Persian Literature: A Bio-bibliographical Survey*, vol. I, part 1, *Qur'anic Literature; History*, London 1927-39. Valuable additional material and a commentary is provided by Khaliq Ahmad Nizami, *Supplement Elliot & Dowson's History of India*, vols. II and III, Delhi, 1981; idem, *On History and Historians of Medieval India*, Delhi, 1983.
3. *Tabaqat-i Nasiri*, edited by 'Abd al-Hay Habibi, vol. I, 2nd edn., Kabul, 1963, pp. 131-2.
4. Khwaja Ni'mat ullah, *Ta'rikh-i Khan Jahani*, vol. II, edited by S.M. Imam al-din, Dacca, 1960, pp. 548-9.

5. *Tar'ikh-i Firuz Shahi*, Calcutta, 1862, p. 510.
6. 'Abd-Allah, *Tar'ikh-i Da'udi*, Aligarh, 1969, p. 2.
7. Ahmad Yadgar, *Tar'ikh-i Shahi*, Calcutta, 1939 edn., p. 1.
8. Shaikh Ilahdad Faizi Sirhindi, *Akbar Nama*, British Library, Or. 169, fol. 4a-4b.
9. See Harbans Mukhia, *Historians and Historiography during the Reign of Akbar*, Delhi, 1976, pp. 74-9.
10. See P. Hardy, *Historians of Medieval India*, London, 1960, pp. 22-3.
11. *Tar'ikh-i Firuz Shahi*, pp. 324-5.
12. Ziya al-din Barani, *Fatawa-i Jahandari*, Lahore, 1972 edn., pp. 142-3.
13. Abu'l Hamid Lahauri, *Padshah Nama*, vol. I, Calcutta, 1867 edn., pp. 4, 5.
14. Shams al-din ibn Siraj al-din 'Afif, *Tar'ikh-i Firuz Shahi*, Calcutta, 1891 edn.
15. For example, Muhammad Bakhtawar Khan, *Mir'at al-Alam*, Lahore, 1979 edn., vol. I, p. 1; Musta'id Khan, *Ma'asir-i Alamgiri*, Calcutta, 1870 edn., p. 2.
16. Such histories as the *Burhan-i Ma'asir* by 'Ali b. 'Aziz Tabataba, Hyderabad, Deccan, 1936, on the Sultans of Gulbarga, Bidar and Ahmadnagar in the Deccan show signs of (unconscious?) structuring of this sort.
17. See Muhammad Umar, 'A Comparative Study of the Historical Approach of Muhammad Qasim and Khafi Khan', in Mohibbul Hasan (ed.), *Historians of Medieval India*, Meerut, 1968, pp. 156-64.
18. Abu'l Fazl, *Akbar Nama*, vol. III, Calcutta, 1884-7, pp. 290ff.
19. *Akbar Nama*, vol. I, Calcutta, 1877, pp. 18-19.
20. For example, Mu'tamad Khan, *Iqbal Nama-i Jahangiri*, Calcutta, 1865 edn., p. 2; Muhammad Salih Kambu Lahauri, *'Amal-i Salih*, Calcutta, 1923 edn., vol. I, p. 7; Musta'id Khan, *Ma'asir-i 'Alamgiri*, p. 8; Khwaja Kamgar Husaini, *Ma'asir-i Jahangiri*, New York, 1978 edn., p. 3.
21. *Tabaqat-i Nasiri*, vol. I, p. 449.
22. Barani, *Ta'rikh-i Firuz Shahi*, pp. 233, 235.
23. 'Afif, *Ta'rikh-i Firuz Shahi*, p. 47.
24. Khwandamir, *Qanun-i Humayuni*, Calcutta, 1940 edn., pp. 36-7.
25. Yusuf ibn Abu'l Qasim, *Mazhar-i Shahjahani*, Karachi, 1962 edn., pp. 250, 251, 254.
26. Khafi Khan, *Muntakhab al-Lubab*, part II, Calcutta, 1874, p. 704.
27. Yahya ibn Ahmad ibn 'Abd-Allah al-Sirhindi, *Ta'rikh-i Mubarak Shahi*, Calcutta, 1931 edn., p. 222.
28. Khafi Khan, *Muntakhab al-Lubab*, p. 704.
29. Muhammad Hadi Kamwar Khan, *Tazkirat al-Salatin Chaghta*, Bombay, 1980 edn., p. 143.
30. 'Abbas Khan Sarwani, *Ta'rikh-i Sher Shahi*, vol. I (Persian text), Dacca, 1964, pp. 154-5.
31. *Ta'rikh-i Shahi*, p. 336.
32. Ibid., pp. 228-9.

33. 'Abd al-Qadir Bada'uni, *Muntakhab al-Tawarikh*, vol. II, Calcutta, 1865 edn., p. 62.
34. Yusuf 'Ali Khan, *Ta'rikh-i Bangala-i Mahabatjangi*, Calcutta, 1969 edn., p. 2.
35. 'Abd-Allah, *Ta'rikh-i Da'udi*, pp. 65-7, 76-7.
36. *Ta'rikh-i Khan Jahani*, vol. I, Dacca, 1960, p. 303.
37. 'Ali Muhammad Khan, *Mirat-i Ahmadi*, part II, Baroda, 1927 edn., p. 53.
38. *Tabaqat-i Nasiri*, fol. II, Kabul, 1964 edn., pp. 90ff.
39. *Ta'rikh-i Firuz Shahi*, p. 468.
40. *Muntakhab al-Tawarikh*, vol. II, p. 255.
41. 'Afif, *Ta'rikh-i Firuz Shahi*, pp. 95-6.
42. Mubarak Allah Wazih, *Ta'rikh-i Iradat Khan*, Lahore, 1971 edn., pp. 2-3.
43. 'Time in Islamic Thought'; pp. 108-10 *passim*.
44. *Ma'asir-i 'Alamgiri*, p. 305.
45. Cf. *Ta'rikh-i Firuz Shahi*, p. 521 and *Fatawa-i Jahandari*, p. 247.
46. *Ma'asir-i Jahangiri*, p. 62.
47. *'Amal-i Salih*, vol. I, p. 2.
48. *Ta'rikh-i Sher Shahi*, vol. I (Text), pp. 238-9.
49. *Ta'rikh-i Firuz Shahi*, pp. 372, 374.
50. *Ta'rikh-i Sher Shahi*, vol. I (Text), p. 53.
51. P. Hardy, 'Force and Violence in Indo-Persian Writing on History and Government in Medieval South Asia', *Islamic Society and Culture: Essays in Honour of Professor Aziz Ahmad*, Delhi, 1983, pp. 173-5, 177.
52. On occasionalism in Islamic thought see: Majid Fakhry, *Islamic Occasionalism*, London, 1958; Harry Austryn Wolfson, *The Philosophy of the Kalam*, Cambridge, Mass., 1976, pp. 466-544; Lenn Evan Goodman, 'Did Al-Ghazali Deny Causality?', *Studia Islamica*, XLVII, 1978, p. 109.
53. Muhsin Mahdi, *Ibn Khaldun's Philosophy of History*, London, 1957, pp. 140-1.
54. Bayazid Biyat, *Tazkira-i Humayun wa Akbar*, Calcutta, 1941 edn., p. 64.
55. Rizq Allah Mushtaqi, *Waqi'at-i Mushtaqi*, British Library, Add. 11, 633, fol. 79a.
56. Yahya ibn Ahmad al-Sirhindi, *Ta'rikh-i Mubarak Shahi*, p. 15.
57. 'Aqil Khan Razi, *Waqi'at-i Alamgiri*, Lahore, 1936 edn., p. 50.
58. Abu'l Fazl, *Akbar Nama*, vol. II, Calcutta, 1879 edn., p. 369.
59. *Ta'rikh-i Firuz Shahi*, p. 399.
60. 'Afif, *Ta'rikh-i Firuz Shahi*, p. 456.
61. *Akbar Nama*, vol. III, pp. 233, 393.
62. *Ta'rikh-i Bangala-i Mahabatjangi*, p. 137.
63. Muhammad Kazim, *'Alamgir Nama*, Calcutta, 1868 edn., p. 432.
64. *Ta'rikh-i Iradat Khan*, p. 133.
65. William J. Courtenay, 'The Critique of Natural Causality in the Mutakallimun and Nominalism', *Harvard Theological Review*, 66, 1973, pp. 77-94; Lenn

Evan Goodman, 'Did Al-Ghazali deny Causality?', *Studia Islamica* (Paris), XLVII, 1978, pp. 83-120; Ilai Alon, 'Al-Ghazali on Causality', *Journal of the American Oriental Society*, C, 4, 1980, pp. 397-405; Binyamin Abrahamov, 'Al-Ghazali's Theory of Causality', *Studia Islamica*, LXVII, 1988, pp. 76-98.

66. Muhammad Abu'l Quasem, *The Ethics of Al-Ghazali*, Selangor, 1975, pp. 45 ff.
67. *The Babur Nāma in English*, tr. A.S. Beveridge, London, 1969 (2nd ptg.).
68. Al-Kufi, *Chach Nama*, Hyderabad, Deccan edition, 1939, pp. 30, 35, 41, 46, 48.
69. See Zahiruddin Malik, 'Persian Historiography in India during the 18th Century', in *Historians of Medieval India*, ed. Mohibbul Hasan, Meerut, 1968, pp. 142-55.
70. Muhammad Qasim Aurangabadi, *Ahwal al-Khawaqin*, British Library Add. 26244, fol. 196b. (Original not seen, but translated passage in: Muhammad Umar, 'A Comparative Study of the Historical Approach of Muhammad Qasim and Khafi Khan', in idem, *Historians of Medieval India*, p. 158.)

REFERENCES

'Abd-Allah, *Ta'rikh-i Da'udi*, edited as *Ta'rikh-i Daudi of Abdullah*, by Shaikh Abdur Rashid, with Introduction and Analytical Summary by Iqtidar Husain Siddiqi, Aligarh, 1969.

Abrahamov, Binyamin, 'Al-Ghazali's Theory of Causality', *Studia Islamica*, LXVII, 1988, pp. 76-98.

Abu'l Fazl, *Akbar Nama*, ed. Agha Ahmad 'Ali and 'Abd al-Rahim, *Bibliotheca Indica*, Calcutta, 1873-87.

'Afif, Shams al-din Siraj al-din, *The Ta'rikh-i Firoz Shahi of Shams Siraj 'Afif*, ed. Maulavi Vilayat Husain, *Bibliotheca Indica*, Calcutta, 1891.

'Ali Khan, Yusuf, *Ta'rikh-i Bangala-i Mahabatjangi*, ed. Abdus Subhan, *Bibliotheca Indica*, Calcutta, 1969.

Alon, Ilai, 'Al-Ghazali on Causality', *Journal of the American Oriental Society*, C, 4, 1980, pp. 397-405.

Babur, Zahir al-din, *Tuzuk-i Baburi*, A.S. Beveridge as *The Babur Nama in English*, 2nd ptg., London, 1969.

Badauni, 'Abd al-Qadir, *Muntakhab al-Tawarikh*, ed. W.N. Lees and Ahmad 'Ali, *Bibliotheca Indica*, vol. II, Calcutta, 1865.

Barani, Ziya al-din, *Fatawa-i Jahandari*, ed. Afsar Salim Khan, Lahore, 1972.

———, *Ta'rikh-i Firuz Shahi*, edited as *The Tarikh-i Feroz-shahi of Zia al-Din Barani* by Saiyid Ahmad Khan, *Bibliotheca Indica*, Calcutta, 1862.

Bhakari, Yusuf Mirak Namkin, *Ta'rikh Mazhar Shahjahani*, ed. Saiyid Husam al-din Rashidi, Karachi, 1962.

Biyat, Bayazid, *Tazkira-i Humayun wa Akbar*, edited as *Tadhkira-i-Humayun wa Akbar of Bayazid Biyat* by M. Hidayat Hosain, *Bibliotheca Indica*, Calcutta, 1941.

Courtenay, William J., 'The Critique of Natural Causality in the Mutakallimun and Nominalism', *Harvard Theological Review*, 66, 1973, pp. 77-94.

Fakhry, Majid, *Islamic Occasionalism and its Critique by Averroes and Aquinus*, London, 1958.

Goodman, Lenn Evan, 'Did Al-Ghazali Deny Causality?', *Studia Islamica*, XLVII, 1978, pp. 83-120.

Hardy, P., *Historians of Medieval India: Studies in Indo-Muslim historical Writing*, London, 1960.

———, 'Force and Violence in Indo-Persian Writing on History and Government in Medieval South Asia', in Milton Israel and N.K. Wagle, eds., *Islamic Society and Culture: Essays in honour of Professor Aziz Ahmad*, Delhi, 1983, pp. 165-208.

———, 'Didactic Historical Writing in Indian Islam: Ziya al-Din Barani's Treatment of the Reign of Sultan Muhammad Tughluq (1324-1351)', *Islam in Asia*, vol. I, *South Asia*, ed. Yohanan Friedmann, Jerusalem, 1984, pp. 38-59.

Husaini, Khwaja Kamgar, *Ma'asir-i Jahangiri*, ed. Azra Alavi, New York, 1978.

Juzjani, Minhaj al-din Siraj al-din, *Tabaqat-i Nasiri*, ed. 'Abd al-Haiy Habibi, vol. I (2nd ptg.), Kabul, 1963; vol. II, Kabul, 1964.

Kamwar Khan, Muhammad Hadi, *Tazkirat al-Salatin Chaghta*, ed. Musaffar Alam, Bombay, 1980.

Kazim, Muhammad, *'Alamgir-Nama*, ed. Khadim Husain and 'Abd al-Haiy, *Bibliotheca Indica*, Calcutta, 1865-73.

Khafi Khan, Muhammad Hashim, *Muntakhab al-Lubab*, ed. Kabir al-din Ahmad, vol. II, *Bibliotheca Indica* (in 2 parts), Calcutta, 1860-74.

Khan, 'Ali Muhammad, *Mirat-i Ahmadi*, ed. Syed Nawab Ali, *Gaekwad's Oriental Series*, part II, Baroda, 1927.

Khwandamir, *Qanun-i Humayuni*, ed. M. Hidayat Hosain, *Bibliotheca Indica*, Calcutta, 1940.

al-Kufi, 'Ali b. Hamid b. Abu Bakr, *Chach Nama*, ed. as *Fath-nama-i Sind known as Chach Nama* by 'Umar ibn Muhammad Da'udpota, Hyderabad, Deccan, 1939.

Lahauri, Abu'l Hamid, *Padshah Nama*, ed. as *The Badshah-Namah by 'Abd al-Hamid Lahawri* by Kabir al-din Ahmad and 'Abd al-Rahim, *Bibliotheca Indica*, Calcutta, 1866-72.

Lahauri, Muhammad Salih Kanbo, *'Amal-i Salih*, edited as *'Amal-i-Salih or Shah Jahan Namah of Muhammad Salih Kambo* by Ghulam Yazdani, *Bibliotheca Indica*, Calcutta, 1912-23.

Lucas, J.R., *A Treatise on Time and Space*, London, 1973.

Mahdi, Muhsin, *Ibn Khaldun's Philosophy of History*, London, 1957.

Malik, Zahiruddin, 'Persian Historiography in India during the 18th Century', in ed. Mohibbul Hasan, *Historians of Medieval India*, Meerut, 1968, pp. 142-55.

Massignon, Louis, 'Time in Islamic Thought', *Man and Time: Papers from the Eranos Yearbook*, London, 1958, pp. 108-14.

Mukhia, Harbans, *Historians and Historiography during the Reign of Akbar*, Delhi, 1976.

Mushtaqi, Rizq-Allah, *Waqi'at-i Mushtaqi*, British Library, Ms. 11, 633.

Musta'id Khan, *Ma'asur-i Alamgiri*, ed. Agha Ahmad Ali, *Bibliotheca Indica*, Calcutta, 1870-3.

Mu'tamad Khan, *Iqbal-Nama-i Jahangiri*, edited as *Iqbalnamah-i Jahangiri of Motamad Khan* by 'Abd al-Haiy and Ahmad Ali, *Bibliotheca Indica*, Calcutta, 1865.

Ni'mat ullah, Khwaja, *Ta'rikh-i Khan Jahani wa Makhzan-i Afghani*, ed. S.M. Imam al-din, vol. I, Dacca, 1960, vol. II, Dacca, 1962.

Nizami, Khaliq Ahmad, *Supplement to Elliot & Dowson's History of India,* vol. II, *Ghaznavids & the Ghurids*, Delhi, 1981; *Supplement to Elliot & Dowson's History of India,* vol. III, *The Khaljis and the Tughluqs*, Delhi, 1981.

———, *On History and Historians of Medieval India*, Delhi, 1983.

Qasim, Muhammad, *Ahwal-i Khawaqin*, British Library, ms. Add. 26, 244.

Quasem, Muhammad Abu'l, *The Ethics of Al-Ghazali*, Selangor, 1975.

Razi, 'Aqil Khan, *Waqi'at-i 'Alamgiri*, ed. M. Abdullah Chaghtai, Lahore, 1936.

Sarwani, 'Abbas Khan, *Ta'rikh-i Sher Shahi*, ed. as *The Tarikh-i Sher Shahi of Abbas Khan Sarwani*, vol. I (Persian Text) by S.M. Imam al-din, Dacca, 1964.

Seddon, Keith, *Time: A Philosophical Treatment*, London, 1987.

al-Sirhindi, Yahya ibn Ahmad ibn Abdallah, *Ta'rikh-i Mubarak Shahi*, edited as *Ta'rikh-i Mubarak Shahi of Yahya bin Ahmad bin 'Abdullah As- Sirhindi* by M. Hidayat Hosain, *Bibliotheca Indica*, Calcutta, 1931.

Shaikh Ilahdad Faizi, Sirhindi, *Akbar Nama*, British Library, Ms. Or. 169.

Storey, C.A., *Persian Literature: A bio-bibliographical Survey*, vol. I, part 1, *Qur'anic Literature: History*, London, 1927-39.

Tabataba, 'Ali b. 'Aziz Allah, *Burhan-i Ma'asir*, Hyderabad, Deccan, 1936.

Umar, Muhammad, 'A Comparative Study of the Historical Approach of Muhammad Qasim and Khafi Khan', *Historians of Medieval India*, ed. Mohibbul Hasan, Meerut, 1968, pp. 156-64.

Wazih, Mubarak Allah, *Ta'rikh-i Iradat Khan*, ed. Ghulam Rasul Mihr, Lahore, 1971.

Whitrow, G.J., *The Natural Philosophy of Time*, 2nd edn., Oxford, 1980.

Wolfson, Harry Austryn, *The Philosophy of the Kalam*, Cambridge, Massachusetts, 1976.

Yadgar, Ahmad, *Ta'rikh-Shahi*, edited as *Ta'rikh-i-Shahi* (also known as *Tarikh-i-Salatin-i-Afghani*) by M. Hidayat Hosain, *Bibliotheca Indica*, Calcutta, 1939.

Muslim Intellectual Life in India

IQTIDAR HUSAIN SIDDIQUI

Thirteenth and Fourteenth Centuries

The independent Muslim Sultanate in north India, founded in the beginning of the thirteenth century, attracted soldiers, scholars and men of sciences and arts to India. Every town and city was studded with institutions of learning (*madrasas*). Since the immigrants came mainly from Persian-speaking lands of Khurasan and Central Asia and, with the exception of the *ulama* (religious divines), they could not directly benefit from Islamic literature in Arabic, the important works on Islam, ethics, philosophy and history were translated into Persian. Generous support was extended by the ruling elite to scholars, and thus ensued an efflorescence of learning and culture during the fourteenth century.

A little evidence available in contemporary sources suggests that cultural traditions, religious and quasi-religious, that had been maintained and patronized by Muslim rulers outside India influenced the foundation of Muslim rule in India, and led to the rise of the cities of Uchh, Lahore, and Delhi (also Lakhnauti in Bengal) as centres of Islamic religious, scientific and intellectual culture. The association of scholars, scientists, poets and *ulama* (religious divines) with the royal court was a distinctive feature of the polity developed in Central Asia since the eleventh century.[1] Heirs to the Central Asian traditions, the architects of the sultanate in India tried to turn their courts into centres of intellectual culture. This helped in the maintenance of Islamic identity and in the integration of Muslims in Indian society. It also needs to be stressed that the *ulama* were part of the ruling elite as they were entrusted by the state with the administration of justice (as judicial officers) and legislative functions (as *muftis* or expounders of law). There was a clear-cut division of power between the Sultan and the *ulama*, at least since the time of Mahmud of Ghazna (*d.* AD 1030). The Sultan exercised military, executive and financial powers, while judicial and legislative powers lay with the *ulama*. The Sultan was allowed discretion only in dealing with crime against the state.[2]

A large number of Muslim scholars from Central Asia, Iran and Western

Asia settled in the cities and towns of north India. The literature they produced in Persian provides insights into the intellectual life and religious thought of the Muslim elite in the sultanate during its early phase. Many of the *ulama*, besides being employed in the civil administration, were teachers in *madrasas* established by the state. Those *madrasas* that were established in the capital cities were higher seats of learning and served by the scholars of eminence. The first of these was started by Qutbuddin Aibek in Delhi after he had made it his headquarters before his accession to the throne in AD 1206. It was named the *Madrasa-i-Muizi*[3] after his master, Sultan Muizuddin Muhammad bin Sam. Later, his successors founded *madrasas* in their respective capitals. Nasiruddin Qubacha, who declared himself sultan and seized the territorial units of Lahore, Multan and Sind, founded the *Madrasa-i-Firuzi* in Uchh;[4] Ghyasuddin Khalji founded *madrasas* in Bihar and in Lakhnauti,[5] his capital. Some time after AD 1230 Shamsuddin Iltutmish founded a large *madrasa* for the educational needs of an expanding city and named it the *Madrasa-i-Nasiriya* after his deceased son, Nasiruddin Mahmud.[6] The *madrasas* and mosques constructed in every town and city where Muslim colonies and garrisons were planted functioned as civilizing institutions. Even in small localities mosques and *madrasas* were built. Balban is reported by Ziya uddin Barani to have established a number of *thanas* (police posts) along the highways for the suppressions of highway men. Every *thana* had its mosque and *madrasa*.[7] These *thanas* often developed into important townships. Besides *imams* and teachers, *khatibs* were posted there to provide the soldiers and civilian Muslims with religious leadership.[8] The syllabus chalked out by the Saljuq Wazir Nizam ul-Mulk Tusi in Baghdad and other cities was followed. This system encouraged specialization only in theological sciences, *tafsir* (exegesis of the Koran), *hadith* (the Prophetic traditions) and *fiqh* (Islamic jurisprudence) of each of the four Sunni school, Hanafi, Maliki, Shafi'i and Hanbali.[9] The *madrasas* were open to all. As a result, by the end of the later half of the thirteenth century educated men who came of the families of low-caste converts to Islam had begun to compete with the *ashraf* (social elite) in state service. In fact, Islamic culture represented by the *ulama* and the Sufis to whom religious service was a genuine concern continued to be marked by an egalitarian undercurrent at odds with the *ashraf* of foreign origin; the *ashraf* had monopolized state service and wanted to safeguard their interest by supporting hierarchical ideals.[10]

Some words are also in order about the religious and intellectual dimensions of the Persian translation of Arabic classics on Islamic religion, philosophy, *fiqh* and history, for it inspired writers of subsequent periods. The first Arabic classic to be translated into Persian was Qazi al-Tanukhi's *Kitab ul-Faraj ba'd ul-Shidda*. Sadiduddin Muhammad Awfi, a Bukhara-born emigrant, translated and dedicated this to Nasiruddin Qubacha in Uchh. This work contains authentic traditions about Islamic faith, morality and state craft, besides giving valuable information on the road systems, oceans and geographic features of different countries.[11] This translation impressed the Sultan so much that he persuaded Awfi to compile another work like it into Persian, bringing it down to his own time.[12] Thereupon, Awfi set to compile his *magnum opus*, the *Jawami'ul-Hikayat wa-Livami'ul-Rivayat*. The latter is of encyclopaedic range, based on Arabic classics and early Persian historical literature produced under the patronage of the Ghazanavids and Saljuq Sultans, his own observations, and information collected from traders about life and conditions in countries as far as China. The compendium soon gained popularity among the *ulama*, sufis, historians, and bureaucracy. In fact, historical traditions contained therein about the Prophet, pious caliphs, early sufis, and political and social institutions developed in different Islamic countries made it a reference book.[13]

In Delhi, Nizam ul-Mulk Junaidi, the *wazir* of Shamsuddin Iltutmish, persuaded Majduddin Jajarmi to translate from Arabic into Persian Imam Ghazzali's celebrated *Ihya-i-ulum id-din*.[14] This work was considered extremely important for it has countered the influence of the teachings of philosophers like Bu Ali Sina and had revived the popularity of traditional Islamic science. In translating the Arabic text the translator incorporated Koranic verses, *hadith* and the utterances of the Prophet's companions in original Arabic with translation and explanations of the subtle points therein. There were also additions and alterations made by the translator; where Imam Ghazzali quotes rulings from the Shafi'i sources regarding legal problems, he replaces them by those of the Hanafi school. It reveals the indifference, if not hostility, of the orthodox Hanafi *ulama* towards the Shafi'i school of religious thought.[15] Jajarmi's translation made a great impact on the religious thought of Muslims in India. According to Amir Khusrau, his Persian prose, with its flow and gentle expression, was emulated by new writers, particularly the doctors of law.[16] Ziya uddin Barani includes this translation in the list of Arabic and Persian treatises studied and discussed by the educated *murids* of Shaikh Nizamuddin Auliya in his *Jama't Khana*.[17]

Likewise, the Persian translation of Shaikh Shihab uddin Suhrawardi's *Awarif-ul-Ma'arif* is an important contribution to Islamic literature produced in Persian. Sultan Tajuddin Abu Bakr of Multan (1243-4) asked Daud Khatib to translate it from Arabic into Persian in order to promote a spiritual temper among Persian speaking Muslims. A key text for the sufis, this contains traditions of the Prophet and teachings of the early sufis relating to the organization of Islamic spiritual life. Daud Khatib being the *murid* of Shaikh Bahauddin Zakariya, sought his Pir's permission to make the translation. The Pir is said to have helped him translate explaining difficult passages.[18] This is the earliest translation of the *Awarif-ul Ma'arif*, done ten or eleven years after the death of Shaikh Shibabuddin Suhrawardi. In it we see the development of Persian as an effective vehicle of expression of religious and metaphysical ideas.

As for the presence of the different schools of Islamic thought in India in the thirteenth century, Amir Khusrau would have us believe that only the Hanafi school of thought was followed by all Muslims. He states in his *mathnavi*, *Qiranu's Sa'dain*:

> Muslims here belong to the Hanafi creed, but sincerely respect all the four schools. They have no enmity with the Shafi'is and no fondness for the Zaidis, with heart and soul are they devoted to the path of the community and the *Sunna*. It is a wonderful land, producing Muslims and favouring religion, where even the fish comes out of the stream as a Sunni.[19]

In India Hanafi law was adopted as state law, but there was no dearth of the followers of Shafi'i school in the sultanate. Even the ruling dynasty of Ghur who migrated to India after the Mongol expansion in Central Asia and Khurasan (AD 1219-20) were divided among Hanafis and Shafi'is. Sultan Ghyasuddin Muhammad bin Sam of Ghur became a Shafi'i while his younger brother, the conqueror of north India, Muizuddin Muhammad bin Sam, followed Hanafi law.[20] According to Majduddin Jajarmi, many educated Muslims belonging to the schools other than the Hanafi had settled in Lahore.[21] In Delhi itself, the Shafi'is maintained their separate *madrasas*[22] and appear to have influenced young Hanafi scholars. Amir Khusrau incorporates with disapproval in an epistle related to jurisprudence in the *Ijaz-i-Khusravi*, the discussion on a legal point between a grandfather and his grandson, both being *danishmands* or scholar doctors of law. The grandson quoted a ruing from the *Shafi'i fiqh* and his grandfather who happened to be a staunch supporter of Hanafi school lost his temper.[23] This indicates that interaction between the followers of different schools had created tension. But the Sunni orthodoxy was in complete control of religious affairs of the sultanate. They suppressed all innovations, even those not at variance with Islamic teachings. They banned the *Sama'* (sufi song), so popular among sufis who considered it helpful in heightening their cosmic consciousness. The sufis had to listen to *Sama'* secretly. Shaikh Nizamuddin Auliya tells us that the ban was lifted when Minhaj-i-Siraj Juzjani, the historian, took over as the chief qazi of the sultanate during the reign of Muizuddin Bahram Shah (1240-2).[24] Minhaj Juzjani was a theologian of moderate views but he seems to have been an exception. He supported even Raziya's accession to the throne. He blames male bias for her overthrow.[25] He was unlike other *ulama* in government service.

When faced with a new situation that called for a solution, *sharia* (canonic law) experts would sit together, and seek guidance from precedents. They would refrain from giving a judgement if there was no guidance, provided the practice adopted or use of something begun by Muslims was not at variance with Islamic teachings. In such a situation their silence was taken as consent. Shaikh Sharafuddin Yahya Maneri, the greatest of metaphysical thinkers of medieval India, tells us that people were in the habit of chewing betel and the lime used by them was made of the ash of shells. The *ulama* condemned this, because shell was forbidden food. Perplexed, people referred this to the *muftiyan* (expounders of law). The *muftis* discussed the problem and realized that great hardship would be caused to thousands of people if they would agree with the *ulama*, and did not write any judgement. Shaikh Sharafuddin Maneri said 'The *Muftis* made things easy for the people, for the path of Islam is a wide open one. It is not lawful to pass a law which would be a burden for the people.'[26]

In passing the intellectual and cultural dimension of the metropolis of Delhi may be discussed. According to Minhaj-i-Siraj Juzjani and Isami, Delhi rose from a *pargana* headquarters of no consequence into a centre of learning and cosmopolitan culture in the reign of Iltutmish. It became a haven for the learned from all parts of the world.[27] Doing homage to the memory of Iltutmish Isami mentions the arrival of painters from China besides the migration of *ulama*, poets and men of piety from different Muslim countries.[28] Barani tells us that by the time of Balban (1261-87) Delhi had acquired the status of *Misr-i-Jami'* (a perfect city). It contained the largest number of *ulama*, *mashaikh*, *mufassiran* (exegists of the Quran), *muhadithin*, *hufaz* (those who commit the Quran to memory), *muzakiran* (who deliver religious sermons), *fazilan* (intellectuals) and master artists and craftsmen.[29] Amir Khusrau says that Arabic verses composed by the poets of Delhi could put to shame the leading poets of Arabia.[30] During this period Islamic influence began to bounce back to Central Asia and Iran.[31] Isami corroborates Khusrau in these words: 'If any crisis developed in Bukhara or confusion arose in Samarqand, the jurists of those places turned to the divines of Delhi and acquired *fatva* (decree) from them.'[32]

Some words are also in order about the progress in astronomy and astrology in Central Asia and Khurasan before the foundation of the sultanate of Delhi, by which Indian Muslims were influenced.[33] One common feature of the historical literature produced in India by the emigrant writers is that, with the exception of Minhaj-i-Siraj Juzjani, all seem to have believed in the effect of stars and planets on the fate of man and the universe. In fact, astrology had become a part of astronomy in Central Asia, under Buddhist influence. Fakhr-i Mudabbir opens the introduction to his *Shajra-i-Ansalb* (Book of Genealogy) with a description of the dome of the heavens with their seven skies, each with its presiding planet—all testifying to the glory of the Creator. Hasan Nizami mentions the zodiac and the seven planets influencing man's destiny.[34] Sadiduddin Muhammad Awfi calls Nizam ul-Mulk Junaidi a *Sahib-i-Qiran* or one born during the conjunction of two auspicious stars.[35] Minhaj-i-Siraj Juzjani, however, as a rationalist theologian was free from such influence. Like other orthodox *ulama*, he considered it blasphemous impertinence. But he considered the study of astronomy a cultural pursuit.[36]

Under the benevolent rule of the Khalji Sultans after AD 1290 occurred an intellectual efflorescence. Now intellectuals were free to overcome local and contemporary prejudice and investigate facts afresh. The freedom of thought allowed by the Khalji Sultans encouraged the *ilm-i-Ma'qul* or rationalist sciences to attract young scholars and incite their curiosity. Thus an atmosphere congenial to intellectual progress was created; attempts to rethink Islam or Islamic *sharia* in the light of changed circumstances could not be ruled out by orthodoxy in the name of conformity. Of the historians of that age, Ziya uddin Barani, though critical of Alauddin Khalji's indifference to the *sharia* in dealing out punishment for crimes against the state, provides us with a complete picture of religious and intellectual life during his reign.[37] According to him the Sultan consulted the rationalists and acted accordingly. He mentions Sa'd Mantaqi, a distinguished logician and rationalist who had become the Counsellor of the Sultan. Besides him, some other scholars of *ilm-i-Ma'qul* are also mentioned. According to Barani, Sa'd Mantaqi, Maulana Najmuddin Intishar (also a poet), Maulana Alimuddin and Ubaid Sha'ir enjoyed prestige.

These four persons belonged to the rationalist-school (*ilm-i-Ma'qul*). They had complete mastery over rationalist sciences. Maulana Alimuddin, Sa'd Mantaqi and Najmuddin Intishar, the poet had become the distinguished scholars both of *ilm-i-Kalam* (scholasticism) and logic. No one could rival them in having mastery over these sciences. They were found most of the time pre-occupied with studying philosophical literature. As for Ubaid, the poet, he was without any faith in religion.[38]

Barani also mentions sixty-six leading scholars associated with the Sultan's court. 'Every one of them', says he, 'had a style and distinction in poetry. They had to their credit their *diwans* and were celebrated for their mastery over prose and verse both.' They also taught the popular sciences.[39] In fact, this was the time when the court at Delhi became a centre of intellectual culture; it was to become a model or reference point for rulers in subsequent centuries.

By this time Delhi had also grown as the largest city of the Islamic world. Barani says that no reign could be compared with Alauddin Khalji's as regards the expansion of Delhi and construction of grand buildings.[40] Isami was corroborated by Ibn Battuta calling Delhi the largest and most beautiful city of the World of Islam.[41] Another contemporary Arab geographer historian, Shihabuddin al-Umari adds, 'There are one thousand madrasas in Delhi, one of which is meant for the Shafi'is and the rest for the Hanafis. There are about seventy *bimaristans* (hospitals); in India the *bimaristan* is called *darul-Shifa*.'[42]

In addition, the seminaries of India attracted students from foreign countries who returned with testimonials from renowned Indian teachers. Barani writes that the scholars of Bukhara, Samarqand, Baghdad, Cairo, Khwarazm, Damascus, Tabriz, Safahan and Ray and Rum (in Anatolia) recognized Indian scholarship for its authoritative knowledge of sciences, no matter whether it was *manqulat* (traditional Islamic science), or *ma'qulat* (rational sciences) or *tafsir*, *fiqh* (Islamic jurisprudence), *Usul-i-Din* (principles of *fiqh*), or *nahv* (grammar), articulation, lexicography, meanings, oratory, rhetoric, *ilm-i-Kalam* (scholasticism) or logic.[43] Often Indian scholars issued *fatvas* to Muslims in neighbouring countries. Scholars of Central Asia and Iran are reported to have visited India to learn from them. Sometimes they came with their books and sought the opinion of Indian experts. The recognition of a literary work by Indian *ulama* was considered a source of prestige in the scholar's own country.[44]

Like the Muslims of foreign countries, Indian Muslim scholars also regarded foreign travel useful for the enrichment of man's understanding. Scholars of Delhi and Multan appear to have travelled widely. The sons and grandsons of Shaikh Bahauddin Zakariya were widely travelled scholars. One of them, Maulana Alimuddin, is said to have visited several countries of Western Asia. On his return he settled in Delhi and engaged in the diffusion of knowledge.[45]

Some evidence available in the contemporary sources shows the passion of some scholars for knowledge about the intellectual heritage of Hindus, especially astronomy, medicine, mathematics and yoga. Amir Khusrau speaks highly in his *Mathnavi Nuh Siphr* of the contribution of Brahmins to logic, prognostication, scholasticism and physics. He emphasizes the indebtedness of the world to Hindu India for *Ilm-i-Hindsa* (arithmetic). According to him, Hindu sages had made a substantial contribution in every branch of learning except of *fiqh*.[46]

Astronomers and astrologers also received royal patronage. Barani tells us that women of the *haram* of Alauddin Khalji lavishly rewarded Hindu and Muslim astrologers for drawing horoscopes on the birth of princes. They were held in favour for their expertise and experience. 'The elite of Delhi', says Barani, 'could not start any work or undertake any project without consulting the astrologers.' In fact, the astronomers also practised astrology to earn their keep.[47]

The condemnation of astrology by the Islamic orthodoxy was justified, for it was contrary to the teachings of Islam. However, its condemnation of astronomy could not be justified. In defence of astronomy, Shams Siraj Afif, the late fourteenth-century historian rightly observes:

> Astronomy is one of the fourteen sciences known to scholars. But the study (of astrology) has been forbidden by the Prophet. It is, however, permissible to know the rules concerning the shadow of the sun and that in a particular month in what degree of what sign of the zodiac the sun would be, the hours of the short night and the long night and when (the night) turned into the day.[48]

It was really the curiosity and perseverence that enabled Amir Khusrau to talk with conviction about the centrality of the sun in a solar system, with the earth revolving around it. In his *Qiran ul-Sa'dain*, he says: 'The movement of the earth has been linked with time, hence day and night, the seasons of spring and autumn. These changes constitute the source of life and comfort for living beings.[49] Again, he expresses the same view in his *Ijaz-i-Khusravi*; people moved around the court of the ruler as the earth moves round the sun; that the moon is dark but shines on account of the reflected light of the sun.[50] Likewise, the Muslim intellectuals appear to have held to the concept of linear time and opposed to view of cyclic time. They also argued that the past did not always have superiority over the present in terms of piety, religious morality or progress. Once Muhammad bin Tughluq (AD 1324-51) remarked in the course of a chat with his scholars that superiority is either in point of time or in matter of position, or in degree of essence, and, therefore, it is not right to say that superiority consists on any one of them. The Sultan held, says the author of *Masalik ul-Absar*, that 'this argument was contrary to that of rationalist thinkers because the past never has superiority over the present for any of these reasons.[51] Similarly, he differed from the 'Asharites and supported the point of view of philosophers regarding the role of causality in history.

As regards the concepts of political economy and public welfare held by the elite of Delhi, the reference to them in contemporary literature suggest that the political thinkers of the sultanate were ahead of their time. In his critique of Alauddin Khalji's reign in the *Ijaz-i-Khusravi*, Amir Khusrau says that the Sultan stood unrivalled as regards his mastery over *ilm-i-ma'ishat* (economic science), and that 'he had gained precedence over the kings of the past (by introducing far-reaching economic reforms)'. The allusion made to *ilm-i-ma'ishat* tends to reveal that economics formed part of political philosophy of the elite and the standard of education and learning was high. For Barani the working of the economy is important and could not be left to economic forces. In his *Fatawa-i Jahandari* a work containing his political philosophy, he displays his awareness of an economic demand in Delhi, while he talks about interdependence of the livelihood of people, soldiers, commoners and others and the state. For the creation of a stable social and political order in the country, the king had to exert to his utmost to control prices of essential commodities. He also says that prices should be settled by kings in accordance with the principle of the cost of production.[52] Barani's account in his celebrated *Tarikh* of the price control and rationing systems introduced by Alauddin Khalji casts light on his grasp over market mechanisms as well as his competence for economic analysis.[53]

The best product of the efflorescence of the age was Muhammad bin Tughluq. Contemporary writers who were not biased against him for his religious policy portray him as a remarkable man on several counts. According to Shihabuddin al-Umari, the Sultan had committed the Quran to memory, was punctual in offering prayers five times a day and observing fasts during the month of fasting. He was a supporter of reason and showed preference for rationalist sciences (*ilm-i-ma'qul*) instead of *ilm-i-manqul* (traditional sciences). At the same time, he considered *hadith* the source of *sharia* and patronized scholars of *hadith*.[54] Ibn Battuta refers to the visit by Maulana Abdul Aziz Ardawili, the disciple of Imam Ibn Taimiya, to his court. The Maulana was a scholar of *hadith*. When the Sultan referred to him a certain *hadith* for comment, he reeled off so many on that subject, that the delighted Sultan poured a thousand gold *dinars* from a gold tray over him and said, 'They are yours and the tray as well.'[55] Barani also calls the Sultan the *hafiz* of the Quran and that he could quote rulings from *Hidaya* off hand.[56] The *Hidaya* was a standard work on Hanafi *fiqh*, compiled after *Bazdawi* and *Qaduri*. Ikhtisan, the author of the romance *Basatin-ul-Uns* and the *Dabir-i-Khas*, calls his royal patron *Nauman-i-Sani* or Imam Abu Hanifa of his age. He also informs us that the Sultan being a liberal and enlightened ruler lifted a ban on Shi'ism, with the result that the Jafri faith began to bloom.[57] Ibn Battuta corroborates Ikhtisan when he refers to the Shi'i immigrants from Iraq and Yemen enjoying royal patronage and holding important positions in the sultanate.[58] Isami calls the Sultan an enemy of Islam because he killed Muslims and participated in the Hindu festival of Holi; this testifies indirectly to his liberalism.[59] But in his personal life the Sultan was orthodox, never drank wine nor maintained a large *haram*. He does not seem to have married more than once. However, the orthodoxy turned against him when he tried to replace the traditionalist *ulama* by rationalists at his court. So he could not enforce his new rules and regulations for social progress. Barani informs us that the Sultan was a man of high spirit and wanted to combine within himself the functions of Caliph and Sultan,[60] i.e. the role of temporal and spiritual leader. The orthodox *ulama* were not willing to concede him the right to interfere with religious law (*sharia*). Thus a clash of ideas and ideology took place. The *ulama* issued *fatvas* justifying rebellion.[61] The nobility of the provinces took advantage, and rebellions were widespread and the economy shattered. Efforts of this ruler to free Muslim minds from dogma and superstition could not succeed.[62]

Firuz Shah had to make compromises with the orthodoxy and the nobility. The *ulama* were allowed a free hand in suppressing innovations. But the projects undertaken by Firuz Shah for public welfare and the diffusion of knowledge, such as the constructions of canals for irrgation,[63] construction of a grand college, *Madrasa-i-Firuz Shahi*, with a spacious hostel for the comfort of students and the establishment of a large *darul-Shifa* with separate wings for the treatment of people, animals and birds show that Firuz Shah and his wazir, Khan Jahan Maqbul, were influenced by the late Sultan.[64] In short, the legacy of Alauddin and the first two Tughluqs was discernible in subsequent centuries.

Last, a word may be added about the social role of the sufis during the thirteenth and fourteenth centuries. No discussion of Islam in India is complete without a reference to sufism. The sufi *silsilahs* (orders) that emerged in the beginning of the sultanate period were the Suhrawardi, Chishti and Qalandarya *silsilahs*. The latter, with the exception of a few, had generally walked out of their legacy of renunciation, abstention and discipline. Unlike them, the Suhrawardi, Chishti and the Firdausi sufis performed an important social role; their large-hearted tolerance irrespective of birth and creed paved the way for interaction between the followers of different religious traditions.[65] In fact, they were pioneers of the inter-religious dialogue that led Hindus and Muslims to understand each other strengthening the foundations of pluralist society. The *Malfuzat* of Shaikh Nizamuddin Auliya and Shaikh Sharafuddin Yahya Maneri contain interesting information about religious conversions. They considered conversion through inducement or persuasion immoral. They were certainly the forerunners of modern comparative religionists. The contribution of the sufi *khanqahs* and *dargah* to the development of a composite culture in India is by no means less important.

NOTES

1. The Ghaznavid and Ghurid Sultans are reported to have had mosques and *madrasas* (colleges and schools) constructed in their dominions. These were civilizing institutions, diffusing learning and knowledge. The Sultans of India emulated them in this respect. They made land grants for the maintenance of teachers, students and the educational institutions. The scholars turned out by these *madrasas* did not only work as teachers but were also employed by the state to man the civil, judicial and revenue departments. Cf. Abu Said Gardezi, *Zain al-Akbar*, ed. Abdul Hai Habibi, Iran, 1347 Shamsi, pp. 179-81; Muhammad bin Mansur Fakhr-i-Mudabbir, *Muqadimah-i-Shajrah-i-Ansab*, ed. E. Danison Ross under the misleading title *Tarikh-i-Fakhr Uddin Mabarak Shah*, London, 1927, pp. 16, 18, 21, 22, 26. It may be recalled that E. Denison Ross wrongly identified Muhammad bin Mansur Fakhr-i-Muddabir with his contemporary scholar Fakhr Uddin Mubarak Shah Marvarudi who was the court poet of Ghur and the author of *Bahr ul-Ansab*. Therefore, the *Muqadimah*, ed. Deninson Ross separately may be called *Tarikh-i-Fakhr-i-Muddabir*.
2. Barthold states, 'the concept of the state was brought to its extreme expression under the Ghaznavids, and especially under (Sultan) Mahmud'. It should also be added that the Sultan only exercised executive, military and financial powers while judicial and legislative functions were the concern of the *ulama* who were employed but not interfered with by the Sultan. Cf. V.V. Barthold, *Four Studies in the History of Central Asia*, Eng. tr. V. Minorsky and T. Minorsky, Leiden, 1956, vol. I, p. 70.
3. Minhaj-i-Siraj Juzjani refers incidentally to the *Madrasa-i-Muizi* in his account of Sultan Raziya's reign. Shaikh Nizamuddin Chishti also refers to it. *Tabaqat-i-Nasiri*, op. cit., vol. I, p. 461; Hasan Sijzi, *Fawaid ul-Fuad*, Lucknow, 1885, p. 23.
4. *Tabaqat-i-Nasiri*, vol. I, pp. 419, 420.

5. Ibid., pp. 427, 436.
6. This *Madrasa-i-Nasiriya* has also been incidentally mentioned by Minhaj-i-Siraj. Minhaj-i-Siraj was appointed by Sultan Raziya as the Principal. Cf. *Tabaqat-i-Nasiri*, vol. I, p. 460.
7. Ziya uddin Barani, *Tarikh-i-Firuz Shahi*, Calcutta, 1862, pp. 57-8, hereafter cited Barani.
8. *Khatibs* (preachers) commissioned in each territory to provide people with religious guidance and deliver religious sermons at court. They were highly educated people. Some of them left behind literary works of historical importance. Cf. Iqtidar Husain Siddiqui, *Perso-Arabic Sources on the Life and Conditions in the Sultanate of Delhi*, New Delhi, 1992, pp. 50, 64, for the thirteenth-century *Khatib*, Daud Khatib and Shaikh Jamaluddin of Hansi.
9. Cf. Umaruddin, *The Ethical Philosophy of al-Ghazzali*, Aligarh, 1962, p. 15.
10. Amir Khusrau and Ziya uddin Barani are critical of Sultans who preferred merit to birth in recruiting state officials and promoting people to high positions. Before the advent of the Khaljis to power, important posts seem to have been reserved for men of aristocratic birth. Cf. Amir Khusrau, *Ijaz-i-Khusravi*, vol. 4 (Newal Kishore Press, Lucknow, 1876), p. 236; *Tarikh-i-Firuz Shahi*, pp. 38-9.
11. Cf. *Perso-Arabic Sources on the Life and Conditions in the Sultanate of Delhi*, pp. 3-4.
12. Cf. Sadiduddin Muhammad Awfi, *Jawami'ul Hikayat wa-Livami'ul Rivayat*, vol. I, part 1, ed. M. Nizamuddin, Hyderabad-Deccan, 1965, pp. 3-16.
13. Cf. *Perso-Arabic Sources on the Life and Conditions in the Sultanate of Delhi* pp. 9-11.
14. Majduddin Abul Ma'ali Muaiyid Jajarmi, *Tarjuma-i-Ihya -i-ulum-id-din*, Ms., British Library, London, no. Or. 8194, ff. 1a-2b.
15. Cf. *Perso-Arabic Sources on the Life and Conditions in the Sultanate of Delhi*, pp. 48-9.
16. *Ijaz-i-Khusravi*, vol. 1 (Newal Kishore Press, Lucknow, lithograph), pp. 56-7.
17. *Tarikh-i-Firuz Shahi*, p. 346.
18. Qasim Daud Khatib, *Tarjuma-i-Awariful-Ma'arif*, Ms., University Collection, Maulana Azad Library, Aligarh, no. 320, ff. 4a-b.
19. These verses have been translated by Annemarie Schimmel in *Islam in the Indian Subcontinent*, Leiden, 1980, p. 10.
20. *Tabaqat-i-Nasiri*, vol. I, pp. 362-3.
21. Majduddin Abul Ma'ali Muaiyid Jajarmi, *Tarjuma-i-Ihya-i-ulum-id-din*, Ms., British Library, London, no. Or. 8194, f. 3a.
22. Cf. Shihabuddin al-Umari, *Masalikul Absar in Perso-Arabic Sources on the Life and Conditions in the Sultanate of Delhi*, p. 116.
23. *Ijaz-i-Khusravi*, op. cit., vol. 4, pp. 177-8.
24. Cf. *Fawaid ul-Fuad*, op. cit., pp. 239, 240-1.

25. *Tabaqat-i-Nasiri*, vol. I, 457.
26. Zain Badar Arabi, *Khwan-i-Pur N'imat* (collection of utterances of Shaikh Sharafuddin Yahya), Patna, 1321 AH, p. 14.
27. *Tabaqat-i-Nasiri*, vol. I, pp. 440-1.
28. Isami, *Futuh-us-Salatin*, ed. M. Usha, Madras, 1948, pp. 108-9.
29. Barani, pp. 130-2.
30. Amir Khusrau, *Muqidma-i-Ghurat ul-Kamal*, Ms., British Library, London, no. Add. 21, 106, f. 184b.
31. Cf. *Ijaz-i-Khusravi*, vol. 4, p. 170.
32. *Futuh-us-Salatin*, p. 452.
33. Cf. Iqtidar Husain Siddiqui, 'Science and Scientific Instruments in the Sultanate of Delhi', *Hamdard Islamicus*, Karachi, Autumn, 1994, vol. XVII, no. 3, pp. 1-18.
34. Iqtidar Husain Siddiqui, 'The Origin and Growth of Islamic Historiography in India: Analysis of the Thirteenth Century Indo-Persian Historians' Approach to the History of the Foundation of Muslim Rule in South Asian Sub-continent', *Journal of Objective Studies*, vol. I, nos. 1 and 2, July-October 1989, p. 88.
35. Sadiduddin Muhammad Awfi, *Jawami'ul-Hikayat-wa-Livami'ul Rivayat*, ed. Amir Bano Musaffa and Mutahir Musaffa (Bunyad-i-Farhang, Iran), vol. III, pp. 401, 402.
36. *Tabaqat-i-Nasiri*, vol. I, pp. 331-2.
37. Barani, pp. 297-9.
38. Barani's admiration of the rationalist thinkers of Alauddin's reign is found in the account of Muhammad bin Tughlaq's reign available in the unrevised first version of his *Tarikh-i-Firuz Shahi*. In this version, Barani's approach is more rationalist and free of the didactic element. It was brought to completion in the fifth regnal year of Firuz Shah. Cf. *Tarikh-i-Firuz Shahi* first version, ms. Bodleian Library, Oxford, Elliot-collection, no. 353, ff. 189 a-b; also Peter Hardy, 'Didactic Historical Writing in Indian Islam: Ziya uddin Barani's Treatment of the Reign of Sultan Muhammad Tughluq', in *Islam in Asia*, ed. Friedmann, Jerusalam, 1984, pp. 51-7.
39. Barani, pp. 361-2.
40. Barani, first version, Bodleian Ms., f. 125a; printed text, pp. 325-6.
41. *Futuh-us-Salatin*, pp. 452, 504-5; Ibn Battuta, *The Travels of Ibn Battuta*, tran. Hamilton Gibb (Hakluyt Society, Cambridge, 1971), vol. III, p. 618.
42. Shihabuddin Al-Umari in *Perso-Arabic Sources on the Life and Conditions in the Sultanate of Delhi*, pp. 116-17.
43. Barani, pp. 352-3.
44. Ibid., pp. 354-5.
45. Ibid., p. 354.
46. Amir Khusrau, *Nuh Siphr*, ed. Muhammad Wahid Mirza (Calcutta, 1950), pp. 162-3; also 224-6, for the horoscope drawn by him.
47. Barani, pp. 363-4.
48. Shams Sirraj Afif, *Tarikh-i-Firuz Shahi*, Calcutta, 1891, p. 258.

49. Amir Khusrau, *Qiran ul-Sa'dain*, ed. Ismail Meeruti, Aligarh, 1918, p. 5, lines 25-6, also editor's introduction in Urdu, p. 99.
50. *Ijaz-i-Khusravi*, vol. 2, p. 158.
51. *Perso-Arabic Sources on the Life and Conditions on the Sultanate of Delhi*, p. 123.
52. In vol. 4 of the *Ijaz-i-Khusravi*, Amir Khusrau writes on different popular sciences of his time, such as *Iilm-i-ma'ishat* (economics), prosody, grammar, logic, philosophy, etc., displaying his erudition. Cf. *Ijaz-i-Khusravi*, vol. 4, (Lucknow, AD 1876), pp. 236-318.
53. Barani, *Fatawa-i-Jahandari*, ed. Mrs. A. Salim Khan, Lahore, 1972, pp. 131-3.
54. Ikhtisan, *Basatin ul-Unr*, Ms., British Library, London, Add. 7717, ff. 30 a-b, also *Perso-Arabic Sources on the Life and Conditions in the Sultanate of Delhi*, p. 96.
55. *Perso-Arabic Sources on the Life and Conditions in the Sultanate of Delhi*, p. 107; also *Travels of Ibn Battuta*, Eng. tr. Sir Hamilton Gibb, Cambridge, 1971, vol. II, p. 676, for Abdul Aziz Ardawili.
56. *Masalik ul-Absar*, in *Perso-Arabic Sources of Information on the Life and Conditions in the Sultanate of Delhi*, p. 123.
57. *Basatinul-Uns* in *Perso-Arabic Sources on the Life and Conditions in the Sultanate of Delhi*, p. 96.
58. Ibn-i-Battuta, *Ajaib-ul-Asfar*, Urdu translation, Islamabad, 1983, p. 453.
59. *Futuh-us-Salatin*, pp. 424, 425, 426.
60. Barani, Bodleian Ms. (1st version), f. 187a; in the revised version Barani revises his statement, saying that the Sultan wished to join Prophethood with kingship.
61. *Futuh-us-Salatin*, pp. 447-9.
62. Cf. *Perso-Arabic Sources on the Life and Conditions in the Sultanate of Delhi*, pp. 154-6, for the details in the unrevised version of Barani's *Tarikh*.
63. In the first version of his *Tarikh*, Barani indirectly refers to the elimination of Muhammad bin Tughluq's favourites. Their assets were declared forfeit to the state exchequer but their servants were allowed to join service elsewhere. In the second revised version he refers incidentally to his own imprisonment because he was also one of the counsellors of the late Sultan. Bodleian Ms., f. 217a; printed second revised text, p. 554; also Iqtidar Husain Siddiqui, 'Water Works and Irrigation System in India During Pre-Mughal Period', *Journal of the Economic and Social History of the Orient*, Leiden, vol. XXIX, pp. 52-77.
64. *Sirat-i-Firuzshahi* (Khuda Baksh Oriental Public Library, Patna, 1999), pp. 235-41; Barani praises the beautiful surrounding of the *madrasa* and tells that many residents of the city moved from the city, had houses constructed in its vicinity and began to reside there permanently. Barani, p. 563.
65. Cf. Iqtidar Husain Siddiqui, 'Rise of Syncretic Trends among Sufis in India', *Indian Journal of Secularism*, vol. III; no. 1, April-June 1999, pp. 1-11.

Learning and Intellectual Thought in the Sultanate of Delhi during the Lodi Period

IQTIDAR HUSAIN SIDDIQUI

The dissolution of the sultanate of Delhi, caused by Timur's invasion in AD 1398, was paradoxically paralleled by the diffusion of its imperial culture in north India. A number of independent regional sultanates and principalities arose, the founders of which were the erstwhile governors and army generals of the Sultan of Delhi. Being heirs to the Cultural legacy of the imperial court of Delhi; they emulated zealously their former masters in extending munificent patronage to the men of learning and talent; their *karkhanas* (workshops-cum-store houses) attracted men of arts and crafts. The aesthetic standards set by the Delhi Sultan and elite in literature, fine arts, architecture, dress, and also in social gathering during the preceding centuries inspired people and provided a cultural reference. As a result, the migration of the people of talent and learning caused by the sack of Delhi by Timur to safer places in the new regional Kingdoms and principalities helped their rulers to found Centres of Culture in place of Delhi. The emigrants introduced their traditions of higher culture. Consequently, Ahmedabad in Gujarat, Burhanpur in Khandesh, Shadiabad alias Mandu in Malwa, Nagaur in Rajasthan, Kalpi in Bundelkhand and Jaunpur in eastern Uttar Pradesh emerged as centres of learning and culture. Each one attracted men from different parts of India and foreign countries as well. As regards Delhi it was left as a place of no cultural importance. The entire period during which it was ruled by Khizr Khan and his successors (AD 1414-51) is historically and culturally uneventful; Delhi and the area around continued to suffer from anarchy.

With the advent of Bahlul Lodi to the throne in AD 1451 an era of economic recovery and cultural progress began in the history of the Delhi sultanate. His liberal patronage to teachers and scholars led to the revival of the old seats of learning in Delhi and the establishment of new *madrasas* and seminaries in the provincial towns. Notwithstanding the fact that social developments of historical importance provided building material to the Sur and Mughal empires, no serious attempt has been made by modern scholars to analyse the social life and culture of pre-Mughal times. The apparent reason seems to be the paucity of relevant information in the so-called Afghan chronicles. However, we get interesting pieces of information about cultural life and intellectual activities available in the contemporary literature. The hagiographical traditions, even when anecdotes predominate, give us insights into the promotion of learning and the proliferation of urban culture. Similarly, the circumstantial evidence and impressions provided by the literary sources enlighten us and we can draw a fairly accurate picture of cultural life and intellectual thought during the Lodi period. The aim of this paper is to analyse the relevant evidence, regarding the intellectual history of the period.

Evidence that has seeped into the standard sufi sources and the *Waqi'at-i Mushtaqi*,[1] provides us with insights into the cultural life and intellectual activities and elements of continuity and change in thought and cultural institutions. This also tends to reveal that the city of Delhi which could not sustain its elite on lucrative jobs for want of royal patronage under the rule of the last Sayyid rulers,[2] was again put by Sultan Bahlul on the road to rapid recovery. The land-grants and stipends given by the Sultan went a long way to promote the cause of learning and growth of literature both in Persian and Arabic. Shaikh Jamali Kanbu's eye-witness account of the Sultan's visit to the *khanqah* of Shaikh Sama' uddin Kanbu suggests that he was full of zeal to befriend the cause of the *ulama* and *masha'ikh*.[3] Likewise, evidence of anecdotal nature contained in the *Waqi'at-i Mushtaqi* confirms the impression that *ulama* were provided with the means of livelihood by Bahlul Lodi, so that they could carry on their traditional work of disseminating knowledge in the cities and towns. Every *alim* (scholars) had direct access to the Sultan and secured either a land-grant or a stipend.[4] As a result, Delhi attracted students from different places for the completion of their higher education. The students who graduated from its revived *madrasas* were able to get important positions in the administration, for the expansion and consolidation of the Sultan's authority created job opportunities for them. Maulana Minhaj is worth mentioning in this regard. He came from the Lahore region for higher education and got the post of *mufti* of Delhi after he specialised in Islamic jurisprudence.[5]

Among the scholars who seem to have made great impact on the intellectual life and religious thought, mention may be made of Shaikh Sama'uddin Kanbu, the leading Suhrawardi saint. Notwithstanding the fact that he was a sufi missionary, primarily interested in the spiritual training of his *murids*, he also spared time to deliver lectures to *ulama* and students. In fact, Shaikh Sama'uddin combined the role of an orthodox *alim* and the spiritual excellence of a *dervish*. Born in Multan in 1405, he completed his education at an early age. It is said that he acquired full knowledge of all the Islamic sciences, *fiqh*, scholasticism (*ilm-i-kalam*) and *hadith* when he was only twelve.[6] For his education and early training, he seems to have remained orthodox, in spite of conversion to sufism and attachment to Ibn al-Arabi's philosophy of *Wahdat al-wujud* (unity in the essence of the Creator and the created). Emphasizing the Shaikh's role as an *alim*, Shaikh Jamali Kambu states that everyday in the morning he (Sama' uddin) delivered lectures to the scholars and students. In these he spoke on *tafsir*, *hadith* and the principles of Islamic jurisprudence. Further, he adds that many of the students who attended his lectures belonged to the class of *danishmands* (scholars of Islamic jurisprudence).[7]

Similarly, the little relevant evidence available about the education of the princes also casts light on Sultan Bahlul's attitude towards learning. He was very particular about the selection of scholars for the education of his sons. He treated prisoners of war kindly if they happened to be learned men and employed some of them to educate his sons in popular arts and sciences. The Sharqi wazir, Qutlugh Khan who was singular for his learning and experience of statecraft and whom Bahlul had captured in a battle near Delhi in 1478, was engaged to teach the Crown Prince, Nizam Khan (later Sultan Sikandar).[8]

Sikandar Lodi for his part was a cultured and highly educated man. Basically interested in rational sciences, he sought to overcome contemporary prejudice and investigated facts for himself in order to find out the truth. During his reign scientists were encouraged to apply their knowledge to practical use, suggest new ideas to modify old concepts and introduce new crafts. The Sultan's love of the company of the learned and his interest in knowledge created an environment of trust and dignity for men of learning. He collected a fairly large number of scholars and intellectuals at his court. People sent their children to schools for education. Mushtaqi says that education was carried with such zeal that the sons of the nobility and soldiers applied themselves to gaining knowledge.[9] Nizam al-Din Ahmad also refers to educational progress during this reign: 'Learning gained popularity during his auspicious reign. The sons of nobles and soldiers seriously pursued their study.'[10]

Describing his close association with Sikandar Lodi, Shaikh Jamali Kambu incidentally informs us about the prestige and position enjoyed by scholars at the court. Sultan Sikandar Lodi was gifted with noble qualities and excellent behaviour. He had cultivated tastes and was respectful to men of learning and piety.[11] Shaikh 'Abd al-Haqq *Muhăddith* who had access to all types of literary work produced during the Lodi period, states:

'The reign of Sultan Sikandar was an age of virtue, piety, honesty, clemency, dignity and security. He (the Sultan) was favourably inclined towards the '*ulama*; men of piety, culture and refinement. Consequently, scholars came from different parts of the world, including the Arabian lands. Many were invited by the Sultan, others came of their own accord. All settled in or near Delhi.[12] 'Abd ullah, the compiler of the *Ta'rikh-i Da'udi*, corroborates the *Muhaddith* in these words: 'Having been attracted by his (Sultan's) affection and patronage, the grandees, saints and scholars came from Arabia, 'Ajam (Iran) and the parts of India. They took permanent abode either in Delhi or Agra during his reign.'[13] The details are given in the *Najat al-Rashid* about the life and teachings of Shaikh Hussamuddin Muttaqi of Tulanba. Having heard about Shaikh Hussamuddin's devotion to learning and teaching, Sikandar Lodi offered him a large land grant but the Shaikh declined it because he had adopted a life of extreme austerity.[14]

Odd bits pieced together from various sources reveal that efforts were made by the state to provide educational facilities to people even in small towns. Scholars who were comparatively less known and settled in the interior find mention in the sources. In fact, the maintenance land-grants made by the Sultan to the *ulama* and sufis in the vicinity of towns led them to settle there. As a result, teachers appear to have been available in every town. For example, Shaikh Hamza, a Chishti saint, is reported to have employed two teachers for the education of certain children of Sayyid origin whose parents were too poor and who had been left uneducated due to the vicissitude of circumstances. The Sayyids are said to have been denied the privileges meant for the *ashraf* for their poverty and illiteracy. Of the teachers, one was a scholar of Arabic while the other taught the children Persian.[15] The town of Phulet (Muzaffarnagar district in UP) deserves to be mentioned in this regard. It was an ordinary town without much charm of social life. Shaikh Ahmad bin Yusuf, a favourite of Sikandar Lodi, was given in *madad-i-ma'ash* a few villages near Phulet. As expected, the scholar settled down in the town and founded a *madrasa* to train theologians in that region. Shortly afterwards, other scholars and sufis also settled in Phulet and it soon developed into a centre of learning.[16] Ni'mat ullah Harvi writes about the educational institutions of Samana town (district Patiala) that they were properly maintained by Malik Bustan Kakar, the *wajahdar* (officer-in-charge). Maulana Ahmad was appointed by the *wajahdar* to supervise the teaching in every *madrasa* in his town.[17]

We also find in the *Ta'rikh-i Sher Shahi* and *Lata'if-i Quddusi* interesting information bearing on the system of education at different levels. An account is furnished by 'Abbas Sarwani about Miyan Farid's (later Sher Shah Sur) education in the small town of Sahsram (district Shahabad in Bihar). Though Miyan Farid's father, Hasan Sur, himself does not seem to have been an educated man, he was very much interested in the education of his children as learning and sophistication were the means to state service and a prerequisite for association with the high-ups in the society. For higher education, a student had to go to a city, where he studied under the guidance of celebrated scholars. Miyan Farid went from Sahsram to Jaunpur that was the provincial headquarters of the region and had famous colleges and seminaries since the days of the Sharqi Sultans. In Jaunpur *madrasa*, Farid is said to have studied *Kafiya*[18] along with the commentary, written in Persian by Shihabuddin Dawlatabadi, classics of Persian poetry, Islamic jurisprudence, and historical literature, in addition to work bearing on the way and manners of the princes and statecraft.[19] Like Miyan Farid Sur, Shaikh Rukn uddin, son of Shaikh 'Abd al-Quddus Gangohi, came to Delhi from Shahabad (district Karnal) for the completion of his education. In Delhi he specialized in logic, jurisprudence, *tafsir* and *hadith* under the guidance of master scholars. Student at a higher level attended lectures of masters singular for their command over special branches of Islamic learning.[20] But such facilities for the students to benefit from a number of eminent teachers specialized in particular branches of knowledge were generally available only in the large cities.

In passing it may also be mentioned that travel by a scholar to foreign countries in quest of learning was encouraged. Some of the scholars, associated with the royal court had been to the famous centres of learning and culture in different Islamic countries. Mention may be made of Shaikh 'Abd al-Wahhab Bukhari and Shaikh Jamali Kanbu. Both of them are reported to have visited as scholars the countries of Western and Central Asia.[21] Emphasising the importance of travel undertaken by a student in search of knowledge, Badauni refers to an age-old tradition among the Muslims in India as elsewhere. He states that a student not only got into the habit to endure hardships in course of his journey but also gathered experience, learnt manners, and became a highly cultured man.[22]

It will not be out of place to make a brief reference to the education of girls during this period. The evidence, though brief and laconic, shows that in aristocratic families girls were educated like boys. Learning had become popular among the Afghan women. Influenced by the Delhi aristocratic culture, they observed strict *purdah* and learnt the ways of refined ladies. Some of them gained fame for their knowledge of Islamic sciences. Bibi Surat, the daughter of Malik Bustan Kakar, acquired profound knowledge of Hanafi *fiqh*. Women of aristocratic background called on her and sought her advice on legal problems.[23] Even in middle-class families, girls were taught to recite the Quran and read Persian.[24]

Unfortunately, prominent scholars and scientists of the age have not received due attention. There are, however, brief references to some of them scattered in miscellaneous sources that not only contain insights into the social milieu of the scholars but reveal the atmosphere, bursting with intellectual activity at the royal court, in the cities and towns as well.

Shaikh 'Abd Ullah Tulanbi and his brother, Shaikh 'Aziz Ullah Tulanbi were considered the greatest intellectuals of their age. Attracted by the munificence and affection of Sikandar Lodi, both brothers came from Multan to Delhi. Educationists by profession, they are said to have played an important part in reviving the traditions of scholarship in Delhi. Shaikh 'Abd Allah settled down in Delhi while his brother, 'Aziz Allah, selected Sambhal for his permanent stay. According to al-Badauni, they introduced the systematic study of the rational sciences (*ilm-i-ma'qul*). Before their arrival, with the exception of *Sharh-i Shamsiya* and *Sharh-i Saha'if*, no works treating of logic and scholasticism were recommended to students. Shaikh 'Abd Ullah trained more than forty *danishmands* and every one of them later disseminated knowledge in the tradition of their masters. Sikandar Lodi also attended Shaikh 'Abd Ullah's lectures in Delhi. It is said that the Sultan entered the hall quietly and sat where nobody could see him, so that his presence could not cause any stir and the Maulana's lecture be interrupted. As soon as the lecture was over, the Sultan discussed problems with the Maulana.[25]

Badauni mentions the names of four *danishmands*, Miyan Ladan, Jamal Khan Dehlavi, Miyan Shaikh Gawaliari and Miyan Sayid Jalal Badauni, among the disciples of Shaikh 'Abd Ullah Tulanbi.[26] Other Persian works contain a bit of useful information about Miyan Ladan and Jamal Khan Dehlavi. Both of them enjoyed privileged positions in their times. Miyan Ladan was the son of Shaikh Sama' uddin Kanbu and was born in 1455. His father, a leading Suhrawardi Sufi, loved him more than his other children on account of his devotion to his studies. Shaikh Jamali heard Shaikh Sama' uddin Kanbu say repeatedly that Miyan Ladan was the light of his family.[27] Mushtaqi also mentions Miyan Ladan as a *danishmand* and the son-in-law of 'Umar Khan Kanbu, the *amir-i akhur* of Sultan Sikandar. In his account of the death of the Sultan, he also includes him among the royal *nadims* and charged with the duty of leading prayers at the court. He was also consulted by the Sultan on religious issues.[28]

As regards Jamal Khan Dehlavi, he was the grandson of Shaikh Sama' uddin Kanbu and born in Siri (Delhi) in 1490 during the reign of Sikandar

Lodi. For his mastery over the rational sciences and strict adherence to the law of *sharia*, Islam Shah Sur appointed him chief *qadi* of his empire. On his death, 'Abd Ullah Sultanpuri, generally known as Makhdum al-Mulk, led the funeral prayer and then remarked: Today *Imam-i A'zam* (the title of Imam Abu Hanifa, the founder of the Hanafite school of law) has passed away from the world, and with him the understanding of the book *Hidaya* (one of most important works written by al-Marghinani of Hanafi *fiqh*) and the science of Islamic jurisprudence and scholasticism have disappeared.'[29]

'Aziz Ullah who had settled down in Sambhal also trained scholars as *danishmands* and, in addition delivered public lectures. He possessed such intelligence and power of recollection that he could quote actual passages from books in his lectures as well as to his pupils, no matter how difficult or minute the subject or problem. At times his senior students came and made difficult queries in order to test his memory, but the master could always satisfy them. Badauni writes: 'When they came up for examination, and propounded the most inscrutable problems, the learned Shaikh would explain them on the instant while giving his lesson.'[30] One of his distinguished pupils was Miyan Hatim Sambhali who enjoyed immense prestige during the Sur period and Akbar's reign.

Mention should be made of the Delhi born *alim*, Maulana Shu'ayb who is paid homage by the contemporary scholars for the diffusion of Koranic knowledge in Delhi and the region around it. He was the son of Maulana Minhaj, the Mufti of Delhi during the reign of Bahlul Lodi. Shaikh Ruknuddin, who attended his lectures in Delhi, and was deeply impressed by his knowledge and personality, says that he possessed eloquence as well as knowledge. He delivered lectures on the *tafsir* of the Divine word from the pulpit of his mosque. The gathering of listeners was mostly composed of *Huffaz* and other learned persons.[31] Shaikh 'Abd al-Haqq Muhaddis adds:

> He (the Maulana) was angelic both in character and appearance. His sweet voice had such an effect on people that even pedestrians stopped on the way as soon as it reached their ears. The grandees and scholars of the city came to listen to his lectures. He was also a teacher and most of the scholars of Delhi and the places around had been his students in the beginning of their student life.[32]

Another eminent teacher who produced a number of books on different sciences was Shaikh Allah Diya of Jaunpur. His commentary on the *Hidaya*, running into several volumes, was indicative of the range of his encyclopaedic knowledge. His commentary on the *Kafiya* was also widely-known in medieval times. Besides, he wrote notes upon the *Tafsir-i Madarik* and a number of treatises on various subjects which were read up to the time of Akbar. It was indeed his fame that induced Sultan Sikandar Lodi to invite him to Agra along with other scholars from various places, so that he could benefit from the discussion of religio-philosophical subjects. Badauni says: Sultan Sikandar collected together scholars of his empire, placed on one side Shaikh 'Abd Ullah and Shaikh 'Aziz Ullah Tulanbi and on the other Shaikh Allah Diya and his son Shaikh Bhikari, and engaged them in discussion. Eventually, it became clear that the former were superior in oratory, while the latter were better writers.[33]

In Chanderi, Shah Ahmad alias Shara-i Turk, a learned *danishmand*, also played an important role in maintaining the traditions of learning and scholarship. He had command over different branches of learning, including rational sciences. Though he was a teacher by profession, he spared time to compile books on various subjects in which he defended the cause of Islamic orthodoxy and Sunni point of view with regard to religious practices and concepts. Amongst his disciples was Shaikh 'Abd ul-Ghani Sonipati who collected his master's works and imparted instruction to his students on their basis. Shah Ahmad passed away in 1521 at the age of ninety.[34]

There appear to have been many other scholars of distinction who flourished during this period, but information about their achievements is wanting. Shaikh Ruknuddin refers to a number of them in his *Lata'if-i Quddusi*, implying that they enjoyed prestige for their erudition. In particular, he makes mention of Muhammad Mubarak Jaunpuri, Maulana Ibrahim, Qazi Danishmand Thanesari and Maulana 'Abd Ullah Danishmand Dehlavi who were familiar with sufi philosophy and doctrines and also held scholarly discussions with the learned representatives of sufism. Unlike Shaikh Ruknuddin, Mushtaqi does not mention the members of the fairly large sprinkling of scholars whom Sultan Sikandar Lodi had collected in his service. He simply states that the group of scholars employed by the Sultan remained in attendance daily till late at night. They were served dinner in the evening from the royal kitchen. Every one of them had his servants waiting outside the palace. They attended their respective masters when the court was adjourned.[35] Food was also sent to the scholars in the colleges and seminaries.[36]

The most outstanding foreign scholars who seem to have made an impact on the intellectual life were Sayid Rafiuddin Safavi and Shah Muhammad Jalaluddin bin Muhammad Shirazi. Sayid Rafiuddin Safavi belonged to an illustrious family of famous *ulama* in Shiraz (Iran). He came to India after he had studied in a number of Islamic countries. In India, he first settled in Delhi but afterwards shifted to Agra at the persuasion of Sikandar Lodi. He is reported to have studied rational sciences under the guidance of Maulana Jalal al-Din Dawwani while Shaikh Muhammad bin 'Abd ur-Rahman had supervised his study of *hadith* literature.[37]

Master of rational and religious sciences, Sayid Rafi 'al-Din soon became a prized courtier of the Sultan. Apart from learning, the Sayyid was famous for other personal charms; compassion always radiated from his personality. Shaikh 'Abd ul-Haqq Dehlavi says that he was an *alim* attached to the royal court, yet he could give away all his belongings to people on occasions in the tradition of a devout sufi. Like common people, scholars also benefited from his large heartedness. They got financial assistance and also improved their knowledge of different sciences under his guidance.[38] Even Abul Fazl who was almost niggardly in praise of the orthodox, is all praise for the Sayid because his father had been helped by him in more than one way.[39]

Sayid Rafiuddin Safavi was consulted by Sultan Sikandar on state matters. His scholarship, integrity and association with the Lodi court enhanced his influence in the country. The Afghan grandees held him in reverence even after the fall of the Lodi dynasty. Sher Shah Sur made him his counsellor and called upon him for advice from time to time.[40] The Sayid is reported to have died in 1547.[41]

Shah Muhammad Jalal'unddin bin Muhammad Shirazi came from Mecca in the company of al-Hajj Shaikh 'Abd ul-Wahhab Bukhari (a prominent Suhrawardi sufi saint) and settled down in Agra. He possessed both the piety of a sufi and the erudition of a devoted scholar. On his arrival in Agra, Sultan Sikandar Lodi honoured him with royal favours. The dishes of food that were supplied to him on the first day of his visit to the court, were continued to be sent to him daily without any change till the end of his reign. Though the Shaikh was at home in every branch of knowledge, he was particularly interested in sufi poetry. He delivered lectures on Maulana Rum's *Masnawi*, and explained the meanings of spiritual terms and points raised therein to the scholars. He had food and *firni* always ready for the entertainment of visitors.[42]

The intellectuals and scientists who came from Malwa and sought refuge at the Lodi court in 1510 also deserve to be mentioned in some detail. They were the favourites of Nasiruddin Shah Khalji. On their patron's death, conditions deteriorated and they found it difficult to stay in Malwa. Mushtaqi furnishes the following details about them: 'During the period of chaos and anarchy, many gifted persons left (Malwa) for different places. Malik al-Hukama (chief of the physicians), Malik al-Fuzala (chief of the scholars), 'Alam Khan and (the lady) Dildar Aghacha the *Nadima-i Majlis* (female courtier), who happened to be the distinguished scholars and leading intellectuals of the age, sought refuge at the court of Sultan Sikandar Lodi. 'Alam Khan passed away soon later, but Malik al-Fudala' and Malik al-Hukama' survived for long. Once Khwajgi Sa'id Farmuli (Sikandar Lodi's confidant) informed the Sultan about the qualities of *Nadima-i Majlis* and got permission to conduct her into the royal presence. Having interviewed her the Sultan remarked , 'She is, no doubt, intelligent and worthy, yet her sex does not permit her to be a courtier. It would be better if she stays inside the purdah.'[43] Amongst these intellectuals, the Malik al-Hukama enjoyed immense prestige for his knowledge of medicine and medical science. He not only treated people but also knew about the diseases in the plants, trees and animals. Mushtaqi informs us about his clinical experience: The Malik al-Hukama diagnosed diseases by reading the pulse of the patient or by examining urine. One day Nasir Shah tested his knowledge. The Sultan sent three bottles, each containing urine, one of them of a sick woman, the others of a monkey and a buffalo. 'When they were brought to the physician, the latter asked the bearer to show them one by one. As he examined them, he smiled and dictated the prescriptions. That one of the patients be given such and such medicine with warm water, the monkey boiled cotton seeds mixed with certain other things, and the buffalo freedom.'[44]

It may be recalled that the Lodi period witnessed the revival of orthodox learning with emphasis laid on the study of *fiqh*, *tafsir*, *hadith* and *ilm-i-kalam*. But the intellectual pursuits of Sikandar Lodi and some of his nobles give us a clue to the fact that the study of *ilm-i-ma'qul* was also popular. In fact, the Sultan and his favourites had become an inspiration to others. The keen interest evinced by Sikandar Lodi in rational sciences, poetry and literature led to a qualitative change in thought process, intellectual pursuits and learning. The *hukama* and *fuzala* were encouraged to carry on experiments, produce literature and work for the diffusion of knowledge in the empire. The achievements of certain scientists and scholars among the Sultan's courtiers are by all standards quite important. Let us analyse the available evidence in this regard.

Sikandar Lodi had a cultivated taste for Persian poetry and encouraged the study of rational sciences, he was fond of composing poems. The medieval writers quote his Persian verses by way of specimens which shed light on his refinement and personal sophistication. His pseudonym was Gul Rukh (rose faced)[45] Ni'mat ullah Harvi quotes Sultan Sikandar's versified letter addressed to Shaikh Jamali Kanbu. In this letter the royal invitation to the poet was versified with literary charm.[46] Badauni, who was a critical scholar of literature and whose judgment about different poets is accepted as just and fair even by modern scholars, says about these verses that they 'are written with the utmost regard to poetical form.'[47] He quotes the following couplets:

سروی کہ سمن پیرہن وگل بدنستش
روح است مجسم کہ درآں پیرہنستش
مشک ختنے چیست کہ صد مملکت چیں
درحلقۂ آں زلف شکن درشتش
گل رخ چہ کند جو ہر دندانِ ترا وصف
ہم چوں درسیراب سخن دردہنستش
درسوزنِ مژگاں بکشم رشتۂ جاں را
تا چاک بدوزم کہ درآں پیرہنستش

That cypress whose robe is the jasmine, whose body the rose,
Is a spirit incarnate whose garment the body provides.
How matters the Khutani musk? All the kingdoms of China,
Are conquered, and bound in the chains of her clustering curb
Could Gul Rukh essay to discover the charm of her teeth,
He would say they are water-white pearls of the Ocean of Speech.
In the eye of her eye-lashes needle the thread of my soul,
I'll fasten and swiftly repair every rent in her robe.[48]

Likewise, the hints available in biographical details of intellectuals, *mashaikh* and orthodox *ulama*, help us analyse the various streams of thought among the social and religious elite. It is worth recalling that the *ulama* who came to India in the wake of Turkish conquest towards the close of the twelfth century belonged to the Hanafi school of thought with leanings towards Ash'arite philosophy. They stood for a strict adherence to the *sharia* implying thereby that salvation lay only in complete surrender to the Divine Will as expressed in the Quran and further interpreted by the founders of the Hanafite School of law.[49] They were also opposed to the study of rational science and works written by the Mu'tazilites, Abu 'Ali Sina and others and condemned their advocates as heretics.[50] But their opposition seems to have softened with the passage of time, and it began to be realized that familiarity of a scholar with rational sciences would sharpen his intellect and as well increase his sophistication. For instance, Shaikh Jamali Kanbu, who was an orthodox Suhrawardi sufi and criticises in his *Tazkira* the influence of the philosophers, 'Ubayd Samarqandi, Maulana 'Ali Mantiqi and Dabir Ikhtisan, stating that the latter had abandoned the right path of *sharia* under their influence,[51] does not recommend a ban to be imposed on the study of philosophy. He rather implies that besides the Greek philosophy, a prince should also be familiarized with the *hikma* of Abu 'Ali Sina, so that an all round development of his personality would be possible.[52]

Like the Hikmat-i Abu 'Ali Sina or rationalist philosophy, Hikmat-i Ishraq propounded by Shaikh Shihabuddin Suhrawardi al-Maqtul (*d.* 587/1191) that regarded Being and Knowledge as irradiations of the Pure Light[53] also held fascination for certain intellectuals in India. Besides the sufis, some of the orthodox *ulama* also felt attracted by the *Ishraqi* philosophy and acquired acquaintance with it through reading and discussion with its scholars. The case of Shaikh Mubarak Nagauri may be cited. He went from Nagaur to Ahmedabad in order to perfect his understanding of *Ishraq* under the tutelage of Khatib Abul Fazl Gazaruni. The latter originally hailed from Shiraz and had come to Gujarat on the invitation of a certain Sultan in the fifteenth century.[54] Likewise, the philosophy of *Wahdat-al-wujud*, advocated by Shaikh Ibn al-Arabi was very popular among the sufis or *masha'ikh*. Generally the *ulama* condemned it as heresy and prevented the young scholars from studying it.[55] However, their severe opposition to this metaphysical philosophy aroused the curiosity of certain scholars and, in certain cases, it won converts.[56] It may be stressed that the patron-saint of the Lodi dynasty, Shaikh Sama'uddin Kanbu who was more of an orthodox *alim* than a sufi,[57] also subscribed to the philosophy of *Wahdat al-wujud*. The passages quoted by Shaykh 'Abd ul-Haqq *Muhaddith* from his *Miftah ul-Asrar*, reflect on his commitment to the philosophy of *Wahdat al-wujud*. He says,

> The followers of *Wahdat al-Wujud* hold that there is no limit to man's spiritual progress. If man were to survive for a thousand years and to keep himself preoccupied with devotion and worship, every day new light and secret would dawn on him that he did not experience previously because Divine Wisdom and Knowledge are limitless. According to this philosophy, man is the best of all Creation.[58]

As regards Sikandar Lodi's interest in different schools of thought, he got into close touch with their representatives, listened to them, and derived amusement and also satisfied his curiosity yet, the circumstantial evidence accessible to us tends to reveal, was himself a rationalist in every matter, literary and religious. He was unorthodox in his personal life, in spite of the fact that he had collected a fairly large number of orthodox *ulama* and sought advice from them over legal matters faced by him. He secretly sipped alcohol, shaved his beard and questioned the validity of age-old beliefs that did not appeal to reason. He also advocated the cause of *ilm-i-ma'qul* (rationalism) instead of *manqul* (traditionalism). We may now briefly summarize the details available in the *Waqi'at-i Mushtaqi*.

One day, the Sultan asked the learned gathering whether the birds understood each other's tongue. Some of the scholars said: 'the exegesis indicate that birds do understand one another's tongue'. In the meantime, Khwaja Sa'id Farmuli arrived there. The Sultan turned to Khwaja Sa'id and told him of his query to the scholars along with their answer. Khwaja Sa'id said that it was enough otherwise further discussion would amount to questioning the very faith in religion. The Sultan retorted: 'O yes! I have also got the same feeling but I wanted to discuss it on the basis of *ma'qul* (rationalism), but in vain. You tell me whatever you have got in your mind.' Again the Khwaja repeated: 'One should not apply *ma'qul* (reason) to *manqul* (traditional explanation).' The Sultan insisted, saying: 'I have also held the same point of view but you should tell me whatever you think about it.' Thereupon, Khwaja Sa'id observed: 'apparently, it seems that certain birds may understand each other's tongue but, in actual fact, all of them do not have this capacity. For example, whenever the fowler sets the net, he keeps the blades of grass under his teeth and makes a sound, the birds are attracted and trapped. The birds cannot understand this much that the sound does not come from their own species.

Similarly, the fowler stitches the eyes of a sparrow, places it on the net, and when it is pricked (from below) it cries for help. Hearing its cry, the birds flock to it and are entrapped. They do not understand this much that the cry has been caused by pain and helplessness and, therefore, other birds should not go near it. They do not avoid the risk (of being caught). Some of the birds, such as crows and those which make their nests on the trees and mountains, such as crane and pheasants gather at the call of their species and then disperse for safety. But most of the birds do not possess this capacity.[59]

Of the nobles who had been singular for their learning and scientific learning, Miyan Taha Farmuli and Masnad-i-'ali Miyan Bhu'a, the *wazir* of the empire also deserve mention. Miyan Taha Farmuli is reported to have been familiar with all the arts and sciences practised in his day. Sikandar Lodi paid him homage for his chemical and technological inventions in these words, 'Miyan Taha is equal to one thousand intellectuals.'[60] Miyan Taha lectured to scholars on morality and religion, imparted instruction to students, and taught different arts to his slaves. He supervised their study of the *diwans* of Khaqani, Anwari and the *Shahnama* of Firdausi. He had no rival in his knowledge of music. The *Sarogians* (experts of classical Indian music) of his age considered him unrivalled in their art and also confessed their inferiority to him.[61]

Miyan Taha was also acknowledged master of *ilm al-tib*. It is said that he had committed to memory four thousand *ashloks* (formulas of Ayurvedic system of medicine) relating to ailments and their treatment. Brahmins who were considered masters of Ayurveda came to consult him. Nobles and their children came to him for treatment. Moreover, the Miyan was interested in scientific and technological inventions. One of his inventions was the production of paper of extreme whiteness made of pulp mixed with ivory. It was not broken even when it was rolled or opened and no stripes or scars could be caused thereon in the process. He made a flag of an elephant's tusk which was in no way inferior to flags of fine cloth. It was much whiter than the usual. He made another flag of material mixed with wax which too was not damaged on being folded or opened.

Miyan Taha also acquired sufficient knowledge and experience of metallurgy. He manufactured swords of steel, particularly the Indian sword (called *langvani*), the edge of which could be spoilt neither by fire nor by sharpening. He trained slaves to manufacture different types of weapons. In his *karkhana* the slaves produced under his instructions swords like the imported ones from Western Asia and Europe.[62]

Masnad-i-'ali Miyan Bhu'a was celebrated for his vast knowledge of sciences and humanism. He was a statesman and administrator. Being the wazir of the sultanate, he utilized his resources and position in gathering a fairly large number of knowledgeable persons around him. It is also said that he collected books bearing on various sciences and employed expert calligraphists to make copies. Moreover, the scholars who enjoyed his patronage came from different parts of the world, including Khurasan, Iraq and Central Asia. The most important achievement of Masnad-i-'ali Miyan Bhu'a is the compilation of the *Ma'dan al-Shifa-i Sikandar Shahi.*[63] It is based on Sanskrit classics on ancient medicine.[64] According to Mushtaqi, it was considered matchless both in standard and value in the whole of India.[65]

Besides, Masnad-i 'ali also encouraged scholars in his service to compile literary works. Unfortunately, these compilations have not survived the ravages of time. The *Lahjat-i-Sikandar Shahi*, however, compiled by 'Umar bin Yahya al-Kabuli, a Persian translation of a Sanskrit work dealing with Indian music, has survived.[66]

Another development of great importance, resulting from the administrative and cultural reforms introduced by Sikandar Lodi was the learning by Hindus of Persian language and literature. The Sultan is reported to have banned the use of Hindi in the state departments in favour of Persian for accounts and records. Nizam al-Din Ahmad writes that after the promulgation of the royal order, Hindus began to learn Persian.[67]

The Hindus seem to have acquired proficiency in Persian within a short time and some of them emerged as distinguished scholars.[68] Badauni informs us about the Brahmin Dunkar, a gifted poet and a scholar of traditional Muslim sciences. He gave Muslim students instruction in science. Badauni also quotes the following *matla* of his *ghazal* that Dunkar had composed in the metre of Mas'ud Beg's popular poem as a *jawab* (reply):[69]

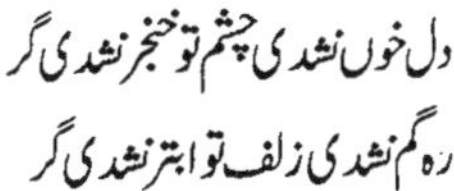

Had not thy glance been the dagger, my heart had not bled today;
Had not thy lock been the serpent, I never had lost my way.

Biographical details furnished by Nizamuddin Ahmad and Badauni about Shaikh 'Abd Ullah Badauni add to our knowledge that middle-class Hindus became conscious of the advantages of learning Persian and, in consequence, made arrangements for teaching their children Persian. Shaikh 'Abd Ullah was born in a Hindu family of Samana. His father engaged a Muslim scholar to teach him Persian language. In course of his study the student was impressed by the life and teaching of the Prophet and was attracted to Islam. Ultimately he decided to embrace Islam.[70] His parents did not prevent him from renouncing their faith. The convert, now named 'Abd Ullah, moved to Delhi. There he joined the circle of Miyan Ladan Danishmand, the *nadim* of Sikandar Lodi. Later, he moved to Badaun where he studied with Sayid Jalal Badauni. After the death of the latter 'Abd Ullah took his place.[71] Badauni says: 'he taught and imparted instruction for many years in Badaun, and many well-known *danishmands* who became famous had been his pupils. People from the surrounding country and from the utmost parts of (other) countries by waiting upon him attained eternal felicity.'[72]

Badauni was one of his students. He studied *Sharh-i Saha'if*, scholasticism, and the principles of jurisprudence. Closely associated with his master, Badauni was deeply impressed by his simplicity, piety, religiosity and knowledge. He writes:

His (Shaikh 'Abd Ullah's) unceremoniousness and humility are such that he goes on foot in the tradition of his predecessors and successors to the market and shops to buy household goods, whether in small or large quantities, and to purchase all necessary supplies for his kitchen, and carries them back to where he dwells. On the way, too, he teaches a number of students, and howsoever much they may say, 'Master, there is no need for you to trouble yourself in this way, we will perform this duty', he does not consent thereto . . . notwithstanding that a class of pupils of copious attainments and students of clear intellect were engaged in study, and brought subtle difficulties for his elucidation, I never saw him, in the course of his teaching, to be under the necessity of referring to a book for the purpose of solving those questions and obscure subtleties, for whatever he had once seen he had on the tip of his tongue.[73]

Sultan Ibrahim Lodi also appears to have been a patron of scholars like his predecessors. But the information furnished by our sources about his relations with the *ulama* is brief and one-sided. Shaikh Jamali, who failed to win the new Sultan's confidence and lost his official position, is bitter in his criticism of Ibrahim Lodi and his favourites. Jamali is, however, corrected by other sources. For instance, the Sultan not only renewed and confirmed land grants held by the scholars but also favoured new applicants in a large number in an attempt to earn a good name. In fact, he seems to have surpassed his father and grandfather in this.[74] The relevant evidence contained in the *Akhbar al-Akhyar* also tends to confirm that he desired to collect scholars of distinction at his court for prestige. For instance, he offered the post of *hajib* to Maulana Zain al-'Abidin alias Miyan Adhan, but the later did not accept.[75] The teacher of Ibrahim Lodi, Shaikh Farid Bukhari, whom the Sultan elevated to the post of sadr,[76] seems to have espoused the cause of all those scholars who could be of help and service to the state. Shaikh Jamali, however, accuses him of having been the main cause of estrangement between Ibrahim and the nobles of Sultan Sikandar.[77]

Equally interesting are the references found in the sources to libraries built by individual scholars. These libraries shed light on the affluence in which scholars lived. The possession of a rich collection of books by an individual was thought the sign of learned man. Consequently, almost every scholar who was seized with a passion for knowledge appears to have possessed his own library. Libraries existed in cities as well as towns. Shaikh Ruknuddin's testimony to this is of immense significance. Mentioning Babur's invasion of the Panjab in 1523-4, Shaikh Ruknuddin says that the invaders did not even spare libraries in the towns of the Panjab; all of them were plundered along with residences.[78] Babur himself describes the library of Ghazi Khan Lodi, son of Daulat Khan in the town of Milvat.[79] In this the invader found a huge collection of books relating to different subjects. Babur states:

I went into Ghazi Khan's book room, some of the precious things found in it, I gave to Humayun, some sent to Kamran (in Qandahar). There were many books of learned contents, but not so many valuable ones as had at first appeared.[80]

Incidentally, Mushtaqi also provides hints about the libraries of scholars of average means and educated grandees in key positions in the Delhi sultanate and the provincial kingdoms. Describing the close and cordial ties between Miyan Zain Uddin (the *Muqta*ʻ or governor of Badaun) and his servants, he makes allusion to the library possessed by his father, a man of average means. He states that on the dismissal of Zain Uddin by Ibrahim Lodi (1517), many of the former's old servants, officers as well as soldiers, stayed with him. One of these was Mushtaqi's father, Shaikh Saʻd Ullah Dehlavi. He performed the duty of *imam*. Zain Uddin had showered special favours on him. A few years after the dismissal of Zain Uddin, the relations of Shaikh Saʻd Ullah advised him to seek employment with some other noble as his friend was no longer able to support his servants financially. The Shaikh did not accept their advice, because he did not consider it becoming to part company with old benefactors in their time of adversity. But he also told them for their satisfaction, 'I have got a residential building that I would dispose of for the sustenance of my family. In addition I also have a *kitab khana*, the sale proceeds of which would suffice for long. I have no worry so long as these belongings last. All these were acquired during my association with him (Miyan Zain Uddin).'[81]

It seems that the maintenance of libraries by the scholars and nobles was thought a part of culture and learning in all of India. In the Bahmani kingdom also the scholars and nobles owned private libraries. The Wazir Khwaja Jahan (Mahmud Gawan) is reported to have collected hundred thousands of books for his personal collections along with other valuables.[82]

In the final analysis, it may be stated that the Lodi period not only witnessed the revival of old educational institutions but also the proliferation of culture and learning. The seminaries and *madrasas* founded and maintained by state grants turned out distinguished scholars who rose to prominence. The *ulama* and literati of Akbar's reign, with a few exceptions, were the productions of the intellectual efflorescence that can be described as the renaissance of the Delhi elite culture during the Lodi period. In short, the elite of the Lodi period made substantial contribution to Indian aristocratic culture and provided building material for the construction of the edifice of Mughal culture.

NOTES

1. Shaikh Rizq Allah Mushtaqi, *Waqi'at-i Mushtaqi*, Ms. British Museum, London, Add. 11, 633; also Iqtidar Husain Siddiqui, 'Shaikh Rizq Allah Mushtaqi: A Sufi Historian of Medieval India', *Islamic Culture*, Hyderabad-Deccan, October 1969, pp. 277-93, for an evaluation of the source material.
2. 'Ali bin Mahmud al-Kirmani, known as Shihab Hakim, the compiler of the *Ma'athir-i Mahmud Shahi* states that in 1447 Sultan Mahmud Khalji of Malwa was informed about the plight of the religious divines and scholars in Delhi. Thereupon out of sympathy with the scholars he sent his emissaries with money for them and invited them to his capital, Mandu. On their arrival, one of the scholars, Shaikh Nizamuddin Mahmud, was selected by the Sultan as his *nadim* (counsellor) for the former's learning and culture.

   Rizq Ullah Mushtaqi mentions Shaikh Mahmud as Mahmud Nu'man and also adds that he was raised to the position of *hajib* (chamberlain) by Mahmud Khalji's son and successor. Sultan Ghiyath al-Din Shah; *Ma'athir-i Mahmud Shahi*, ed. Nurul Hasan Ansari, Delhi, 1968, pp. 67-8; *Waqi'at-i-Mushtaqi*, f. 75a.
3. Shaikh Jamali Kanbu, *Siyar al-Arifin*, Delhi, 1311 AH, p. 176.
4. *Waqi'at-i Mushtaqi*, op. cit., ff., 6a-b.
5. Shaikh 'Abd al-Haqq Muhaddith, *Akhbar al-Akhyar*, Delhi, 1283 AH, p. 243.
6. Ahmad Khan, *Shajra-i Suhraward*, Ms. Reza Library, Rampur, no. 365, ff. 12a-13b.
7. *Siyar al-Arifin*, op. cit., p. 176. The term *danishmand* was generally used for a man of learning well-versed in *fiqh*, scholasticism, *mantiq* and *hadith*. One of the earliest thirteenth-century writers, Sadiduddin Mahmud 'Awfi used the term *danishmand* in the sense of a jurist who could be appointed *qadi*. The *malfuzat* of Shaikh Nizamuddin Awliya also contain references to *danishmands* which tend to show that they were the scholars known for their command over *fiqh*, logic and other rational sciences. Cf. Muhammad Awfi, *Jawami'al-Hikayat wa Liwami-ur Riwayat*, ed. Bano Mussafa Karimi, Iran, 1352 Shamsi, vol. II, pp. 409-10, 577; Hasan Sijzi, *Fawa'id-al-Fuad*, Newal Kishore Press, pp. 165-6.
8. Nizam al-Din Ahmad, *Tabaqat-i Akbari*, Calcutta, 1913, i/308; Muhammad Qasim Hindu Shah Firishta, *Gulshan-i Ibrahimi*, also known as *Ta'rikh-i-Firishta*, Lucknow, no date, p. 179.
9. *Waqi'at i-Mushtaqi*, f. 8b.
10. *Tabaqat i-Akbari*, Calcutta, 1913, i/170.
11. *Siyar al-Arifin*, p. 138.
12. *Akhbar al-Akhyar*, p. 261.
13. 'Abd Allah, *Ta'rikh-i-Dau'udi*, ed. Shaikh Abdur Rashid, Aligarh, 1971, p. 36.
14. 'Abd al-Qadir Badauni, *Najat ur-Rashid*, ed., Lahore, 1972, p. 413.

15. *Akhbar al-Akhyar*, p. 214.
16. Shah Wali Allah, *Anfas al-Arifin*, Delhi, 1315 AH, pp. 62-3.
17. Ni'mat Allah Harvi, *Tarikh-i Khan-i Jahani*, ed. Imam al-Din, Dacca, 1962, ii/886-7.
18. The title of *Kafiya* is *al-Kifayat fi'l-Nahv*. It is on prose, how it is written and errors in the selection of words avoided. It was written by Jamaluddin bin Abu 'Amr 'Uthman. Shaikh Shihabuddin Daultabadi, the courtier of Sultan Ibrahim Sharqi made a translation of this work in Persian which became very popular subsequently.
19. 'Abbas Sarvani, *Ta'rikh-i Sher Shahi*, ed. Imam al-Din, Dacca, 1964, p. 31.
20. Shaikh Ruknuddin, *Lata'if-i Quddusi*, Delhi, 1311/1894, pp. 47, 61.
21. *Waqi'at i-Mushtaqi*, ff. 26a-b, *Akhbar al-Akhyar*, pp. 253-4, *Siyar al-Arifin*, pp. 69, 139-40.
22. *Najat-ur-Rashid*, op. cit., p. 375.
23. *Tarikh-i-Khan-i-Jahani*, ii/828.
24. *Lataif-i Quddusi*, p. 63.
25. Al-Badauni, *Muntakhab ut-Tawarikh*, Calcutta, 1864, i/323-4; hereafter cited as Badauni, Eng. tr. George S.A. Ranking, i/427-8, hereafter cited as Ranking.
26. Badauni, i/324.
27. *Shajrah-i-Suhraward*, f. 28a-b.
28. *Waqi'at i-Mushtaqi*, ff. 24b, 27b.
29. *Shajrah-i Suhraward*, ff. 9b-10a.
30. Badauni, i/324-5; Ranking, i/428.
31. *Lataif-i-Quddusi*, op. cit., p. 61.
32. *Akhbar-al-Akhyar*, p. 261.
33. Badauni, i/329; Ranking, i/428-9.
34. *Akhbar-al-Akhyar*, p. 254.
35. *Waqi'at i-Mushtaqi*, f. 26a.
36. Ibid., ff. 26a-b.
37. *Akhbar-al-Akhyar*, p. 288.
38. Ibid., pp. 288-9.
39. *A'in-i Akbari*, Eng. tr. Jarret, 3/486.
40. *Ta'rikh-i-Sher Shahi*, p. 191; also Badauni, i/369-71.
41. *Akhbar-al-Akhyar*, pp. 253-4.
42. *Waqi'at-i-Mushtaqi*, ff. 26a-b.
43. Ibid., ff. 79a-b.
44. Ibid., ff. 79-80a-b.
45. Cf. *Tarikh-i-Khan-i-Jahani*, i/244.
46. Ibid., i/226.
47. Badauni, i/323.
48. I have adopted George S.A. Ranking's translation with minor modification in a line. Badauni, Eng. tr. G.S.A. Ranking, i/425-6.
49. The Sunni *ulama* and *mashaikh* who came to India from different countries

in the thirteenth century belonged to the Hanafi School. They were deadly opposed to the Isma'ili Shi'is and philosophers. They were supported in their mission by the rulers and ministers. Nizam al-Mulk Junaydi, the famous *wazir* of Sultan Iltutmish encouraged the scholars of Arabic to translate classical literature on orthodox religion into simple Persian for the benefit of less educated persons. In 620 AH/AD 1223 Mawlana Majd al-Din Abu'l Ma'ali bin Muhammad Jurjami, completed his translation of Imam Ghazali's *Ihya'al-'Ulum al-Din*. This translation was read with the Arabic text during the subsequent period. Majd al-Din Jurjami's translation of Imam Ghazali's *Ihya al-'Ulumid-Din*, Ms. British Museum, London, Or. 8194, Ziya uddin Barani, *Ta'rikh-i-Firoz Shahi*, Calcutta, 1862, p. 346.

50. The orthodox *ulama* and *mashaikh* were so much against the study of literature produced by the Mu'tazilites and other free thinkers, that they issued *fatawa* from time to time that it should be burnt wherever found. Even the *tafsir* literature such as *Tafsir-i-Kashshaf* and *Tafsir-i-Ijaz* were not spared. Hasan Sijzi, *Fawa'id al-Fuwad* (collection of the sayings of Shaikh Nizamuddin Auliya), Newal Kishore, p. 109, also Barani, pp. 444, 465, for his condemnation of the rationalist philosophers.
51. Jamali Kanbu, *Siyar al-Arifin*, Ms. Habib Ganj Collection M.A. Library, Aligarh, f. 147a.
52. Jamali Kanbu, *Mahr-o-Mah*, ed. Hussam al-Din Rashidi, Rawalpindi (Pakistan), 1974, p. 92.
53. Cf. R. Arnaldez, *Ishrak*, in *The Encyclopaedia of Islam*, New edition, vol. IV, Fasc. 61-2, Leiden, 1973, p. 120a.
54. Abu'l Fazl, *A'in-i Akbari*, Lucknow, 1892, iii/205; Eng. tr. H.S. Jarret, Calcutta, 1948, iii/484.
55. *Akhbar-al Akhyar*, pp. 223-4, particularly the account of Shaikh Hasan Tahir.
56. Shaikh Rukh al-Din, *Lata'if-i Quddusi*, pp. 42-3, 44.
57. *Siyar al-Arifin*, Rizvi Press, Delhi, 1893, pp. 173-8.
58. *Akhbar al-Akhyar*, p. 245.
59. *Waqi'at i-Mushtaqi*, ff. 66a-67a; and also *Ta'rikh-i Da'udi*, pp. 56-7.
60. *Waqi'at i-Mushtaqi*, f. 68a.
61. Ibid., f. 68b.
62. Ibid., ff. 68a-70a.
63. Ibid., ff. 33a-b.
64. Miyan Bhu'a, *Ma'dan al-Shifa-i Sikandar Shahi*, Newal Kishore Press, Lucknow, 1877.
65. *Waqi'at i-Mushtaqi*, f. 33a.
66. Umar bin Yahya al-Kabuli, *Lahjat-i-Sikandar Shahi*, Ms. Madras University Library, PMS, no. 518, ff. 6b-7a, for Miyan Bhu'a's patronage to the men of learning in his service.
67. *Tabaqat-i Akbari*, i/71; Badauni, iii/54.
68. *Firishta*, p. 188.
69. Badauni, i/323; Eng. tr. Ranking, i/426; Firishta, p. 188.

70. *Tabaqat-i-Akbari*, ii/473; Badauni, iii/54.
71. Badauni, iii/55.
72. Ibid., iii/55-6.
73. *Siyar al-Arifin*, pp. 138-9.
74. Iqtidar Husain Siddiqui, *Wajh-i ma'ash* grants under the Afghan Kings (1451-1555), *Medieval India: A Miscellany*, Aligarh, 1972, vol. 2, pp. 29-31, 259.
75. *Akhbar al-Akhyar*, p. 259.
76. Shaikh Nur al-Haqq, *Zubdat al-Tawarikh*, Ms., India Office Library, London, no. 1805, ff. 79b-80a.
77. *Siyar al-Arifin*, pp. 138-9.
78. *Lataif-i Quddusi*, p. 64.
79. The town of Milvat is situated in the Salt Range in 32° 42' in Jhelum district (Pakistan).
80. *Baburnama*, Eng. tr. Mrs. Beveridge, ii/460.
81. *Waqi'at i-Mushtaqi*, ff. 30b-31a.
82. Ibid., f. 85a.

Khwaja Shah Mansur: The Tragic Career of an Intellectual Finance Minister

AFZAL HUSAIN

The execution of Khwaja Shah Mansur in 1581 casts a persistent shadow over Akbar's otherwise enviable reputation as a humane sovereign. The execution is particularly poignant since Shah Mansur was one of the major architects of his financial reforms. Yet there is no biography of the victim, and certainly no full discussion of the evidence about his fall.

Khwaja Shah Mansur began his profession as a clerk from Shiraz, apparently his native place.[1] He migrated to India and joined Mughal service in the royal perfumery department in the early years of Akbar's reign. Subsequently he was promoted to the office of *Ashraf-i Itriyat*, 'accountant of the perfumery department'. Muzaffar Khan, who was not only the *Diwan* but also held the overall charge of administration in general, is said to have become jealous of his capacities, and sought to entangle him in various intrigues.[2] Ultimately, he got him arrested and dismissed from service. Mansur then went to Jaunpur and obtained appointment as *Diwan* under Ali Quli Khan Zaman.[3] Sometime afterwards, apparently after the revolt of Khan Zaman and the appointment of Mun'im Khan to Jaunpur, Khwaja Mansur joined his service and assumed charge of his establishment. From Bayazid Bayat's memoirs it appear that Shah Mansur served as *Diwan* of Mun'im Khan from 1570 to 1572. Afterwards he was appointed *Bakhshi* by Mun'im Khan in place of Dost Muhammad, who was removed from the office on a charge of taking bribes from soldiers. Mansur served Mun'im Khan as *Diwan* and *Bakhshi* till the latter's death in 1576.[4] He visited the imperial court several times in connection with the affairs of his master. On one such occasion, when he had appeared at the court to plead that Mun'im Khan be assigned *jagirs* in Bengal in exchange for those in Bihar, Akbar was greatly impressed with his knowledge of financial matters and his businesslike attitude.[5]

After the death of Mun'im Khan, when Raja Todar Mal started making enquiries into the finances of Mun'im Khan, Khwaja Mansur, the person in charge of his affairs, was arrested and even tortured, apparently in an attempt to make him divulge the full assets of his master.[6] When the imprisonment was reported to the emperor, however, he immediately ordered his release, summoned him to the court and appointed him *Wazir*.[7] With regard to his sudden and direct appointment to this high office, Abu'l Fazl offers the remark that he was raised to this position 'without the recommendation of courtiers which is what helps most men, and without the experience which the experts regard as evidence for promoting servants.'[8] This clearly indicates that the appointment was seen as an assertion of imperial power and Akbar's high opinion of Mansur's abilities. It is, however, not surprising in the circumstances, that he was not given independent charge of the department. Raja Todar Mal was recalled and appointed *Mushrif-i Diwan* and Muzaffar Khan was made *Wakil* in the following year (1577), so that Mansur had, in effect, two superiors watching over him; superiors, moreover, who were by no means friendly to him. In the appointment order of Muzaffar Khan it was stated that he should enquire into the affairs of the empire and Todar Mal and Mansur were to perform their duties in consultation with him.[9]

Very significant administrative reforms were introduced by this collegium of officers.[10] It was in the implementation of these that serious differences developed among them. To give Mansur a free hand, Muzaffar Khan was sent in 1579 as governor to Bengal and Todar Mal, soon afterwards, to Bihar.[11] Clearly, Akbar had shown a preference for Mansur over the others. Mansur was not in a position to carry out the reforms without any interference. One of the great reforms of Akbar, the *A'in-i Dah-sala*, whose basic design had been laid with the resumption of *jagirs* in 1574-5, was actually implemented by Khwaja Mansur. Abu'l Fazl acknowledges that 'though the carrying out of this great design was committed to Raja Todar Mal and Khwaja Mansur, the Raja was sent off to eastern provinces and it was the Khwaja who by dint of his sagacity comprehended the sublime instructions and arranged the exquisite plan'.[12]

Khwaja Mansur made another important contribution to Mughal administration by dividing Akbar's empire into twelve *subas* each with a Governor (*sipahsalar*), a *Diwan*, a *Bakhshi*, a *Mir'Adl*, a *Sadr*, a *Kotwal*, a *Mir Bahr*, and *Waqi'a Nawis*.[13] As a matter of fact the arrangements made by Mansur henceforth formed the basis of Mughal provincial administration till the very end of the empire. Khwaja Mansur made special efforts to implement his regulations rigorously. In matters of realizing arrears and effecting economy in finances, he made no distinction between the different nobles, which naturally cost him the goodwill of the leading courtiers.

One reform that Mansur tried to implement and which created a great crisis was the reduction of the allowances of officers posted to Bihar and Bengal. After the conquest of Bihar and Bengal, Akbar had increased the pay of the army by 100 per cent in Bengal and 50 per cent in Bihar, keeping in view the bad climate of the region and continued Afghan resistance.[14] Khwaja Mansur in 1580 reduced this to 50 per cent in Bengal and 20 per cent in Bihar.[15] He also wrote strong letters to Tarsun Muhammad Khan and Ma'sum Khan Farankhudi in this connection. Muzaffar Khan further complicated the situation by preparing the accounts from the beginning of the year and demanding refund of the excess payments from the affected officers.[16] The political situation in Bengal and Bihar was already fluid, and these demands brought matters to a head. Todar Mal, looking for an opportunity to humiliate Mansur, immediately took up this issue. Making the political consequences of the reduction in allowances a pretext, he accused Mansur of having undermined the entire effort made by him and other officers in keeping officers like Tarsun Muhammad Khan and others loyal to the emperor. He also charged him with unreasonably demanding the payment of revenue that had already been collected by the enemy at a time when the imperial officers were engaged in war with the Afghans.[17] Abu'l Fazl agrees that Khwaja Mansur diverged from the proper course and was imprudent in his efforts to increase the revenue at such a time.[18]

The situation in the east was truly serious and rebellion could break out any moment. Therefore, to conciliate the officers and rebels, Akbar dismissed Mansur from office and handed him to Shah Quli Mahram to be kept a prisoner. Wazir Khan was appointed *wazir* in his place.[19]

These actions failed to prevent the outbreak of rebellion, and so with conciliation no longer seeming to serve any purpose, Mansur was reinstated. Abu'l Fazl's comments on his reappointment are worth quoting: 'It appeared that in writing of accounts and demanding arrears there was no fault of the Khwaja except the thought of increasing the revenue and a failure to recognize the circumstances of the time'.[20] In other words, the suspicion of treasonable conduct had no basis—Mansur's measures might well have had Akbar's own sanction. It was only to quieten discontent that he had been made a scapegoat. A number of references in the *Akbarnama* and other contemporary sources nevertheless underline the fact that Shah Mansur had been widely unpopular among the nobility. Badauni writes that such harsh measures were adopted by Mansur that 'people forgot the tyrannies of Raja Todar Mal and Muzaffar Khan and kept showering on him an abundance of abuses'.[21] The *Tabaqat-i Akbari* also tells us that his harshness had in various matters been repeatedly brought to the notice of the emperor.[22] Abu'l Fazl, writes that 'he was always laying hold of trifles in financial matters and displaying harshness; and sympathy for debtors never touched the hem of his heart'.[23]

Mansur's unpopularity obviously derived from what he felt was the call of duty. The eighteenth-century *Ma'asir-u'l Umara*, tells us that the Khwaja greatly improved the administration and cleared up outstanding matters: he excelled in astuteness, knowledge, effecting economies and strict observance of rules and regulations.[24] More significant is Abu'l Fazl's admission that 'there is seldom found such an acute accountant and a man so hard working, so discriminating and so plausible of speech'. Akbar too was to remark sadly, after Mansur's execution, that 'from that day the market of accounts became dull and the thread of accountancy dropped from the hand'.[25]

At this time the atmosphere at court was tense. The rebels of Bengal and Bihar had read the *khutba* in the name of Akbar's younger brother, Mirza Hakim, and had induced him to invade the Punjab. There was also a feeling that some nobles were secretly working in Mirza Hakim's interest.[26] Faced with the greatest crisis of his career, Akbar decided to march against Mirza Hakim.

At this juncture, Akbar received three letters forwarded by Raja Man Singh, allegedly written by the *munshi* of Mirza Hakim, to Hakimu'l Mulk, Khwaja Mansur and Muhammad Qasim Khan *Mir Bahr*. These letters were found in possession of Shadman, an officer of Mirza Hakim, who had been arrested by Man Singh.[27] Akbar regarded these letters as forgeries and did not show them to Mansur and the other two officers. But when he started on his march, he took the precaution of ordering Mansur to accompany him. When he reached Sonepat, the *Diwan* of Mirza Hakim, Malik Sani, arrived at the camp and stayed with Khwaja Mansur. Under the circumstances, this action of Mansur was incredibly indiscreet. Abu'l Fazl says that it was suspected that Malik Sani had come on a spying mission and, as he had stayed with Mansur, the latter was suspended from service and placed under arrest.[28] The court then moved on through Panipat and Thanesar to Shahabad. Here two letters were produced for the emperor. From these it appeared that Shah Mansur's *shiqqdar* (revenue-collector) of Firozpur (which lay in Mansur's *jagir*) had personally established contacts with Mirza Hakim.[29] At this, Akbar was enraged; he ordered Mansur to furnish security and suggested that if Khwaja Sulaiman, who was related to him, could offer such security it could be accepted. Since Sulaiman did not come forward to offer the security, Mansur was hanged on 28 February 1581.[30]

It appears that it was the last set of letters that led to Mansur's execution. However, the entire evidence against him is circumstantial. Abu'l Fazl in the *Akbarnama* (final version) nowhere categorically states that Mansur was really guilty of treason. A careful reading of his account shows that he is in fact labouring to excuse the execution by pleading that, it was partly an equitable retribution for the excesses committed by Mansur as *Diwan* and partly a casualty of the great stress brought about by a major rebellion. The fact that there was a conspiracy against Mansur is not denied.[31]

Other contemporary accounts, the *Tabaqat-i Akbari* and the *Muntakhab al-Tawarikh* expressly allege that the letters were forged and Mansur was executed on a trumped-up charge.[32] Akbar himself was later convinced that he was not guilty. After reaching Kabul, he made an enquiry and found that Raja Todar Mal, with the help of Karamullah, brother of Shahbaz Khan, had forged the letters and the last letter, which had been the cause of his execution, was also forged.[33] On the other hand, Father Monserrate, who was with the camp, following perhaps the popular rumour mill, considered Mansur the ring-leader of a conspiracy against Akbar and guilty of treason. He fully justifies the execution.[34]

Two pieces of evidence not previously examined in this context are now available and shed valuable light on the episode. One comes from a collection of letters of Hakim Abu'l Fath Gilani.[35] The Hakim accompanied Akbar on his march to Kabul and took part in the proceedings against Khwaja Mansur. A *farman* of Mirza Hakim addressed to Mansur had been discovered in which a reference to his *'arzdasht* (petition) to the Mirza was made, indicating Mansur's attachment to Mirza Hakim. The emperor handed over the document to Abu'l Fath to read aloud. After he had read the letter, the Hindu and Muslim nobles present, numbering six or seven, unanimously asked for Mansur's execution. No one dared say anything in opposition. Abu'l Fath says that he also could not say anything except to remind Akbar that His Majesty himself used to say that in times of war letters were often forged in the names of nobles of rival armies, and not much reliance could be placed on them. Akbar did not like this and said that there were no doubts now in this particular matter. After that Mansur was arrested and handed over to Zain Khan Koka. His entire property was confiscated, but he was not condemned to death.[36] In a subsequent letter Gilani mentions that two *parwanahs* addressed to Khwaja Mansur and Hakimu'l Mulk had now been intercepted; and this finally led to the unfortunate man's execution. The same letter informs us of the arrival of Shaikh Jamal and Bir Bal at the imperial camp. At the end of the letter he writes that Mansur was not an ordinary person and he was not guilty of the crime he was charged with.[37]

The other evidence is from Abu'l Fazl, whose final version in the *Akbarnama* we have examined above. An earlier rescension of the *Akbarnama* is also available to us.[38] A careful study of this version shows that many modifications have been introduced in the final version concerning this episode. Abu'l Fazl tells us in the earlier version that the last batch of letters was obtained by Malik 'Ali from the enemy camp, and, two days before Shah Mansur's execution, Payag Das was made the *Diwan*. We are further told that Akbar wanted to keep Mansur in captivity, but on the pleading of Bir Bal and others he ordered him to be hanged. Abu'l Fazl here admits that the charges against Mansur were not fully confirmed and it was quite possible that his enemies had laid a plot against him. He also points out that Mansur's uncompromising nature turned leading nobles against him.[39]

In the light of these two independent accounts there is definite room for the suspicion that the execution of Shah Mansur was the result of a well-laid conspiracy in which leading nobles of the empire were involved. Man Singh (who sent the first set of letters to Akbar), Bir Bal (who persuaded the emperor to execute him) and Todar Mal (who got the final letters forged with the help of Karamullah, brother of Shahbaz Khan) were the leading figures in this conspiracy.

The role of Shahbaz Khan's brother in forging the evidence against Shah Mansur brings under suspicion Shahbaz Khan himself. It cannot be overlooked that, left at Fatehpur Sikri, Shahbaz Khan had begun dismantling the centralized administration of Shah Mansur. Only a little while Shah Mansur's execution Shahbaz Khan began to offer *jagirs* in lieu of salary to the nobles. This is first reflected in Hakim Abu'l Fath's letter to Humam from the imperial camp at Lahore, 30 March 1581, where he enjoins the latter not to accept a *jagir* from Shahbaz Khan without imperial permission. The imperial camp had just crossed the Chenab, when Abu'l Fath was writing to his brother about 'a harsh *farman*' having been sent to Shahbaz Khan, for 'having a mad enhancement in people's monthly pay and *jagirs*'.[40] But Shahbaz Khan seems to have disregarded these instructions; when Akbar, returning from his expedition, received him at Panipat, he found him unrepentant, leaving it to Akbar to decide whether to undo what he had done.[41] Obviously, Shahbaz Khan had not only taken advantage of Mansur's dismissal and execution, but was satisfied that his defiance of orders had much support among 'the soldiery', an euphemism, in the present case, for the great nobility. On the basis of both circumstantial evidence and the application of the maxim *cui bono*, he must, then, be judged guilty, along with his other three colleagues at court.

Abu'l Fazl tells us that Akbar always regretted his energetic finance minister's tragic end: 'The market of finance', he admitted, 'became cold thereafter'.[42]

NOTES

1. Nizamuddin Ahmad, *Tabaqat-i-Akbari*, ed. B. De and Hidayat Husain (3 vols.), Calcutta, 1913-14, II, p. 436 (hereafter cited as *Tabqat*) calls him *navisanda-i Shiraz*. Also see Abdu'l Qadir Badauni, *Muntakhab al-Tawarikh*, ed. Ali Ahmad and Lees, Bib. Ind. Calcutta, 1864-9, II, p. 240 (hereafter cited as Badauni).
2. Abu'l Fazl, *Akbarnama*, ed. Maulvi Abdur Rahim, Asiatic Society of Bengal, 1877, III, p. 193; *Tabaqat*, II, 436; Badauni, II, p. 240 (hereafter cited as Badauni).
3. *Akbarnama*, III, p. 193; Shahnawaz Khan, *Ma'asir-u'l Umara*, ed. Ashraf Ali, Bib. Ind., Calcutta, 1888, I, pp. 653-4.
4. Bayazid Bayat, *Tazkira Humayun o Akbar*, ed. Hidayat Husain, Calcutta, 1941, pp. 326-7; *Ma'asir-ul Umara*, I, p. 653. *Akbarnama*, III, pp. 193-4, makes no reference to his holding the office of *Bakhshi* under Mun'im Khan.
5. *Akbarnama*, III, p. 164. See Bayazid, p. 341, for more details.
6. Bayazid, p. 349; *Akbarnama*, III, pp. 193-4.
7. *Akbarnama*, III, pp. 193-4; *Tabaqat-i Akbari*, II, p. 494; Badauni, II, p. 240. Cf. *Ma'asir u'l Umara*, I, pp. 653-4.
8. *Akbarnama*, III, pp. 193-4.
9. Raja Todar Mal was appointed *Mushrif-i Diwan* in the twentieth year (1575), but was sent to Bengal in the same year.
10. For details of the reforms carried out by them, see Ibn Hasan, *The Central Structure of the Mughal Empire*, pp. 154-5.
11. *Akbarnama*, III, p. 291.
12. Ibid., p. 293.
13. Ibid., p. 282.
14. Ibid., p. 293.
15. Loc. cit.
16. Ibid.
17. *Akbarnama*, III, pp. 315-16; *Tabaqat-i Akbari*, II, pp. 354-5.
18. *Akbarnama*, III, pp. 315-16; also Badauni, II, p. 287, and *Tabaqat-i Akbari*, II, p. 356.
19. *Akbarnama*, III, pp. 315-16.
20. Ibid., p. 328. Abu'l Fazl at another place (III, pp. 315-16) affirms that the reductions were made by Mansur on his own.
21. Badauni, II, p. 240.

22. *Tabaqat-i Akbari*, II, pp. 546-7.
23. *Akbarnama*, III, pp. 343-4.
24. *Ma'asir-u'l Umara*, I, pp. 853-4.
25. *Akbarnama*, II, pp. 343-4.
26. We have no direct evidence for this, but from a careful reading of the contemporary accounts one gets this impression. Monserrate specifically mentions a conspiracy and considers Mansur as its ringleader. *Commentary on his Journey to the Court of Akbar*, tr. J.S. Hoyland and S.N. Banerjee, Cuttack, 1922, p. 92. The letters of Hakim Abu'l Fath Gilani also hint at this. See *Ruq'at-i Hakim Abu'l Fath Gilani*, ed. Dr. Bashir Husain, Lahore, 1968, p. 13.
27. *Akbarnama*, III, pp. 342-3. Other contemporary sources give more details about the event: *Tabaqat-i Akbari*, II, pp. 535-8; Badauni, II, pp. 292-5. The account of Shah Mansur in Farid Bhakkari, *Zakhirat al-Khawanin*, ed. Moinul Haq (3 vols.), Karachi, 1961, I, p. 185, begins from this event.
28. *Akbarnama*, III, p. 343.
29. Ibid., does not mention the name of the *shiqqdar*.
30. Ibid., p. 343.
31. Ibid., pp. 343-4.
32. Badauni, II, pp. 292-5, concludes that Mansur fell victim to the conspiracy, although he himself is a great critic of Mansur. He ridicules Akbar for feeling sorry for the execution after discovering that the letters were forged (II, p. 295). The *Tabaqat-i Akbari*, II, p. 553, makes no direct comment in this regard, but its account is the most detailed; and Badauni has taken much of his information from it. One gathers the impression from it too that Mansur was executed on the basis of forged letters.
33. *Tabaqat-i Akbari*, II, p. 553; Badauni, II, pp. 294-5.
34. *Commentary of Father Monserrate*, pp. 64-70. Smith largely agrees with Monserrate and considers Shah Mansur guilty of treason (V. Smith, *Akbar The Great Mughal*, 1919, pp. 93-6).
35. *Ruq'at-i Hakim Abu'l Fath Gilani*, ed. Dr. Bashir Husain, Lahore, 1968.
36. *Ruq'at*, pp. 12-14. The letter was written from Shahabad.
37. Ibid., pp. 18-20. This letter was also written to Hakim Humam and sent from Sirhind.
38. B.M. MS, Add 27, 247, f. 246.
39. Ibid., ff. 316-17.
40. *Ruq'at*, pp. 26-7, 34.
41. Badauni, II, p. 296.
42. *Akbarnama*, III, p. 344.

Munajat (Invocation to God) of Shaykh Abu'l Fazl Allami (1551-1602)

SYED ATHAR ABBAS RIZVI

Although Shaykh Abu'l Fazl Allami's *Akbarnama* with the *Ain-i Akbari*, the *Makatubat-i-Allami* and the *Iyar-i Danish* are well known, his *Munajat* (Invocation to God) is little known. It is included in the *Lataif-i Fayzi*, also as *Lata'if-i Fayyazi* compiled by Nuru'd-Din Muhammad, son of Hakim 'Aynu'l Mulk. In his preface, Nuru'd-Din says that the poetical works of Fayzi such as *Markaz-i Adwar* and others were collected and arranged by Abu'l Fazl, but that Fayzi's prose compositions had been neglected. To save them from oblivion, he had compiled them into a volume divided into five *latifas* (pleasantries or sections) and three *mantuqas* (expressions, or chapters). The Persian letters of the title *Lata'if-i Fayyazi* yield the date of compilation as 1035/1625. The five *latifas* comprise letters that Fayzi wrote between 24 August 1591 and 7 May 1593 to the emperor as his ambassador to the Deccan, the rest comprise his letters to sufis and ulama, physicians, Sayyids and amirs and to his relations. The first *mantuqa* comprises the *Munajat* and the remaining two *mantuqas* contain miscellaneous anecdotes. The *Lata'if-i Fayyazi* has recently been published in Lahore but the present author had published the *Munajat* in the *Medieval India Quarterly*, Aligarh in 1951 (vol. I, nos. 3 & 4, pp. 1-37 text, and pp. 116-23, with English introduction). Here I re-examine the *Munajat* using a Persian text published in the *Medieval India Quarterly*. The Lahore edition does not comprise the *Munajat*.

According to F. Steingas' *Persian-English Dictionary*, *munajat* means telling a secret, speaking privately with another, prayers, recommendations, an address to the Deity, a silent and fervent prayer, inward converse with God. Along with the obligatory prayers, the Quran calls upon Muslims to earnestly invoke Allah. 'And your Lord hath said; Invoke Me and I will respond to your invocations. "*Uduni astajib lakum*" ' (XL, 60). A different verse says, 'Allah's are the fairest names (*Asma al-Husna*). Invoke Him by them' (VII, 18). Invocations re-kindle the inscrutable mystery of relations between Allah and his servants. The name Allah itself brings home His sole, unlimited and incommunicable sovereignty (*rububiyya*). No wonder that in *munajats* the name Allah is incessantly repeated. Other names such as Rahman (Benefactor), Rahim (Merciful), Ghafur (Forgiving) and Ghaffar (Everforgiving) are frequently mentioned. A verse invokes God thus: 'Our Lord! Give unto us in the world that which is good and in the Hereafter that which is good, and guard us from the doom of Fire.' (II, 201).

Invocations repeated by the Prophet and his companions, family members and early sufis constitute the best specimens of Arabic devotional literature. They read like dialogues between Creator and creature. The rhythm of the Dawn invocations of the fourth Caliph, Ali ibn Abi Talib (d. 661) and that of his disciple Kumayl ibn Ziyad transport readers to a state of ecstasy. In their inimitable lyrical style they invoke the protective, beneficent and merciful attributes of Allah and explain his perfection and transcendence. They answer many problems which seemed insoluble to the later Muslim thinkers. Their principal aim is to strengthen *birr* (piety) and *taqwa* (reverent fear) among the devotees and enable them to show their gratitude to Allah.

On their pattern Persian poets and mystics also composed *munajats*. The masterpiece is the *munajat* of Khwaja Abu Isma'il 'Abdu'llah Ansari (d. 481/1089) of Herat. For example, he writes:

> O God! Two pieces of iron are taken from one spot, one becomes a horse-shoe and one a king's mirror. O God! Since Thou hadst the Fire of Separation, why dist Thou raise up the fire of Hell? O God! I fancied that I know Thee, but now I have cast my fancies into the water. O God! I am helpless and dizzy; I neither know what I have, nor have what I know![1]

Abu'l Fazl also follows the pattern of his predecessors who composed their *munajats* in Persian. It is partly in prose and partly in verse. In it Abu'l Fazl juxtaposes verses from mystic poets such as Sana'i (d. 525/1130-31), Farid-ud Din Attar (d. 671/1220), Jalal-ud Din Rumi (d. 672/1221) and Fayzi (d. 1004/1595), which he seems to have frequently recited with his own prose sentences and paragraphs. Most remarkable is the lucidity of the entire composition. It was not designed to be submitted to the emperor or to any worldly authority, so that the sincerity of Abu'l Fazl's feelings in it cannot be questioned. Although the major portion of the *munajat* comprises devotional and mystic topics, references to Akbar are of considerable historical interest.

Abu'l Fazl was fully aware of the fact that his contemporaries were sharply divided in their assessment of his personality and religious views. He says:

Although the son of Mubarak is present the object of contrary views and a warning to mankind and a strife of love and hate is kindled in his regard, the truth-seeking worshippers of God call him Abu'l Wahdat (the father of Unity of Being or an adherent of Wahdat al-Wujud) and account him a unique servant of the Supreme Being. The valorous men of the realm of bravery style him Abu'l Himmat (father of resolution) and deem him one of the wonders of carnal self-denial. Wisdom proclaims him Abu'l Fitrat (father of inventive genius) and consider him a choice specimen of that family. In writings of common people, which are the noisy dens of ignorance, some attribute worldliness to him and hold him to be one of those plunged into this whirlpool, while others regard him as given to heresy and *ibahat*,[2] and band together in repro of and condemnation.[3]

Shah Nawaz Khan, the author of *Ma'asir-u'l Umara*, writes,

Shaykh Abu'l Fazl's infidelity is commonly known. Some reproach him with being a despised Brahman (i.e. a Hindu), some call him a sun-worshipper, and another group calls him a materialist. Some even carry their disgust so far as to call him a *mulhid*[4] and a *zindiq*.[5] Others, attempting to be more fair, such as the followers of sufis, who belong to the category of those who defame a few virtuous souls—attribute to him the beliefs in universal concord (*sulh kul*), broadly based religious views, the pretence of believing in *Hama Ust* (All is He), freedom from the obligation of the *shari'a* and following the path of *ibahat*.

One of Abul Fazl's contemporaries, Shah Abu'l Ma'ali Qadiri the Sufi (d. 1024/1615), a leading disciple of Shaykh Dawud Chati (d. 982/1574-5), says that he was hostile to whatever Abu'l Fazl had done. One night, however, he saw in a dream that Abu'l Fazl was produced in the assembly of the Prophet Muhammad. The Prophet, casting his blessed glance upon him, gave him a place in his assembly and condescended to observe, 'This man during part of his life did evil things, but his invocation saying, 'O God! Exalt the virtuous for their virtues and comfort the wicked for the sake of Thy graciousness',[6] became the cause of his salvation.[7] Indeed Abu'l Fazl's *Munajat* sets the records straight and is an invaluable source for the assessment of both Abu'l Fazl and Akbar.

Abu'l Fazl invokes God with some of His Koranic names, Ilah (God), al-Samad (Eternally Besought), al-Rabb (Supreme Sovereign), al-Ahad (One), al-Qadir (Almighty), Zu'l Jalal (Lord of Majesty), al-Rahman (the Benefactor), al-Rahim (Merciful), al-Hadi (the Guide), al-Karim (Munificent), al-Hakim (the Wise) and al-Nur (the Light). He also coins Persian titles in keeping with his text, such as Bi-Niyaza (O! Independent One), Dana-i Ahwal (Knower of states), Khata Push (Concealer of faults), M'a'zirat Niya'ush (Hearer of apologies), Gharib Nawaz (Comforter of destitutes), Dil Nawaz (Comforter of heart) Nigaranda-i Surat wa-ma'ani (Designer of form and meaning).

Addressing God as one who has neither names nor signs, who is both manifest and hidden, Abu'l Fazl says: 'How can I call Thee *'Alimu'l Ghayb* (knower of invisible) for the *ghayb* (invisible) has no access to Thy court. Further, how can I call Thee creator of things, for things have no value to Thy holy sanctuary.'[8] Since no single name could be applied to God, Abu'l Fazl had no hesitation in commencing his translation of the Gospels with the formula 'Ainam-i wal Zhizh wa Kristo' (O He! whose name is Jesus and Christ). Shaykh Fayzi added to it the line, '*Subhanaka la Siwaka Ya Hu* (Praise be to Thee, there is none like Thee, O He!).[9] Fayzi's line made Abu'l Fazl's ingenious formula more meaningful. Similarly Abu'l Fazl commenced his preface to the translation of the *Mahabharata* with the formula 'Sri Ganesa namh' (Reverence to Lord Ganesa) in consonance with the Sanskrit text of the original.

Wajib'ul-Wujud (Necessary Being) and Absolute Good

Abu'l Fazl yearns to remain firm in the realm of *Tawhid* or *Wahdatu'l Wujud* (Unity of Being), as conceived by Ibn 'Arabi (d. 638/1240) and his school of sufis. This demands the realization of an already existing union or oneness with Reality, which is the One and All. This is not monism or pantheism as commonly understood. Henry Corbin who had studied Avicenna, Ibn 'Arabi and the Ishraqi thoughts thoroughly, says:

> It is perhaps because our age-old Christological habits prevent us from conceiving (of) a union other than hypostatic that so many Western writers have characterized Ibn Arabic as monist. They overlook the fact such fundamentally didactic thinking is hardly compatible with what Western philosophy has defined as monism.

According to Ibn Arabi, the One and many are two aspects of One. To the ulama *tanzih* meant Divine transcendence and *tashbih*, anthropomorphism. But for Ibn Arabi *tanzih* referred to the aspect of completeness in the Absolute and *tashbih* stood for His limitedness (*taqayyud*). In contrast to the finite God of religion, Ibn Arabic asserts without inhibition the importance of the limitless God of mysticism. It is strictly on the pattern of Ibn Arabi that Abu'l Fazl says, praised be Allah there is no God but He:

> O God! In whatever direction I turn, I find Thee manifested; in whatever particle I look, I find Thy light, The *Ka'ba* of clay points to one direction but the *qibla* of the heart in all directions. . . .
>
> It is imperative that we should cast our glance on the path of truth. Always we should watch the eternal sun. Since God is manifested in all directions, to fix the face of submission to one particular direction is *kufr* (infidelity).[10]

In the same strain he wrote an inscription for a place of worship erected in Kashmir, for the followers of Unity of Being, probably by Akbar.

O God, in every temple I see that people seek Thee, In every language I hear spoken, people praise Thee! Infidelity and Islam run after Thee, Each religion says, 'Thou art one, without equal'.[11]

Although Abu'l Fazl was an ardent admirer of Ibn Arabi, in the *munajat* he borrows heavily from the Ishraqi or Illuminationist doctrines of Shaykh Shihabuddin Suhrawardi Maqtul (d. 1191). According to Shaykh Shihabuddin Suhrawardi, *Wajibu'l Wujud* (Necessary Being) subsists in Himself and no existence or attribute is comparable with Him. Anything that can be conceived as contrary to God is non-existent. There is absolutely no similarity between Necessary Being and whatever is created by Him. Shabistary (d. 720/1320), a follower of both Ibn Arabi and Shaykh Maqtul, says:

Know that God Most High created it,
And whatever comes from God is good,
Being is purely good in whatever it may be,
It also contains evil, that proceeds from other.
If the Musalman but knew what is faith, He would see
that faith is idol-worship.
If the polytheist knew what idols are, how would he be wrong in his religion?
He sees in idols naught but the visible creature,
And that is the reason that he is legally, a heathen.[12]

Postulating on the theory that Necessary Being good, Abu'l Fazl was convinced that from *Khayr-i Mahaz* (absolute good) nothing but good emerged. Consequently, there was no reason to be distressed. He observes, 'O Bestower of exaltation on those who are endowed with sincerity, and O Bestower of Excellence on those who have access to His private chamber! Help me in the assemblies of multitude and on the state of *Wahdat* (Unity of Being). Guide me to the private chamber of *Shuhud* (the sight of God).' He implores God to remove from his heart all traces of *ghayr* (other than God).[13]

Zat and Sifat

Controversies surrounding Essence and Attributes are both abundant and perplexing. Muslim intellectuals, however, are convinced that the Essence is primordially one, and each Name and Attribute is identical with the Essence. According to Abu'l Fazl, Essence is indescribable and His hallowed attributes cannot be recounted. He goes on to say, 'Some people, of their ceaseless efforts, come to certain conclusions and take them for granted. They believe that whatever statements they make sound perfect as regards His Essence. Some other people are bewildered and do not dare make any statements.

In letters of Eternity there is no place for metaphors, Letter patents of Timeless One cannot be reduced to any phraseology, close lips from conversation and close eyes from sighting. For here neither does the phraseology nor does allusions serve any purpose.[14]

Surat (Form) and Ma'ana (Meaning)

The outward appearance of a thing is form, its inward and unseen reality is its meaning. Invoking the designer of form and meaning. Abu'l Fazl says:

Although Thou hast created me in the world of form, do not entangle me in it. Give me plentiful portion and abundant share of the world of meaning.[15]

Ma'rifat (Gnosis)

According to the sufis God is independent of the intellect and exalted above perception. One of the great sufis said, 'God made us to know Himself through Himself, and guided as to the knowledge of Himself, through Himself, so that the attestation of gnosis arose out of gnosis through gnosis, after he who possessed gnosis had been taught gnosis by Him who is the object of gnosis'.[16] Abu'l Fazl was convinced that gnosis is a gift of God. He begged God to guide al those who are lost in the wilderness of disappointment to the holy sanctuary of His sanctity and satisfy thirsty inhabitants of the desert of consternation by the wholesome water of ma'rifat.[17]

O Worshipped One of the dwellers of Ka'ba and monastery! O Lord of the wanderers in the forest and lovers of seclusion! Heavenly beings have received no knowledge of Truth and the people inhabiting the earth have no acquaintance with gnosis. Wise men can do no better than to search, and jurists have recourse to nothing but to discussions. In place of worship nothing but stones and walls can be seen, and mosques are nothing but centres of distress and disorder.[18]

Creation and Divine Will

According to Muslim sages, God created the world in order to manifest His own Names and Attributes. God Himself is said to have observed, 'He was a hidden Treasure but He created the World for He loved to be known.' Abu'l Fazl goes on to affirm that the state of *adam* (non-existence) is the realm of Unity and the abode of peace. It was the Divine will which was responsible for bringing into being plurality of existence, a source of perplexity to men. He therefore implores the Divine Mercy to make the heart of a seeker the mirror of His beauty rather than a cause of veiling and separation. He begs God not to entangle him in the material world and to bestow upon him gifts from the domain of spirituality.[19]

Riza (Satisfaction)

Sufi and non-sufi literature discuss the importance of Riza at length. It is the *sine qua non* of a pious life. Bishr bin Hafi asked Fuzayl bin Iyaz (d. 803) whether renunciation was better, or satisfaction. Fuzayl replied, 'Satisfaction, because he who is satisfied does not long for higher stages.'[20] *Riza* wipes out the bitterness arising out of *Qaza* (Divine decree operating from eternity) and *Qadar* (fate). In an attempt to stick to *Riza*, the seeker no longer finds his own personality or power sufficient, and implores God to dominate his life.

Abu'l Fazl says, 'Everybody begs for something from the court of Thy Almightyness but I yearn that Though shouldst be satisfied with me. Keep me firm on the highway of Thy satisfaction (*riza*), protect my life and ignore my mistakes in the material world.'[21]

The Ego and Reason

The Islamic devotional literature identifies that *nafs* (soul) that incites a person to evil with sensuality or ego. It is known as *nafs-i ammara*. It is devoid of luminosity and unable to perceive the light that shines through it. Reason and ego are in perpetual strife and the latter prevents people from making distinguishing between truth and falsehood. Abu'l Fazl fervently prays God to help him overcome this strife and to acquaint him with the domination of *nafs*. He implores God to enable him to forget his own self.[22]

Heart

Devotional literature identifies self-realization and spiritual consciousness with the heart. Darkness and dross make spiritual consciousness opaque. In that state of affairs, heart and ego become identical. Abu'l Fazl submits to the Bestower of Consciousness, '(God), As I am unable to obtain self-realization, how can I gain God-consciousness?' He begs God to make his heart a mirror that reflects God. Abu'l Fazl was convinced that his sins did not emanate from his heart and it was purity of heart that mattered. He begged God to trace back the origin of his action and not to take into consideration what the body had been doing.[23]

State of the Soul after Death

Abu'l Fazl divides religious opinions about the state of the soul into four categories. One group believes in resurrection (All types of Muslims); another group believes in the transmigration of soul (Hindus), a third one thinks that after a fixed time the soul of deceased is born in the same body (Muslims); and the fourth, whom he considers a group composed of disturbed minds, avers that the human body is like a grass (Materialists). He goes on to say that one group is happy in the hope of going to paradise, another is afflicted with the dread of hell. Some are content with the impossible idea of obtaining Divine vision. Some are pleased with the equally impossible idea of arriving, alighting and returning, i.e. transmigration of the soul. Another group is striving to improve its condition and conduct in order to earn Divine satisfaction. Yet others think only of their present state, regardless of their future. A large number of people are busy bargaining to achieve bodily comfort. Abu'l Fazl does not mention of his own inclinations to any one of the above groups and invokes God to grant him knowledge of the Reality and to guide him along the right path.[24] He goes on to say that people hold different views about the heaven and hell but there is not much difference between the real heaven and hell. The former is identified with the realization of Divine truth and the latter is contained in remoteness from Divine reality.[25]

Taqlid

As was the case with other Muslim thinkers Abu'l Fazl also strongly resented *taqlid* (imitative knowledge or blind following). He implored the source of all knowledge God to give him *tahqiqi* (realized) knowledge or ability to arrive at truth. Reason and intellect were not necessarily guides to the path of Reality, Divine help was the only way out of impasse.[26]

Places of Worship

Abu'l Fazl believed that God cannot be worshipped in a mosque or temple. Neither was the erection of places of worship, according to him, imperative.

He says, 'O creator of the World! Reason does not suggest that rich people and men of wealth should glorify Thee by erecting mud walls. Construction of places of worship is not advisable for finite symbols are in no way related to the infinite.'[27] In his inscription for a place of worship in Kashmir, he wrote, 'If it be a mosque, people murmur the holy prayer, and if it be a Christian Church, people ring the bell from love to Thee. Sometimes I frequent the Christian cloister, and sometimes the mosque. But it is Thou Whom I search from temple to temple.' He added, 'He who from insincere motives destroys this house (of worship), should first destroy his own place of worship; for if we follow the dictates of the heart, we must bear up with all men, but if we look to the external, we find everything proper to be destroyed.'[28]

Man and Divine Love

The *Munajat* throws considerable light on man's position in the hierarchy of universal existence. Adam's primordial knowledge of Divine Names went a long way to making him a theatre wherein the Divine Names and Attributes are reflected. He is an epitome of the whole universe *al kawan al-jami'*, i.e. microcosm. In His essence, God is beyond all needs; yet at the level of His attributes He desired to be known, so He created the world. Consequently, everything in the world participates in God's love. According to the Quran, of the entire creation only man could dare assume the Divine Trust.

Amanat

'Lo! We offered the trust unto the heavens and earth and the hills, but they shrank from bearing it and were afraid of it. And man assumed it. Lo! he hath proved a tyrant and a fool: *Zaluman wa jahula* (XXXIII, 71).'

With this verse in mind, Abu'l Fazl reiterates that *zalum* and *juhul* (tyrant and fool) had no access to God. He says, Our perception cannot penetrate His Being. Our greedy heart cannot fathom Thy depth. Woe to me! We and Thee cannot be identical. Particles of dust as we are, we cannot understand the grandeur of the sun.'[29]

Sin and Divine Forgiveness

Farid Bhakkari, the author of *Zakhirat-ul Khawanin*, was a near contemporary of Abu'l Fazl. He says that the Shaykh used to visit the houses of dervishes at night and distribute *ashrafis* (gold coins) and beg them to pray for the preservation of his faith. Words such as, 'alas what ought to be done' were frequently on his lips. And then he would strike his hands on his knees and heave a deep sigh.[30] The *Munajat* reveals beyond doubt that the consciousness of sin lay heavy on Abu'l Fazl. Both sin and forgiveness are recurring themes of his *munajat*. A sense of sin and self-abasement did not, however, prevent him from placing trust in the efficacy of God's grace and forgiving mercy. Those who lost hope in God's forgiveness, he believed, were miserable. He goes on to stay that he could not look upon God from the point of view of the *faqihs* (Muslim jurists) who failed to appreciate human imperfections. He says, '*Sahiba* (O Lord)! A desolate heart stands in need of no apology for *ushr* or *Kharaj* (land revenue) could not be collected from a desolate village.'[31] Abu'l Fazl states that neither are worshippers nor sinners aware of the Divine mercy. Worshippers are proud of their worship, but sinners find comfort in begging to Thee. He then quotes the following verses.

A recluse does not commit sins for he thinks
 Thee an avenger (*Qahhar*)
We are engrossed in sin for we think Thee
 forgiving (*Ghaffar*)
He invokes Thee as avenger and I as forgiving,
O God! What name pleases Thee most?

Consequently Abu'l Fazl implores God to reward the virtuous and to be gracious in His mercy to wicked people.[32] He seeks forgiveness in the hope that God is in need of nobody's worship and sins do Him no harm.[33]

Abu'l Fazl believed that God's love and mercy are not shown only in His merciful provision for the needs of all, but in His tender forbearance towards men in their follies and errors.

According to Abu'l Fazl, God's majesty and power is not reflected through His justice. It is impossible to understand his mysteries unless He Himself guides the seeker. Thus if He were to make worshippers and ascetics who worship and pray day in and day out suffer perpetual punishment, it would be His justice; but if He were to grant the wishes of the most obstinate sinners it would be an act of His mercy. He prays, 'O bestower of guidance! The road is narrow and night is dark. If I have inadvertently walked on the path of aberration or have by mistake and forgetfulness acted against Thy Riza, do not punish me.'[34]

Object of Abu'l Fazl's Prayer and Invocations

Abu'l Fazl does not invoke God for fulfilment of his needs, for they are granted even before His servants invoke and pray.[35] Abu'l Fazl found himself on the horns of a dilemma, for if he cried out before the Divine court it would amount to madness, and if he kept quiet it would mean indifference. Nevertheless, he recommends that men pray, for begging before the Divine Court offers special pleasure and satisfaction.[36]

Saints and Sages

Praying God to liberate him from worshipping mankind and to direct him to His Own worship, Abu'l Fazl begged God in the name of the dignity of those 'falcons of the threshold of His glory who have fastened their eyes with the needle of jealousy in order to prevent themselves from seeing other than God and in the name of the dignity of farsighted ones who at the time of their worship have burnt all the ideas of fear of hell.'[37] He prayed for Emperor Akbar's long life and prosperity in the name of the dignity of those who had recognized God and were always devoted to Him. He does not name those saints or sages but that does not mean that Muslim sages and saints were excluded from the list of those whose intercession Abu'l Fazl sought.

Akbar in the *Munajat*

Abu'l Fazl did not consider service to Akbar as an obstacle to their religious and spiritual attainment. He preferred it to the ascetic and meditative life of a dervish. In support of his thesis, he quotes an anecdote attributed to the great sufi, Shaikh Alau'd Dawla Simnani (d. 736/136), an ardent supporter of *Wahdat al-Shuhud* (Unity of Appearance) and an inveterate enemy of Ibn 'Arabi's *Wahdat al-Wujud*. The eminent Shaikh was a vizier when he was young and under the spell of mystic ecstasy, he resigned and for forty long years practised unimaginably hard ascetic exercises. Then at the end of his life, he saw in a vision that the day of judgement had arrived and people were being questioned. In the Shaikh's case, the Divine command was issued that all his prayers and ascetic exercises should be weighed on the scales against the merit he had acquired by a kindness done to a woman when he was vizier. That single act emerged heavier, making the great Shaykh lament that he had not continued as vizier doing good to people.[38] According to Abu'l Fazl, asceticism helped only those who practised it, but government service enabled one to help a multitude of needy people. In his *Munajat* Abu'l Fazl seeks Divine blessings for the Emperor in order to show his gratitude to him. He says,

> Badshaha! (O King, Lord)! Since through the medium of this Divine Shadow (Akbar) of far reaching importance we have become a theatre of grace and a stage

of bounties, in the name of his (Akbar's) love of Truth, give us the capacity to show our gratitude to him and grant us strength to express our indebtedness to him.[39]

Abu'l Fazl believed that the greatest favour that God showed to his Emperor, the defender of faith (*din panah*), was the latter's liberation from the defilement (*tangna'y*) of *taqlid* (imitative knowledge or blind following) and arrival at the highway of *tahqiq* (realized knowledge or research). He implores God to give right guidance to all who are prisoners of *taqlid* and intellectually blind, so that the world which is full of thorns might be transformed into a rose garden. Inspired by the *tahqiq* of the Emperor, 'Abu'l Fazl goes on to say, 'Oh Lord! Enable me to walk on the road of *Tawhid* (*Wahdat al-Wujud*), make me interested in the joyful abode of solitude, Attach me to *tahqiq*. Liberate me from the prison of *taqlid*.'

Abu'l Fazl did not wish that the knowledge of his Emperor's devotion to God and Truth should be confined to the latter alone but earnestly longed that common people should also be able to follow him. He implores God to make the reality of this true King's and absolute Caliph's devotion to God known to common people and begs Him to direct the nations of the world to the road of truth through submission to this lover of Truth.

Abu'l Fazl refers to the *Chahar Maratiba-i Ikhlas* (four degrees of devotion) too, and begs God to bestow on all those who are not single-minded in their service to the Emperor, the favour of *Chahar Martiba-i Ikhlas* and made every one glorious on the highway of this shadow of God.[40]

Chahar Martiba-i Ikhlas or *Ikhlas-i Chahargana* has been identified by some scholars with the Din Ilahai or the Divine Faith although the former had nothing to do with the latter. Mulla Abdu'l Qadir Badauni refers to *Ikhlas-i Chahargana* five times in the second volume of his *Muntakhab-ut-Tawarikh* and leaves his readers confused. At the end of his account of 988/1581, he says:

> During this time four degrees of devotion to His Majesty were defined. They consisted in readiness to sacrifice to the Emperor, property, life, honour and religion. Whoever had sacrificed these things possessed the four degrees; and whoever had sacrificed one of these four possessed one degree. All the courtiers now put down their names as faithful disciples of the court.[41]

If all the courtiers had become faithful disciples of the court and the discipleship and *Ikhlas-i Chahargana* are identified with the Din-i Ilahi so it would mean that the entire court of Akbar was converted to Din-i Ilahi, H. Blochmann, who does not make any distinction between Din-i Ilahi, *muridi* (discipleship) and *Chahargana Ikhlas*, could not find more than eighteen members of the so-called new religion. A religion comprising only eighteen members does not merit attention, neither can it be called a religious order within the framework of some other religion. In the *Makatubat-i-Allami*, Abu'l Fazl says that he had found it desirable to sacrifice the capital of his existence which comprised four priceless pearls for the furtherance of the interest of his King. Of those four priceless pearls, life was valuable only to those who had no knowledge of their own real nature. Property was prized by those who, like mean-spirited merchants, were plunged in adding up profit and loss of their transactions. Honour was a matter of distinction for those who were not aware of true greatness and whose attention was given to earthly lust and worldly desires. Religion, by which he meant the *taqlidi* religion, was the guide only for those who sought blindly to traverse the road to truth and uprightness. Readiness to make these sacrifices willingly with open eyes for the promotion of the Emperor's interest was according to Abu'l Fazl, the sign of real eminence and nobility.[42]

Abu'l Fazl's historical work exhibits increasing concern with high officers of integrity to effectively handle the complex political and military needs of an expanding empire and keep pace with Akbar's ambitions of conquest and efficient government based on the principles of universal concord (*Sulh kul*). According to the Emperor himself, his political and administrative needs could be met only by a land of devoted followers prepared to give priority to the imperial interest over their own personal and religious ones.[43] The *Chahar Martaba-i Ikhlas* were designed for the imperial dignitaries, whether Rajputs or Mughals, Indian Muslims or Afghans, Turanis or Iranis. Religious prejudices and racial considerations should not be allowed to interfere with the imperial interest in any situation. Akbar was deeply impressed with the loyalty of his Rajput dignitaries and he seems to have believed that they were endowed with all the four degrees of devotion. He pleaded that nobody in the world could conceive of possessing anything beyond property, life, honour and religion, and the readiness to sacrifice these was invariably found among the Rajput *mansabdars*.[44] In December 1587 Raja Man Singh was appointed governor of Bihar and his *jagir* was transferred from the Punjab to the eastern provinces of India. Akbar seems to have thought it necessary to test the Raja's reaction. He summoned him, introduced the subject of discipleship, and proceeded to test him. The Raja answered rather bluntly:

> If discipleship means willingness to sacrifice one's life, I have already carried my life in my hand. What need is there of further proof? If, however, the term has

another meaning and refers to faith, I certainly am a Hindu. If you order me to do so, I will become a Muslim, but I know not of the existence of any other path than these two.[45]

Mulla Badauni says that at that point the matter was closed. Akbar got his answer and further discussion on the subject was fruitless. The tradition of enlisting disciples continued down to Aurangzeb's reign. The Mughal emperors continued to be addressed as *pir wa murshid* (spiritual guide and preceptor) or *pir wa murshid-i din wa dunya* (spiritual guide and preceptor of the faith and the world) or *pir wa murshid-i 'alam wa alamiyan* (spiritual guide and preceptor of the world and its inhabitants).[46]

In his *Munajat*, Abu'l Fazl deemed it necessary to invoke God to guide the perplexed minds of those who were wavering in their loyalties and make them steadfast to the Chahar *Martaba-i Ikhlas*.

As is the case with Abu'l Fazl's historical works the *Munajat* also refers to the sun as the patron of his Emperor. He says,

O Giver of Light (Furogh Bakhsha) What a light is this that Thou give it to the world illuminating sun? What a favour is this that Thou hast sent the greater luminary (sun) for the patronage of the Great Khalifa? Brighten our eyes from a particle of this light. Make our hearts a rose garden by a drop of the grace (of this light) he adds,

Sun is the *qibla-gah* (any place towards which one looks during prayers) of my *nazar-gah* (place of sight). It is the goal and object of my vigilant heart having access to whatever exists, for (sun) is the patron of my Emperor.[47]

Abu'l Fazl goes on to invoke God 'to maintain the Emperor's resplendance over our head so long as the sun lasts and to make the shadow of the benevolence of this world illuminating sun (Akbar) everlasting on our heads'.[48] He goes on to add,

'Thanks to the court of Benevolent and eternal Lord for He has made the sighting of the light of the shadow of God the *qibla* of the humble particles lying on dust like us, and has spread the lofty shadow of the umbrella of the felicity of the Emperor over the humble denizen of earth.'[49]

Abu'l Fazl's exaltation of sun in the *Munajat* is totally consonant with similar statements in the *A'in-i Akbari*. Abu'l Fazl and Akbar strongly repudiated the aspersions of the orthodox Muslims to the effect that Akbar worshipped sun as God. Mulla Badauni says

From early youth, in compliment to his wives, the daughters of the Rajas of Hind, he had within the female apartments continued to offer the *hom*, which is a ceremony derived from sun-worship; but on the New Year of the twenty-fifth year (1579) after his accession, he prostrated himself both before the sun and fire in public, and in the evening the whole court had to rise up respectfully when the lamps and candles were lighted.[50]

In his account of 991/1583-4 Mulla Badauni goes on to say,

No sooner had His Majesty finished saying the thousand and one names of the 'Greater Luminary', and stepped out into the balcony, than the whole crowd prostrated themselves. Cheating, thieving Brahmans collected another set of one thousand and one names of 'His Majesty the Sun', and told the Emperor that he was an incarnation like Rama, Krishna, and other infidel kings. . . .[51]

Akbar himself, however, observed, 'A special grace proceeds from the sun in favour of kings, and for this reason they pray and consider it a worship of the Almighty, but the short-sighted and the ignorant are scnadalized.'[52] In the *a'in* 18 of the first book 'On illumination', Abu'l Fazl gives the following explanation:

His Majesty maintains that it is a religious duty and Divine praise to worship fire and light; surely, ignorant men consider this forgetfulness of the Almighty and the worship.[53]

In connection with *a'in* 72 of the first book relating to 'the manner in which His Majesty spends his time' Abu'l Fazl says,

Indeed, every man acknowledges that we owe gratitude and reverence to our benefactors: and hence it is incumbent on us, though our strength may fail, to show gratitude for the blessings we receive from the sun, the light of all lights, and to enumerate the benefits which he bestows. This is essentially the duty of kings, upon whom, according to the opinion of the wise, this sovereign of heavens, sheds an immediate light. And this is the very motive which actuates his Majesty to venerate fire and reverence lamps.[54]

Abu'l Fazl preferred to dismiss the 'perverseness of those weak-minded zealots who with much concern, talked of His Majesty's religion as of deification of the Sun, and the introduction of fire-worship'.[55] His gratitude to God for enabling him to catch a glimpse of his Emperor is echoed even in one of the sayings of Akbar. 'The very sight of kings has been held to be a part of Divine worship. They have been styled conventionally the shadow of God, and indeed to behold them is a means of calling to mind the Creator, and suggests the protection of Almighty.'[56]

The complete trust in the Infinite God and deep faith in His grace that Abu'l Fazl exhibits in the *Munajat* are also closely linked with Divine mysteries. Like Ibn Arabi, Abu'l Fazl believed that whatever is loved is identical with God, the Beloved. It is only the heart wherein God reveals Himself to man. Confrontations, encounters, conflicts, diversity, differentiations, separation and multiplicity are transcended at the level of Oneness and Being. According to Abu'l Fazl, Akbar's perfection was mirrored in his love for his subjects and their well-being. He had read Shaykh Shihabud-Din Suhrawardi Maqtul's works and seems to have explained the great Ishraqi master's thinking to Akbar in simple language. According to Suhrawardi Maqtul, 'what is conceived metaphysically as existence (*wujud*) coincides with what is grasped in terms of the root experience as Light (*nur*). In this context coexistence is light.'[57] There is no doubt that Akbar was also influenced by the discussions of Hindu sages and Zoroastrian mystics on this subject and worshipped the sun, fire and light in consonance with Hindu forms of worship. But this did not, according to Abu'l Fazl, negates his worship of the *Wajibul ul-Wujud* (i.e. God).

NOTES

1. E.G. Browne, *A Literary History of Persia*, London, 1924, rpt. Cambridge, 1964, II, p. 70.
2. One who considers laws repugnant to Islamic *Shari'a* as permissible.
3. *Abu'l Fazl, A'in-i Akbari*, Lucknow, 1892, III, p. 221. English translation by H.S. Jarrett, revd. by J.N. Sarkar, Calcutta, 1948.
4. One turned away from the truth of Islam.
5. One who maintains the doctrine of two principles; a disbeliever in God and a future slate.
6. *Munajat*, p. 35. 'Nikan ra ba wasila-i niki Sar airazi bakhsh wa badan ra ba muqtaza-i karam dil nawazi kun.'
7. Shah Nawaz Khan, *Ma'asir-u'l Umara*, Calcutta, 1888-91, II, p. 618.
8. *Munajat*, p. 16.
9. Mulla Abdu'l Qadir Badauni, *Muntakhab u't tawarikh*, Calcutta, 1864-9, II, p. 260.
10. *Munajat*, p. 1.
11. *Makatibat-i Inayat Khan*, Abdus Salam Collections, Mawlana Azad Library, Aligarh Muslim University, Ms. no. 332/102; *A'in-i Akbari*, English translation by H. Blochmann, 2nd revd. edn. by D.C. Phillott, Calcutta, 1939, I, p. vii.
12. E.H. Whinfield, *Gulshan-i raz* of Shabistari, London 1880, p. 84.
13. *Munajat*, p. 30.
14. Ibid., p. 20.
15. Ibid., p. 27.
16. A.J. Arberry, *The Doctrines of the Sufis, Kitab al-ta'aruf li madhhab ahl al-tasawwuf*, translated from Arabic of Abu Bakr al-Kalabadhi, Lahore, 1066, p. 56.
17. *Munajat*, p. 27.
18. Ibid., p. 4.
19. Ibid., pp. 27-8.

20. Hujwari, *Kashfu'l mahjub*, English translation by R.A. Nicholson, London, 1936, p. 179.
21. *Munajat*, p. 5.
22. Ibid., pp. 29, 27.
23. Ibid., pp. 8, 9.
24. Ibid., p. 7.
25. Ibid., p. 10.
26. Ibid., p. 4.
27. Ibid., p. 3.
28. Blochmann, *A'in*, pp. LIV-LV.
29. *Munajat*, p. 16.
30. Shaykh Farid Bhakkari, *Zakharitu'l Khawanin*, Karachi, 1961, vol. I, p. 73.
31. *Munajat*, p. 334.
32. Ibid., pp. 33-5.
33. Ibid., p. 31.
34. Ibid., p. 32.
35. Ibid., p. 13.
36. Ibid., p. 5.
37. Ibid., p. 29.
38. Abu'l Fazl Allami, *Makatubat-i-Allami*, Delhi, 1846, III, p. 180, Letter to Qasim Khan Tabrizi.
39. *Munajat*, p. 5.
40. Ibid., p. 4.
41. *Muntakhab-ut-Tawarikh*, II, p. 291, Lowe, p. 299.
42. *Makatubat-i-Allami*, III, p. 225.
43. Ibid., II, 161, Abu'l Fazl's personal letter to Khan-i A'zam Mirza Aziz Koka.
44. *Akbarnama*, III, p. 256.
45. *Muntakhab-ut-Tawarikh*, II, p. 64, Eng. tr., Lowe, p. 375.
46. S.S.A. Rizvi, *Religious and Intellectual History of the Muslims in Akbar's Reign*, New Delhi, 1974, pp. 398-403.
47. *Munajat*, p. 3.
48. Ibid., p. 2.
49. Ibid.
50. *Muntakhab-ut-Tawarikh*, II, p. 261, Lowe, p. 269.
51. Ibid., II, p. 326, Lowe, p. 336.
52. *A'in*, Eng. tr., Jarrett, III, p. 435.
53. *A'in*, III, Blochmann, p. 50.
54. Loc. cit., Blochmann, p. 160
55. *A'in*, I, Blochmann, pp. 163-4.
56. *A'in*, III, Jarrett, III, p. 450.
57. Toshihiho Izutsu, 'The Paradox of Light and Darkness in the Garden of Mystery of Shabastari', in *Anagogic Qualities of Literature*, ed. Joseph P. Strelka (University Park Pa, 1971), p. 299.

Badauni Revisited: An Analytical Study of *Najat ur Rashid*

ISHTIYAQ AHMAD ZILLI

Badauni's reputation as a scholar and historian rests on his *Muntakhab-ut-Tawarikh*. Its portraiture of Akbar and his policies, particularly his religious views, has provoked hostile comments and criticism. Rizvi, for example, begins his discussion on *Muntakhab-ut-Tawarikh* with the remark, 'one could almost believe he wrote to glorify the pettiness of vision and stinginess of soul of the most hard-bound of the traditional ulama.'[1] It is said to have been 'written with a vengeance'.[2] I do not propose to enter here into a discussion on the merits of this assessment but state that in spite of many rough edges of *Muntakhab-ut-Tawarikh*, no balanced history of Akbar's reign could be written without recourse to it. But for Badauni's history, many aspects of Akbar's religious experimentation and the resultant unrest and social tension might largely have remained buried under the blandishments of the master stylist, Abul Fazl.

For an objective assessment of Badauni's personality, basic patterns of his thought and his contributions, it is necessary that our analysis of his views and attitudes be not confined to *Muntakhab-ut-Tawarikh* alone but his other works should also be taken into consideration. It is widely acknowledged that Badauni belonged to that rare class of *ulama* whose academic and intellectual interests went beyond the traditional areas. Besides being an accomplished scholar of the traditional sciences, he was also noted for his secular knowledge. His skill as prose writer of a high degree is evident. He had a refined taste for poetry in Arabic and Persian. Mathematics, astrology, music and chess were included among his other interests. He is said to have had a very good practice of *bin*.[3] Surely this is not the material which goes in the making of most hide-bound fanatics.

It was indeed in recognition of his accomplishments and versatility that Akbar associated him with the project of translation of Indian classics into Persian and he played the most significant role in the activities of *Maktab Khana* (translation bureau).[4] Credit for the translation of the

Ramayana, *Mahabharata* and *Singhasanbatisi* goes to him.[5] He was also associated with the translation of a number of other books. He was 'decidedly one of the best translators associated with the Translation Bureau.'[6] His contribution to the compilation of the *Tarikh-i Alfi* is too well known to need elaboration.[7] These varied interests of Badauni should be given due importance in the final assessment of his views and contributions.

Besides the *Muntakhab-ut-Tawarikh* and translations of a number of Sanskrit and Arabic books, he has left behind only one other complete book—*Najat ur Rashid*—a voluminous work with a text running into 531 printed pages.[8] Unfortunately this book has not received the attention from the historians and scholars it deserves. It is imperative to objectively analyse this book and try to find answers to questions about its social milieu. This will give a more balanced picture of one of the most controversial writers of medieval India. Moreover, it will also help us understand many of the postulates of Badauni in the *Muntakhab-ut-Tawarikh*, for it not only supplements the information therein but also provides the theoretical background for Badauni's stand on Akbar's religious policies and views.

Badauni has referred to his *Najat ur Rashid* in the course of the discussion variously as *ujalah* (hastily produced),[9] *risalah* (treatise)[10] and *jaridah* (volume, register).[11] This would indicate that it is not a properly planned and produced book. It was written during a journey when books for consultation and reference were not available.[12] He was conscious of the fact that some discussions were not as meticulously elaborated as he would have liked.[13] To have produced such a well documented book purely on the strength of memory is indeed testimony to the erudition and scholarship of Badauni. When one looks at the discussions on a variety of subjects and the way these are substantiated and supported by quotations from the Koran, *Hadith*, Arabic and Persian poetry, sufi literature and history, one cannot help admire his extraordinary knowledge.

Najat ur Rashid was written on the request of a friend and benefactor, Khwaja Nizam ud Din Ahmad Bakhshi, author of *Tabaqat-i Akbari*. There is no reason to doubt Badauni's statement to this effect particularly in view of the very intimate relationship that existed between the two.[14] Badauni informs us that Nizam ud Din himself had wanted to write this book and had been taking notes for the purpose and had already prepared an outline. But he then decided to request Badauni to take up this project and handed over to him whatever material (*tumar*) he had with him on the subject.[15] Rizvi's contention that 'a brief work on the subject had already been prepared by some other scholar and that he had merely hurriedly prepared an amplified version of it' is not borne out by the facts of the case.[16] The reasons behind this change of mind are not given. Perhaps Nizam ud Din realized that Badauni was better equipped for this kind of work.

Some scholars are inclined to the view that the more likely reason could possibly have been Nizam ud Din's desire to save himself from a situation in which a book of this nature could have landed him as an important government official.[17] Because of his official position, Nizam ud Din adopted a very cautious policy. While he meticulously stayed aloof from Akbar's religious views, he took care not to criticise them. His own book is almost totally silent about the religious controversies raging at that time.[18] It would, however, seem that in his heart of hearts he was deeply concerned about the developments and felt that something should be done to stem the tide. This might have been the reason behind the desire to write this book but obviously he came to the conclusion that discretion was the better part of valour and hence the request to Badauni, who in any case, was better equipped for this kind of job. One could also argue that unless he agreed with Badauni at least on major points, he could not have possibly entrusted him with this responsibility.

Either this book was, like *Muntakhab-ut-Tawarikh*, kept secret, or it had a selective and restricted circulation. Scarcity of manuscripts is a clear indicative of this possibility. Its editor, Saiyid Moin ul Haq, could locate only two Mss. of the book; one preserved at the library of Asiatic Society of Bengal and the other at Asifiya Library, Hyderabad. Such limited circulation could have been hardly expected to serve the purpose for which it was supposed to have been written.[19] It could reach only those who were already critical of Akbar's policies. Most probably those who were increasingly coming under the influence of these policies and whom Badauni wanted to redeem, would not have had access to it.

Modern scholars too have not given this book the importance it deserve and even those who have studied it have not been able to free themselves from the framework and prejudices which they might have acquired during their study of *Muntakhab-ut-Tawarikh*. It is rather surprising that a book of this kind coming from the pen of one of the most eminent and controversial scholars of medieval India would have received this treatment. It would seem that those who have pronounced their opinions on it have actually not cared to carefully go through it. P. Hardy describes it as 'a work on sufism, ethics and Mahdavi movement of Badauni's days.'[20] S.A.A. Rizvi defines it as a 'theological mystical work,'[21] but elsewhere says that 'the *Muntakhab-ut-Tawarikh* is meant to destroy the faith of the Sunnis in Akbar; the *Najat ur Rashid* seeks to reiterate the principles on which orthodox sunnism can be revived; thus each work complements and supplements the other.'[22] Blochmann has described it as a 'polemical work' and Ivanov says It is a 'sufic ethical treatise, richly interspersed with interesting historical anecdotes, controversial discussions.'[23] Some of these descriptions are only partly true, others mostly off the mark. For understanding the real nature of the work, it is necessary to take into account not only the objectives of the author but also the actual contents of the book and not allow oneself to judge it with predetermined notions. It should also be kept in mind that it is not a properly planned and executed book. It was compiled during a journey and there are flaws both at the level of arrangement as well as discussions. It is still a remarkable book.

Rizvi thinks that *Muntakhab-ut-Tawarikh* and *Najat ur Rashid* were compiled simultaneously.[24] It is true that their contents complement and supplement each other, but obviously both were not written simultaneously. The aims of both the books converged at one level or the other and that was bound to create some kind of similarity between them. The same concerns which had earlier prompted Badauni to accede to the request of his friend to compose the *Najat ur Rashid* ultimately motivated him to write his *Muntakhab-ut-Tawarikh*. It is therefore only natural that a certain similarity of views and ideas, as well as the tenor of arguments, is found in both the books. The *Najat ur Rashid* was compiled in 1591 during a short duration of time; the last date mentioned in the *Muntakhab-ut-Tawarikh* is 1004/1595.[25] *Najat ur Rashid* contains a reference to *Muntakhab-ut-Tawarikh*, which may suggest that the latter was complete by the time the former was being compiled or at least it was being compiled simultaneously. But most probably this reference was added later, when *Muntakhab* was already in circulation. Moreover, *Najat ur Rashid* is a chronogram and would be valid only if the book was completed in 999/1591.[26]

In the very beginning Badauni states that this book deals with the vices of soul and sins, both mortal (*kabirah*, plural *kabair*) and venal (*saghirah*, plural *saghair*), the knowledge of which is imperative for people.[27] It is therefore clear that the book neither deals with Sufism nor ethics. Elsewhere Badauni has expressed his desire to write a separate book on ethics (*ilm-i akhlaq*) but apparently he could not do so.[28]

Besides introductory and concluding sections, the book consists of seven chapters (*fasl*). The introductory section contains a discussion on the importance and imperative need of repentance (*taubah*). Without repentance, one cannot hope to attain divine forgiveness and it is the gateway to piety and a religiously correct life. With the help of quotations from the Koran and *Hadith*, it is sought to impress upon the reader that if one breaks a pledge not to commit sins again and again, even then one should not feel diffident to repent. It is never too late to repent.[29]

This is followed by a discussion on the nature and definition of sin, mortal and venal. Badauni says that there is lack of unanimity about the exact number of mortal sins. He is of the opinion that it has been intentionally kept vague so that, fearful of their consequences, people should strive to keep away from all kinds of sin. The renowned sufi scholar Shaikh Abu Talib Makki in his book, *Qut ul-Qulub*, has given the number of the mortal sins as seventeen and Badauni has followed him.[30]

It is not possible to enter here into a detailed discussion of all the sins and offences discussed in various chapters. But perhaps a survey of the contents of the book would give us some idea about the actual nature of the book.

The first chapter deals with seventeen mortal sins (*kabair*). The list of mortal sins is headed by polytheism (*shirk*, literally making associates with God). In Islam *shirk* is considered the greatest sin and one who commits it is denied divine grace and forgiveness unless he repents.[31] The Koran declares in no uncertain terms that '*Shirk* is the highest wrong doing.'[32] Other mortal sins include persistence in sin, considering oneself secure from the wrath of God, losing hope in God, misappropriating an orphan's property, theft, disobedience of parents, fornication (*zina*), sodomy, consumption of wine, forging witness, magic, usury, unjustified killing of human beings, disobedience of prophets, running away from combat,[33] calumny against God, forsaking prayer (*salat*) and poor rate (*zakat*).[34]

The second chapter deals with forty heinous sins, which lead to open infidelity (*kufr-i sarih*).[35] Though they are discussed in a purely academic manner and polemic has been scrupulously avoided, the accusing finger could be hardly missed as a number of these were openly practised at Akbar's court: idol-worship, worship of the sun, veneration of stars, tying of Brahmanical thread (*zunnar*), application of *qashqa* on the forehead, excessive interest in philosophy, heresy, honouring infidels, marrying infidels, taking infidels into confidence, adopting practices of infidels, destroying mosques, considering what is permissible as impermissible, reading the books of the ancients, abusing *Ahl-i Bait* (Prophet's family), abusing companions of the Prophet, introducing innovation into the religion, sneering at the Muslims, cursing Muslims, having faith in astrologers, prostration before someone other than God, explaining the

Koran without knowledge, and pronouncing opinion on religious matters (*fatwa*) without knowledge.[36]

The third chapter also deals with forty sins. These mostly relate to the practical aspect, while the sins enumerated in the previous chapters, mainly concern belief. The sins included in this chapter relate to non-observance of prayer, fasting, and *zakat*, slaughtering animals without taking the name of God, gambling, highway robbery, rebellion against the king, calumny against the king, lying, cheating, breaking promise, indulging in music, abandoning the duty of *amr bil maruf and nahi anil munkar* (ordering what is good and forbidding what is bad), incantations, taking bribes, giving away secrets, castration and appointment of eunuchs in the *haram*, treachery, fraud, flattery, helping tyranny, and abusing the dead.[37]

The fourth chapter deals with *Huququllah* (obligations due to the Almighty). The sins covered also number forty and include miscellaneous transgressions such as non-observance of *Juma* prayers, various modes of relationship with women not permitted in religion, urinating and decafating on the thoroughfares, urinating in water, easing oneself under the shade of trees, cutting shady trees, slaughtering animals as a profession, selling human beings, painting, delay in paying back loans, taking omens, wishing for one's death, boasting about one's ancestors, begging without dire necessity, living in *darul kufr*, selling musical instruments, beating slaves without fault, wailing, and liking flattery.[38] No particular principle or criterion has been adopted for putting these sins under this head; the author is fully aware of this and apologises for it.[39]

The fifth chapter deals with those offences, which are considered to be inconsistent with civil behaviour (*muruat*), and propriety of conduct (*adab*). These also happen to number forty. It would seem that perhaps because of the significance of the number forty among the sufis; special care has been taken to somehow take the number of the offences discussed under different heads to forty. The offences arranged under this category include wearing silk clothes or cloth woven with threads of gold or silver, wearing clothes dyed with saffron, eating out of utensils of gold and silver, shaving the beard, abandoning circumcision, distilling wine, consuming opium and the like, playing chess, hearing music from strange women, blocking a thoroughfare, setting wrong precedent, keeping animals hungry, throwing excrement on the way.[40] It also includes offences like entering other peoples' houses without their permission,[41] giving cause of grievance to the neighbours,[42] hoarding in the hope of rise in price[43] and selling arms to infidels.[44]

The sixth chapter covers miscellaneous offences and these also number forty. The misdemeanours put under this head include forgetting the Koran after having memorized it, talking during *khutba* and *azan*, conducting business in mosques, praying in mausoleums and *hammams*, insulting elders, beating children, rebuking beggars, oppressing orphans, withholding counsel, using foul language, abandoning friends, not returning greetings, refusing hospitality to a guest, under-weighing, non-payment of wages, proclaiming oneself *shahanshah*, throwing excrement on the way, destroying bridges and wells, shutting the door in the face of beggars, making coarse jokes and imparting education to the unworthy.[45]

The seventh and last chapter also consists of forty offences, termed by the author *taqsirat* (failings, guilts), while in other chapters terms such as *kabair*, *jaraim* and *gunahan* have been used. This would seem to suggest that the offences discussed in this section are considered less serious than the others. But in reality that is not the case. The failings described in this chapter include claiming false parenthood, separating son from mother, usurping *waqf* property, throwing used water in a well, stealing water for irrigation, selling commodities on prices higher than prevalent in the market.[46] It also includes dealings such as *mutaa* marriage,[47] women riding horses[48] and lighting lamps on graves.[49]

The *Khatimah* discusses the correct method of repentance[50] and briefly touches on the spiritual journey and the intrinsic wickedness of the world and the imperative to avoid it at every cost.[51]

It is clear from this brief survey of the contents that this book is basically a theological treatise and deals with the sins, crimes, offences and misdemeanours that Islam forbids. These transgressions militate not only against the spiritual and religious well-being of the individual but also tend to disturb the social equilibrium and generate tension. As such it does have a bearing on ethics, as the author himself has explained. Badauni wanted to write a separate book on ethics, in the tradition of Imam Ghazali and Tusi,[52] but he did not actually do so.

The various issues covered in the book have been discussed in the light of the Koran, *Hadith* and Islamic jurisprudence. For the purposes of further elaboration, stories and anecdotes from history and sufi literature are employed. To heighten the effect, poetry is profusely quoted. Besides occasional references to sufis and Sufism, there are a number of instances where Badauni discusses issues and ideas relating to sufis. For example, the discussion on the prohibition of music contains long discourse on *Sama*.[53] But on the basis of these occasional references, it would not be justified to call the book a treatise on Sufism. Similarly, it would be incorrect to call it a polemical work, because it is not only free from polemics but

Badauni had in fact come down heavily on those who indulge in polemics. At one point he has even singled out polemics as a major cause of the decline of the community.[54] Anyone who will go through the book objectively will find it to be singularly free of polemic. Badauni has certainly noted differences of opinion among scholars, but that is purely at the academic level and mostly free of acrimony.[55] It is clear in the light of the above discussion that Rizvi's assertion that *Najat ur Rashid* 'reiterates the principles on which orthodox Sunnism could be revived'[56] is absolutely off the mark. It defies logic how a book devoted to sin and religious and moral offences and transgressions could provide principles on which orthodox Sunnism could be revived.

Nevertheless there is little doubt that the book is a scathing indictment of Akbar's religious policies, albeit in an entirely indirect manner. Badauni seems to have made a conscious attempt to scrupulously avoid any reference to the contemporary situation, discussing issues in a purely detached and academic manner. Marriage to non-Muslim,[57] applying *qashqa* on the forehead,[58] wearing *zunnar*,[59] the veneration of sun and stars[60] are discussed in an academic manner and the discussion even does not state that some of these practices were in vogue at the court. Only rarely does Badauni drop a hint about the person against whom the discussion was directed. For example, on a few occasions he has referred to the heretics of the age (*mulhidan-i zaman*)[61] and new heretics (*mulhidan-i jadid*).[62] The most detailed discussion in the *Najat ur Rashid* is on heresy. Different kinds of heresies, that appeared at various points of time in the history of Islam, have been discussed. This is one of the exceptional sections of the book. While reading it one has the uncanny feeling that it is a reflection on contemporary conditions and some of the trends of thought in vogue at the court.[63]

It is obvious that the book seeks to reform and reverse the indifference to Islamic prescriptions that was increasingly affecting various sections of society as a direct consequence of Akbar's religious policy.[64] But this is not actually stated anywhere. It is surmised in the light of the contents and discussions of the book and the way it was hastily put together in adverse conditions. The elite at the court, with its vast influence, prestige and power of patronage, had unleashed a sustained campaign to impress upon the people that the traditional religion (*din-i taqlidi wa majazi*) was no more relevant.[65] Therefore for those with faith in the religion it was the need of the hour to do something to resist this trend. As the years rolled on, these tendencies got more and more vociferous and entrenched. It was perhaps realization of this urgency that compelled Nizam uddin not to defer the compilation of the book and ask his friend to do the needful. It was again perhaps a realization of urgency that prompted Badauni to compile this book on his travels and not to wait for leisure, peace of mind, or availability of books.[66]

The *Najat ur Rashid* is remarkable in the sense that while it is an open indictment of Akbar's *sulh-i kul* and *Din-i Ilahi*, it does not refer to these concepts or mention Akbar by name. The names of scholars and dignitaries of the court and the leading lights of the new dispensation are also conspicuous by their absence. Sin and wickedness are discussed, sometimes at quite some detail, in the light of the Koran and *Sunnah* without bitterness or sarcasm, which is the hallmark of Badauni's style elsewhere. In spite of the cursory nature of the book a dignified attitude is maintained and the discussions do not degenerate to personal acrimony or vilification. Many of the practices which were adopted by Akbar such veneration of the sun and fire, are tackled in a scholarly and objective manner.[67] This attitude, it would seem, was the result of deliberate policy. For one thing, a discussion on a purely religious matter by its very nature required to be carried in a manner befitting the theme. Sins and crimes are serious matters and their seriousness could have been compromised if it would have been carried in a lighter vein. Calling names and criticizing and abusing people would have defeated the very purpose of the exercise.

The opinions pronounced by Badauni on issues connected with Hindus indicate that he equates the Hindus with the *mushriks* (polytheists) of the Prophet's time and wants the same laws to be applied to them. Although the issue of the status of the Hindus was settled at the very beginning of Muslim penetration of India in the early years of the eighth century,[68] it would seem that in some circles doubts continued to persist about their position. After the occupation of Sindh around AD 712, Muhammad bin Qasim declared the Hindus *Mushabih Ahl-i Kitab* (those resembling the people of the Book), and they were consequently accorded the status of protected people (*zimmis*) in the Islamic state. This was recognized by the overwhelming majority of Muslim scholars as also the succeeding governments. But occasionally discordant voices were raised. In the Sultanate period we have Zia uddin Barani, who apparently did not agree, and did not recognize Hindus as *zimmis*. In the *Sahifa-i Naat-i Muhammadi* he has approvingly quoted the concern of the *ulama* at the 'affluence, wealth and tranquillity' enjoyed by the Hindus. They observed that 'neither the Hindus have a (divine) book nor did they belong to the category of *zimmis*'.[69] The *ulama* therefore discussed among themselves the possibility of confronting Hindus with the choice of 'either death or Islam'. According to their interpretation of the law, 'Hindus are to be killed or enslaved and their belonging confiscated and they were humiliated and dishonoured.'[70] Ultimately a delegation of *ulama* called on Iltutmish with the demand that the Hindus should be given the choice of death or Islam. The Sultan, of course, did not accede to the demand.[71] It is nevertheless significant that an issue long settled was sought to be opened. Barani has not provided the names of the *ulama* who raised this question with the Sultan. Apparently, the delegation did not consist of eminent men, or he would have bandied their names to strengthen his viewpoint. But he has hinted that they consisted of recent immigrants.[72] Perhaps they were not familiar with conditions in India. Barani himself, however, seems to be in full sympathy with this view. He has expressed the same views elsewhere in different contexts.[73]

Badauni is perhaps not a fanatic like Barani. He concedes that *Kafiran-i Mutiul Islam* (*kafirs* obedient to Islam) share with Muslims the material benefits and loss of the daily life and are one with the Muslims in this regard.[74] But he does not seem to concede them the status of *Mushabih Ahl-i Kitab*. He has not touched on this issue anywhere in the book. In the *Muntakhab-ut-Tawarikh* he observes that the Hindus have many books but are not *Ahl-i Kitab*.[75] About the status of *Mushabih Ahl-i Kitab*, he is totally silent. From the general tenor of his discussion it would appear that he is not prepared to accede them this status. In the discussion on taking infidels into confidence, which he considers a mortal sin, he has quoted a story about Abu Musa Ashari, the companion of the Prophet, and the second Caliph Umar which purports to the fact that an infidel cannot be taken into confidence in matters of governance.[76]

It is surprising that a scholar of the eminence of Badauni was unaware of the legal status of Hindus in a Muslim state. It is difficult to believe that he knowingly and consciously took a position that ran counter to the status granted by the *shariat* and which has been the guiding principle of the Muslim governments down the centuries. It is not possible to enter here into a detailed discussion about the issue, but a brief discussion is in order to dispel at least some of wrong notions that have persisted on the issue not only among non-Muslims but also among some Muslims.

At the very outset, it should be very clearly stated that many commandments of the Koran regarding *Kafirs* and *Mushriks* are specific to Arab infidels of Prophet's time who not only refused to accept him as a Prophet but also attempted to wipe out Islam and annihilate Muslims. It was to them that the choice of 'either Islam or the sword' was given.[77] It would be, therefore, totally unjustified to extend this injunction beyond that period. Those who tried to apply the rule in medieval India were grievously mistaken. It has given birth to many misconceptions and continues to blur our view regarding a matter of crucial importance.

The treatment of non-Muslims in a Muslim state will be determined by the nature of their relationship with the state. The terms and conditions for those conquered by force would be qualitatively different from those who enter into treaty arrangement with the Islamic state. While the former are designated *zimmis* or *ahluz zimmah* (protected people); the latter are known as *ahlus sulh* or *ahlul Muahadah* (people of peace or people of treaty). While the former will be liable to pay *jizya*, the latter would be expected to abide by the terms and conditions agreed between the parties. There are numerous examples of such treaties from the time of the Prophet and Caliphs and these provide clear guidelines for such situations.[78] A basic stipulation, however, would be that the facilities agreed upon could be enhanced and extended but not curtailed or withdrawn. Similarly, liabilities of subjects could be further relaxed but not increased. For example, due to the increase in the fertility of the land the *kharaj* could not be increased over and above the rate agreed upon between the parties.[79] Some other important differences in the rights of the two groups relate to the payment of *jizya* and proprietary rights over the land under their occupation. People of *sulh* could be exempted from the payment of *jizya*. They could pay their contribution towards the cost of protection provided by the state under some other category[80] and continue to enjoy proprietary rights over their lands.[81] On the other hand, *zimmis* had only hereditary rights over their land.[82] There was no bar on selling and buying of that land among them, but theoretically, conquered land belonged to the Muslim community and could not be sold to a Muslim, if sold to a Muslim, it remained *kharaji* land and could not be converted to *ushri*.[83] On the other hand, the people of the *sulh* enjoyed proprietary rights on their lands. It was because of this that when second Caliph Umar decided to transfer the non-Muslim population of the Arabian peninsula, the Christians of Najaran were given alternative lands in other parts of the Muslim state.[84]

The status of *zimmis* was originally given to the people of the Book: Jews and Christians. Later when regions populated by Zoroastrians, Berbers and others were incorporated, they too were given the status of *Mushabih Ahl-i Kitab* (those resembling people of the Book).[85] For all practical purposes there is no difference between their status and that of the people of the Book. The only difference is that while Muslims are permitted to marry the women of the people of the Book and eat the meat of animals slaughtered according to the rites of their religion, this is not allowed about those who resemble the people of the Book.[86] Besides this there is no difference in rights.

When Muhammad bin Qasim conquered Sindh in the beginning of the eighth century, the problem arose as to what status should be given to the Hindus. After due deliberation, they were given the status of those resembling the people of the Book.[87] The legal position of Hindus in medieval India, therefore, was that of the *Mushabih Ahl-i Kitab* and not that of *mushrikun* and *kuffar* of Mecca, notwithstanding the opinions of Barani, Badauni and their ilk. Succeeding generations of Muslim scholars and rulers continued to accept this position and discordant voices were few and far between.

The rights of protected people in a Muslim State include protection of life and property, freedom to practice their religion, and non-interference in their personal law.[88] Moreover, the *Baitul Mal* (treasury) will take care of those among them who, due to old age, illness or penury are unable to take care of themselves.[89] In the assessment of *kharaj* (land revenue), care should be taken that it is within the paying capacity of the people and they are not overburdened. The revenue is to be charged only on land under actual cultivation. Houses and the land attached to them are not included in the assessment. It is also to be noted that for the purpose of realization of *jizya*, clothes, utensils, food, oxen, ploughs and other implements of agriculture could not be confiscated or attached.[90] It is clearly stipulated that the government would make arrangements for direct collection of revenue without taking the help of the intermediaries. In case such arrangement were made on the request of the people themselves, the government should exercise close supervision so that middlemen did not have the opportunity to oppress the people.[91] Similarly, *jizya* will be taken only from those able bodied persons capable of rendering military service. Women and children were exempt, so too the aged, poor and handicapped. Nobody would be tortured for the realization of *jizya*.[92] As the protected people are exempt from military service and the *jizya* is in fact a tax for protection, any one who renders military service or is made to render it, was exempt from *jizya*. Anyone who makes a worthwhile contribution to the welfare of the state was permanently exempt from the payment of jizya.[93]

These are some of the rights of the protected people guaranteed by the *shariat*. It is therefore clear that Badauni is not correct in equating Hindus with the polytheists of Arabia. The impression that he has sought to convey through the story of Abu Musa Ashari, who is said to have wished to associate a non-Muslim with his administration, and the stern warning of Umar not to entertain such ideas in future, is not in tune with the spirit and teachings of Islam. There are examples from the period of Umar himself that non-Muslims who made some contribution to society, their services were duly recognized by the state. Some non-Muslims are reported to have fought along with Muslims in wars against non-Muslim powers and received shares in the booty equivalent to the shares of the Muslims.[94]

It has been noticed earlier that the book is a strong censure of Akbar's policies though he has not been mentioned anywhere by name. However, the few indirect references to him are invariably respectful. He is referred as *Khalifa-i zaman* and *Sahib-i zaman*.[95] Moreover, Badauni has included topics like 'Rebellion against the king'[96] and 'Cursing the king'[97] in the category of heinous sins. He argues that kings are necessary for the peace and tranquillity of society. If there had been no rulers people would have devoured each other. Those who rebel against the kings are like highway robbers and it is the duty of everybody to resist and fight them until order is restored. Obedience to the king has been commanded in the Holy Koran in the same way as the obedience of Almighty and the Prophet. The kings are shadow of God and the shadow has to be familiar with the essence (from which it emanates).[98] And therefore calumny and slander against the kings is not permitted. According to a *hadith*, the birds in the air and the fish in the water pray for the just king. If they happen to be unjust, one must not curse them or speak evil of them since the order and prosperity of the society is connected with them. As the people get the rulers they deserve, there is really no point in speaking evil about them. It is also not proper for one to sit with people who engage in calumny against the king. Coming to his times, Badauni says he has seen those who have transgressed these limits coming to very tragic end.[99]

Rizvi thinks Badauni was not sincere in these pronouncements. He would have us believe that it was part of a well-thought strategy adopted by orthodox Sunnis 'to win their battle against unorthodox elements by arousing a sense of unqualified obedience to the Emperor, thereby gaining his sympathy'.[100] But in the very next breath he says that Badauni was in fact following 'the teachings of Ghazali and other orthodox Sunni supporters of kingship'.[101] Badauni was not, however, saying something new; he was following a well-established tradition, as Rizvi himself agrees. For another, he was writing a religious treatise and therefore he was not at liberty to give vent to his personal views. He was working under certain constraints and self-imposed discipline. Those who will go through the book would agree that Badauni has not generally allowed his personal prejudices and frustrations to colour the discussions. Moreover, by the time he sat to pen this treatise, Akbar was past the stage when he and his cohorts could have thought of winning sympathy by dilating on the importance of obedience to the king.

Badauni extols *ijtihad*. According to him, it is not permissible (*najaiz*) for a *mujtahid* to follow (*taqlid*) others. It is incumbent on him to strive and exert himself to draw his own conclusions in the light of the evidence of the Koran and *hadith* both in matters relating to fundamentals (*usul*) and details (*fara*). In his opinion a *mujtahid* following others would amount to eating alms (*sadqah*). As it is not permitted for a rich man to take alms from others, similarly it is prohibited for a *mujtahid* to follow conclusions and findings of others. If a *mujtahid* arrives at correct conclusions, he will receive ten-fold recompense, but even if he fails he will be entitled to recompense.[102] At a time when *taqlid* was the order of the day and the doors of the *ijtihad* were supposed to have been closed, this strong advocacy of independent thinking and *ijtihad* is indeed refreshing. It gives the lie to those who have sought to present Badauni as a fanatic. And, therefore, he could not have been included among those who, according to Rizvi, were disturbed by '*ijtihadi* and *tahqiqi* Islam advocating independent thinking and reasoning'.[103] Obviously, *ijtihad* to which Rizvi is referring is not the kind of *ijtihad* that Badauni means.

Badauni has expressed his views about the Shia on different occasions in his book but more particularly in relation to 'Cursing the Companions of the Prophet' and 'Introducing innovations in the religion' and *muta* marriage.[104] It is not only highly unbecoming to indulge in any such activity but is also a grave sin.[105] Badauni laments the conditions of his own days. He says that debates and disputations among Shia and Sunnis are the order of the day, and this leads to much acrimony. Nobody seems to have time or inclination to talk about the love of God and His Prophet.[106]

In his discussion on innovations (*bidat*) in religion Badauni finds occasion to talk about some Shia practices. He says that innovations are of three kinds. Some are good (*bidat-i hasanah*) such as inserting dots and diacritical marks in the text of the Holy Koran. Things like this are obligatory (*wajib*).[107] The second relates to eating, clothing and such other usage, which do not go against the *shariat*. These are included among the permitted things (*mubah*)[108] and no harm will attach to those who will take resort to them. The third are wicked innovations (*bidat-i saiyia*), totally prohibited (*haram*): Shia practices such as *Id-i Ghadir*, and addition of words '*Ali waliulalh*' in *azan* and *kalimah*. He says that the statement that Ali is friend of God is perfectly correct in itself but considering it as a part of the *kalimah* and believing that the correctness of faith and prayers depends on it, is to be condemned.[109]

Badauni's own faith in Ali and his descendants is, however, unbounded and he considers them innocent (*masum*). The way he talks about Ali and his descendants clearly smacks of *tafzili*[110] leanings. He makes a strong plea that all the four caliphs be equally revered. He says that if somebody feels more inclined to any one of them, he should not divulge this. Going through this passage one has the uncanny feeling that probably Badauni is referring to himself.[111] This feeling is further strengthened when one reads one of the stories that Badauni had quoted to prove the greatness of Ali. He says that when Ali was going to fight the *Kharjis*, he came to a river and did not know where to cross it. There was a graveyard nearby and Ali called out the name of a particular person buried there. A number of dead replied and wanted to know whom he wanted. He then specified the man whom he wanted and consequently was directed to the river crossing. After describing this story Badauni quotes verses allegedly of Imam Shafii which say that if Ali had revealed his real true self, all the people would have fallen prostrate before him. What better proof of his excellence and virtue than that people thought he was Allah?[112] He quotes all this quite approvingly and does not seem to have any particular reservation about it. It may, however, be stated here that attribution of these verses to Imam Shafii is absolutely without foundation.

Badauni refers to both Hasan and Husain as *Amirul Muminin*.[113] Umayyad Caliphs are referred as *muluk* (kings) and never as caliphs;[114] the only exception is Umar bin Abdul Aziz whom he calls the fifth caliph, i.e. the fifth pious caliph after Abu Bakr, Umar, Usman and Ali.[115] Most of the time he refers to Muawiah as the governor of Syria (*wali-i Sham*), not Caliph.[116]

There is difference of opinion among the scholars about the permissibility of cursing Yazid, the Umayyad Caliph during whose rule Husain, grandson of the Prophet, was killed.[117] Among the eminent Indian sufis, Shaikh Sharfuddin Yahya Maneri does not permit cursing Yazid.[118] Those who advise caution in this regard include Imam Ghazali and Imam Ibn Taimia.[119] Imam Taftazani noted the difference of opinion on this score but at the same time emphatically supported the view that Yazid should be unreservedly cursed.[120] Badauni, however, makes no reference to this controversy. But he has very prominently quoted the opinion of Taftazani who believes that Yazid committed *kufr* (infidelity) when he consented to the killing of Husain and declares 'curse of God on Yazid, his helpers and supporters.'[121] He thinks that cursing Yazid is obligatory (*wajib*) and a source of divine grace. He approvingly quotes scholars to the effect that 'One who curses Yazid attains piety'.[122] He has referred to him as *palid* (impure).[123] But cursing Yazid should not be extended to his father, as the *ulama* do not approve it. He has also cited evidence in support of this stand. But in his heart of hearts he himself does not seem to be convinced. It is perhaps because of this that he always mentions him, as noted earlier, as the governor of Syria and not as the Caliph of the Islamic commonwealth, a position Muawiah had held for quite some time after the abdication of Hasan from the caliphate in 661 AH.

While highly critical of the Shias Badauni nevertheless had praise for Muhammad bin Abdullah Nurbakhsh, founder of *Nurbakhshiyya* order of the Sufis.[124] As is well known, *Nurbakhsh* was a disciple of Shaikh Abu Ishaq Khuttalani and hence a *Nurbakhshiyya* was a branch of the *Kubrawiyya* order.[125] But Nurbakhsh developed his own distinct Shi'i beliefs and therefore his 'may be classed among Shii orders.'[126] According to Badauni he claimed to be a *Mahdi* and succeeded in attracting many followers.[127] His distinct Shi'i leanings do not detract Badauni from speaking highly of him. In the *Najat ur Rashid* is a copy of what he claims to be the *farman* that he sent in all directions calling people to accept him as *Mahdi*. In this so-called *farman* are quoted, besides a number of verses from the Koran, the oft-referred *hadith* regarding the rise of the *Mahdi*. For instance,

Where are you o people who have gone for *hajj*?
Hurry up, hurry up, the Ka'ba is here.

Badauni has reproduced this *farman* approvingly and mentioned the name of Nurbakhsh with respect and high benedictions.[128]

In the same context, Badauni has given a detailed description of Saiyid Muhammad Jaunpuri, his personality and piety as well as the nature of his claim to be the *Mahdi*. According to him those who heard him explain the meaning of the Koran would renounce the world and join his entourage. All those who came under his influence abandoned their sinful ways and adopted a virtuous life. A large number of people attained high spiritual accomplishments under his guidance. Badauni has also enumerated some of the more serious charges levelled against Saiyid Muhammad and his replies to them. The entire discussion seems to be suffused with a deep sense of sympathy and appreciation for Saiyid Muhammad. Moreover, according to him somebody who happened to be present at the deathbed of the Saiyid reported him saying that he was not the promised *Mahdi* (*Mahdi-i Mauud*) but *Mahdi* only in the literal sense, i.e. a rightly guided one.[129]

Claims of being the *Mahdi* aside, Badauni thinks that there could be no doubt about the piety and spiritual accomplishments of the Saiyid. Badauni spent some time in the company of some leading Mahdavi personalities of the time and found them at a very high level of moral character and piety.[130] The way they explained the secrets and wisdom of the Koran without any formal education was astounding. Thus Shaikh Alai of Bayana, whom Badauni calls the Mansur of the age and the Bayazid of the time. He passes no critical remark about Shaikh Mubarak,[131] but castigates the ignorant and fanatic *Mahdavis* who would not accept anything that goes against the stand taken by the *Mahdi* even if it happened to be a saying of the Prophet or a statement of the Koran. Their endeavour would be to interpret it in such a way as to agree with the stand of the *Mahdi*. But at the same time he also cautions others to be reasonable and tolerant about them. Inability to understand their stand should not lead anyone to condemn them.[132]

Those who are familiar with Badauni's sarcasm and exuberant style would find it difficult to reconcile it with the image that emerges from the pages of the *Najat ur Rashid*: a sober, open-minded, and non-sectarian scholar pleading tolerance for others. He abhors polemics. While discussing issues, he scrupulously avoids polemic and confines himself to stating the exact legal position. Badauni has included marriage with non-Muslims among the heinous sins,[133] issue that had clear bearing on the contemporary problems. But he resists the temptation to relate it to the contemporary situation and confines it to quotations from the Koran. He does not even cite quotations from the *Hadith* and *fiqh*, which contain enormous material on the subject. There is nothing whatsoever in the section which can even remotely suggest that the issue has any bearing on the contemporary situation.

On several occasions Badauni pleads for tolerance of the views of others. For example, before discussing the beliefs and claims of Saiyid Muhammad Nurbakhsh and Saiyid Muhammad Jaunpuri, he remarks:

> It is therefore necessary that you should always be cautious and remove all feelings of partiality and sectarian considerations from your heart. Do not lacerate anybody's heart with the thorn of criticism. This is not likely to cause any harm to them; you should, however, take care of yourself. If you happen to notice a head in prostration on the threshold of the Tavern, do not strike it with your foot, after all you do not know its intention.
>
> . . . Justice demands that as the people of God never join issue with you regarding the formal and technical sciences and accept your authority in this field; you should also accept their superiority in the arena of supernatural knowledge.[134]

Elsewhere Badauni makes a strong plea for tolerant and non-sectarian attitudes. He says:

My dear, in a situation when the discerning and the pious, due to the limitless mercy of God, do not think even Pharaoh outside the domain of *iman*, why should you make so much hue and cry. Since all of them are after truth and doubts have led them astray, God willing they will attain to the grace and bliss and their affairs will come to a happy end.
Every one is seeking Him whether sober or drunk.
Everywhere is abode of love, whether it is a mosque or a fire-temple.[135]

Such examples exhorting readers to observe tolerance for those with whom they do not happen to agree can be multiplied from the pages of *Najat ur Rashid*.

Like Barani, Badauni too believed that education should not be imparted to the low and the mean. In the sixth chapter, which concerns miscellaneous offences, he has devoted a section on 'education to the unworthy'. He maintains that educating the unworthy is like giving a lamp to a thief. He attributes the following verses to Ali:

Education is source of grace for the noble.
For the mean and lowly it is a source of reproach and disgrace.
Water turns into a pearl when it falls in the mouth of the shell.
But in the mouth of a viper the same water becomes poison.[136]

According to Badauni his own experience would go to confirm this view. Mean and base people who managed to acquire education during his time, proved to be a source of mischief to the community and the country.[137]

It has been noticed earlier that *Najat ur Rashid* has been designated by some scholars as a polemical work. But the fact is that the book is almost absolutely free from polemics. It goes to the credit of Badauni that he has not only scrupulously avoided polemics in very form but has very severely condemned it. On more than one occasion he has singled out polemics and disputation among the *ulama* as one of the main factors responsible for the decline of the community.[138] He has counted polemics among serious religious offences and devoted a section to it to highlight its ill consequences.[139] He has made a distinction between academic debate (*munazara*) and polemics and disputation (*mujadala*). While the former is to be approved, the latter is to be shunned and avoided. Discussing the requirements of *munazara*, he says that it should always be based on argument and not lung power. if the truth appears to be on the side of the other party, one should not hesitate to accept it and should never make it a point of prestige because it only brings disgrace.[140]

In support of his contention that decline and ruin of the affairs of the community is to be always traced to the polemics among the ulama, Badauni quotes the example of the city of Ray. Ray was a populous and flourishing city but it was totally ruined due to the doings of its *ulama*. Shias, Shafiis and the Hanafis who lived in this city were at loggerheads. First the Sunnis fought the Shia and obliterated every trace of them from the city. Then the two Sunni groups fought each other, which led to the extermination of the Shafiis; only Hanafis remained. Later, the Mongols came and eliminated the Hanafis. When cotton catches fire, neither the wet is spared, nor the dry.[141]

Interesting aspects of Badauni's own personal life also emerge from the pages of the book. For example, he seems to have a life long weakness for the handsome and beautiful. Though like the *Muntakhab-ut-Tawarikh* he has not given juicy details of his romances and escapades as well as romances involving others, not because the subject of the book warranted it, but in different contexts and on different occasions he admits this weakness and laments that this passion did not leave him much time and energy to accomplish anything big in life. He expresses deep remorse and regret and feelings of anguish and repentance about his past that was devoted to these frivolous affairs.[142]

Early in his career Badauni served Husain Khan for about ten years. He praises the Khan for his piety, generosity and other good qualities. He seems to have been well satisfied with this service and would not think of leaving it for another job. But in 1574 he suddenly left the Khan. In the *Muntakhab-ut-Tawarikh*, where he has given an account of his association with the Khan, he briefly mentions the estrangement but has not specified the reason.[143] Rizvi has not mentioned his separation from Husain Khan and maintains that Badauni continued to have friendly relations with him till his death in 1576.[144] But this view is not supported by the evidence contained in the *Muntakhab-ut-Tawarikh*. Mukhia, obviously using Lowe's English translation of the *Muntakhab-ut-Tawarikh*, maintains:

> That the estrangement of Husain Khan from our author must have been on account of some grave personal default of the latter seems certain, for besides laying the blame of this at the door of the heavens, Badauni is reticent in explaining the reason. Badauni also tried to plead with Husain Khan and secured the intercession of a few persons including his mother's.[145]

Badauni's reticence, however, was not due to a grave misdemeanour. Apparently, it was a deep sense of loyalty and respect for a benefactor that prompted him not to mention the reasons for the estrangement. A close examination of the concerned passage in the *Muntakhab-ut-Tawarikh* would clearly suggest that its rendering by Lowe is not accurate. The fault lay with the Khan and it was the Khan and not Badauni who has secured the intercession of some people including Badauni's mother, but without avail.[146] The 'strange matter' that according to Badauni was at the root of this separation, seems to have so thoroughly disheartened him that in spite of his deep regard for the Khan he could not bring himself to resume this association.

Under the section 'Taking omen from the Koran Badauni has given a story in which he says that for some time he had the good fortune of living with a gracious Khan some of whose good qualities have been mentioned in the *Muntakhab-ut-Tawarikh*. The said Khan was highly addicted to consulting omens. Later a person who claimed to belong to the *Ahl-i Bait* joined him and taught him a particular method of taking omens. One day a handsome young man was brought to him as a prisoner and it was reported that he was willing to accept Islam. He also made a declaration in the presence of the Khan that he wanted to become a Muslim. The Khan said that he would have to consult an omen. Badauni protested that omens are not to be relied in the matters concerning life and death particularly when the person in question has also expressed his wish to become a Muslim. But the Khan was not convinced and in spite of all the protestations of Badauni and the pleadings of the hapless victim, he was killed in accordance with the indications of the omen. If the entire situation is kept in mind, there could be no doubt that this episode relates to Badauni's estrangement from Husain Khan. Because the description of the Khan with whom he says he had the good fortune of staying for some time and whose good qualities have been mentioned in the *Muntakhab-ut-Tawarikh* could not apply to any other person but Husain Khan.[147]

These occasional flashbacks apart, which throw much useful light not only on the complex personality of Badauni but also on many other aspects of contemporary life, the book basically deals with sins, transgressions and misdemeanours which a Muslim should avoid in his personal and social life. Badauni seems to have written it with the twin purposes of making a bid to arrest what he perceived was the decline of true religious consciousness as a result of Akbar's religious policy. In other words, he may be said to have placed a mirror before them so that they can see for themselves where they stood in the matter of their religion. The other obvious purpose seems to have been to register, albeit in an entirely indirect manner, his protest against Akbar's religious policy. In keeping with the nature and spirit of the theme he is extremely restrained in his discussions and his usually exuberant and sarcastic style is entirely missing in this book. But he seems to have been thoroughly disappointed and the aims that he had apparently set before him dismally failed to materialize. This appears to have embittered him and he realized that against the might of the empire he could not hope to succeed. It was perhaps at this stage that he decided to say whatever he wanted to say without mincing words. That led to the uncontrolled outpourings of his heart and soul in the *Muntakhab-ut-Tawarikh*. This is not to suggest that his personal frustrations did not play any role in deciding the nature and tenor of the *Muntakhab-ut-Tawarikh*. But it is not justifiable to attribute it entirely to the personal factor. After all, the personal factor was very much there when he was writing *Najat ur Rashid* but he could successfully rise above these considerations and did not allow it to colour his discussions and determine its tenor. To attribute the bitter and sarcastic outbursts of Badauni in the *Muntakhab-ut-Tawarikh* solely to the personal factor would be too simplistic to explain the complex personality and thought patterns of Badauni.

NOTES

1. S.A.A. Rizvi, *Religious and Intellectual History of Muslims in Akbar's Reign*, Munshiram Manoharlal, Delhi, 1976, p. 278.
2. Harbans Mukhia, *Historians and Historiography During the Reign of Akbar*, Vikas Publishing House, New Delhi, 1976, p. 111.
3. The best testimony to Badauni's academic and intellectual accomplishments comes from Faizi's letter to Akbar on his behalf when he was out of grace at the court. Badauni has incorporated this letter in his account of Faizi. See Abdul Qadir Badauni, *Muntakhab-ut-Tawarikh*, ed. Ahmad Ali, College Press, Calcutta, 1869, vol. III, pp. 303-5. Also see Rizvi, p. 279; Mukhia, pp. 90-2. Ranking has put a question mark on Badauni's knowledge of the Koran because of some inaccuracy in two quotations from it, which is apparently a simple orthographical error. See George S.A. Ranking, *Muntakhab-ut-Tawarikh*, trans. Idarah-i Adabiyat-i Delli, Delhi, 1973, vol. I, p. 5, fn. 1.
4. For information regarding the Translation Bureau see Rizvi, pp. 203-22. For the establishment of *Maktab Khana* see Badauni, *Muntakhab-ut-Tawarikh*, College Press, Calcutta, vol. II, p. 344.
5. *M.T.*, vol. II, pp. 336-7, 366, 399-400, 257. Also see Rizvi, pp. 206, 210, 214.
6. Rizvi, pp. 215-16.

7. *M.T.*, vol. II, pp. 301, 318-19. Also see Rizvi, pp. 253-6; Mukhia, pp. 107-8.
8. *Najat ur Rashid* was edited by Saiyid Moinul Haq and published from Idarah Tahqiqat-i Pakistan, Lahore in 1972.
9. *N.R.*, pp. 71, 318, 329, 425, 465, 467.
10. Ibid., pp. 64, 320, 477.
11. Ibid., pp. 235, 53.
12. Ibid., pp. 2-3, 253.
13. Ibid., pp. 225, 235, 253.
14. Ibid., pp. 1-2, 82. Rizvi (p. 440) does not seem to be convinced by the statement of Badauni that the work was undertaken on the request of Nizamuddin.
15. *N.R.*, pp. 1-2.
16. Rizvi, p. 440.
17. *N.R.*, Introduction, p. 7.
18. Compare K.A. Nizami, *Akbar and Religion*, Idarah-i Adabiyat-i Delli, 1989, p. 238.
19. Rizvi (p. 440) remarks that 'the work undoubtedly voices the demands of the orthodox section of the Mughal elite'.
20. P. Hardy, Abdul Qadir Badauni, *Encyclopaedia of Islam*, E.J. Brill, Leiden & Luzac and Co., London, 1960, vol. I, p. 856.
21. Rizvi, p. 284.
22. Ibid., p. 285.
23. Storey, C.A., *Persian Literature: A Bibliographical Survey*, published by the Royal Asiatic Society of Britain and Ireland, Luzac and Co., London, 1970, vol. I, part I, p. 438.
24. Rizvi, p. 285.
25. *M.T.*, vol. II, pp. 406-7.
26. *N.R.*, p. 531.
27. Ibid., p. 2.
28. Ibid., p. 22.
29. Ibid., pp. 2-15.
30. Ibid., pp. 24-5.
31. Ibid., p. 25.
32. Koran: 31/13.
33. *N.R.*, pp. 25-33
34. Ibid., p. 34.
35. Ibid., p. 35.
36. Ibid., pp. 36-173.
37. Ibid., pp. 174-252.
38. Ibid., pp. 253-88.
39. Ibid., p. 253.
40. Ibid., pp. 288-352.
41. Ibid., p. 326.

42. Ibid., p. 335.
43. Ibid., p. 349.
44. Ibid., p. 320.
45. Ibid., pp. 354-424.
46. Ibid., pp. 425-99.
47. Ibid., p. 334.
48. Ibid., p. 460.
49. Ibid., p. 463.
50. Ibid., pp. 502-8.
51. Ibid., pp. 508-28.
52. Ibid., p. 22.
53. Ibid., pp. 210-14.
54. Ibid., pp. 328, 368-9.
55. For example see *N.R.*, pp. 210-14, 430-4.
56. Rizvi, p. 285.
57. *N.R.*, pp. 100-101.
58. Ibid., p. 50.
59. Ibid., pp. 48-50.
60. Ibid., pp. 45-8.
61. Ibid., p. 36.
62. Ibid., p. 89.
63. Ibid., pp. 61-93.
64. In the assessment of Rizvi (p. 440.) *Najat ur Rashid* 'challenges and refutes the new trends of Islam in India'.
65. Muslims wishing to enter *Din-i Ilahi* were required to abjure their faith in traditional and metaphorical Islam (*Din-i taqlidi wa majazi*). See *M.T.*, vol. II, p. 304.
66. '. . . the work (*Najat ur Rashid*) undoubtedly voices the demands of the orthodox section of the Mughal elite.' See Rizvi, p. 440.
67. For practices like wearing *Zunnar*, prostration before the king and application of the *qashqa* on the forehead, *M.T.*, vol. II, pp. 259-61.
68. Ali bin Hamid al Kufi, *Chachnama*, ed. Umar bin Muhammad Daudpouta, Majlis-i Makhtutat-i Farsiya, Hyderabad Deccan, Matba Latifi, Delhi, 1939, pp. 208-9.
69. S. Nurul Hasan, Sahifa-i Nat-i Muhammadi, *Medieval India Quarterly*, vol. I, nos. 3 and 4, pp. 101-2.
70. Ibid., p. 102.
71. Op. cit.
72. Ibid., p. 101.
73. For example see Ziaud din Barani, *Tarikh-i Firoz Shahi*, Bib. Indica, Calcutta, pp. 70, 290.
74. *N.R.*, p. 201. Also see Rizvi, p. 440.
75. *M.T.*, vol. II, 258.

76. *N.R.*, p. 101.
77. See Abu Ubaid al Qasim bin Sallam (d. 224 H.), *Kitab al Kharaj*, Urdu trans. Abdur Rahman Tahir Surti, *Idarah Tahqiqat-i Islami*, Islamic International University, Islamabad, pp. 44-5. Koranic commandments such as 'When the forbidden months are past, then fight and slay the pagans wherever you find them' (Koran: 9/5), etc., concern only the Arab polytheists. Non-Arabs will be included among the protected people even if they are not people of the Book. Also see Amin Ahsan Islahi, *Islami Riyasat-Ghair Muslimun ke Huquq*, Lahore, 1950, p. 9.
78. Islahi, pp. 12-15.
79. *Kitab al Amwal*, pp. 150-1, 212-14. There are many precedents from the time of the Prophet and the early Caliphs which stipulate that the terms and conditions of the treaty are to be strictly followed and it is not permitted (*halal*) to charge anything over and above the agreed terms. While due to penury or any other such reason, liabilities can always be relaxed, they cannot be enhanced. Once Muawiah wrote to the governor of Egypt to marginally increase the liability of the Copts. The governor refused as it was against the terms of the treaty. See *Kitab al Amwal*, p. 214.
80. Most obvious example in this regard is the case of the Banu Taghlib. They were Christian Arabs and Caliph Umar wanted to levy *jizya* on them. But they were not willing to pay *jizya* and considered it humiliating. Umar agreed to exempt them from the payment of *jizya* on the condition that they would be liable to pay twice the amount of *ushr*. Cf. *Kitab al Amwal*, pp. 40-7, 212-14. It is clear from this example that in specific cases requirements of the payment of *jizya* could be dispensed with and some alternative arrangement could be made, provided it did not harm the treasury.
81. *Kitab al Amwal*, pp. 231-2.
82. Qazi Abu Yusuf (disciple of Imam Abu Hanifa), *Kitab al Kharaj*, al Maktabah al Salafiyyah, Cairo, 1352, pp. 73-5; *Kitab al Amwal*, pp. 231-2.
83. *Kitab al Amwal*, pp. 117, 122-6.
84. *Kitab al Kharaj*, pp. 73-5; Islahi, pp. 21-2.
85. Ibid., p. 128; *Kitab al Amwal*, pp. 46-52, 803.
86. Ibid., pp. 129-30; Islahi, pp. 9-10.
87. *Chachnama*, pp. 208-9.
88. Islahi, pp. 32-3.
89. *Kitab al Kharaj*, p. 126; *Kitab al Amwal*, p. 67; Islahi, pp. 39-40.
90. Ibid., p. 123; Islahi, pp. 35-7.
91. Islahi, p. 37.
92. *Kitab al Kharaj*, pp. 12-23, 125.
93. Islahi, p. 39 quoted from the *Muslim Conduct of the State* (p. 101) by Muhammad Hamidullah.
94. Islahi, pp. 48-50. Shibli Numani, *Al Faruq*, Naz Publishing House, Delhi, vol. II, p. 134.

95. *N.R.*, pp. 239, 438, 439, 457, 490.
96. Ibid., pp. 195-7.
97. Ibid., pp. 197-8.
98. Ibid., p. 198. It is couplet and reads as follows:
Badsh saya-i Khuda bashad—Saya ba zat ashana bashad.
Rizvi (p. 440) has given the meaning of this couplet along with the meaning of a *hadith* in such a way that it gives the impression that it is also a part of it. He writes '. . . the *hadis* says that were there no kings man would have devoured man and that obedience to a ruler is imperative as he is God's shadow on earth and identical with the Divine Being.' The last portion is the meaning of the couplet and not the *hadith*, as Rizvi would have us believe. He has also wrongly translated *ashna* is 'identical'.
99. *N.R.*, pp. 197-8.
100. Rizvi, p. 442.
101. Ibid., pp. 442-3.
102. *N.R.*, pp. 37-8.
103. Rizvi, p. 440.
104. *N.R.*, pp. 118-24, 434-8.
105. Ibid., pp. 119-24.
106. Ibid., p. 123.
107. Ibid., p. 128.
108. Ibid.
109. Ibid.
110. Ibid., p 334.
111. Ibid., p. 121.
112. Ibid., p. 411.
113. Ibid., pp. 160, 450.
114. Ibid., p. 482.
115. Ibid., pp. 158, 346.
116. Ibid., pp. 145, 197.
117. Taftazani, *Majmauah al Hawashi al Bahiyyah ala al Aqaid al Nasafiyyah*, Matba Kurdistan al Ilmiyyah, Misr, 129 H., vol. I, p. 202.
118. Sharfuddin Yahya Maneri, *Khwan-i Pur Nimat*, Urdu trans. Muhammad Ali Arshad Firdausi, Bihar Sharif, 1989, p. 105.
119. Mahmudul Hasan Arif, Yazid bin Muawiah, *Urdu Dairah-i Maarif-i Islamia*, Lahore, 1989, vol. XXIII, p. 292.
120. Taftazani, p. 202.
121. *N.R.*, pp. 154-5.
122. Ibid., pp. 154-8.
123. For example see *Najat ur Rashid*, p. 434.
124. *N.R.*, pp. 73-7.
125. J.S. Trimingham, *Sufi Orders in Islam*, Oxford, the Clarenden Press, 1971, p. 57; *N.R.*, p. 74.

126. Trimingham, p. 122. Also see *Akbar and Religion*, pp. 76-7.
127. *N.R.*, pp. 73-4.
128. Ibid., pp. 77-80.
129. Ibid., pp. 82-3.
130. Ibid., p. 82.
131. Ibid., pp. 80-1.
132. Ibid., p. 73.
133. Ibid., p. 100.
134. Ibid., p. 73.
135. Ibid., p. 131.
136. Ibid., pp. 366-7.
137. Ibid., p. 368.
138. Ibid., pp. 328, 368-71.
139. Ibid., pp. 368-71.
140. Ibid., p. 368.
141. Ibid., p. 369.
142. Ibid., pp. 292, 311, 342-3, 456.
143. *Muntakhab-ut-Tawarikh*, vol. II, p. 87.
144. Rizvi, p. 280.
145. *Historians and Historiography during the Reign of Akbar*, p. 95.
146. Compare *M.T.*, English trans. W.H. Lowe, *Idarah-i Adabiyat-i Delli*, Delhi, 1973, p. 88. Lowe was grievously mistaken in his translation of the passage.
147. *N.R.*, pp. 358-9.

A Sufi Psychological Treatise from India

WILLIAM C. CHITTICK

I discuss here a treatise written by one 'Abd al-Jalil of Allahabad, who followed the mainstream of the school of Ibn al-'Arabi. He is probably identical with 'Abd al-Jalil ibn Sadr al-Din Ilahabadi, the author of the *Irshad al-salikin*, which is a collection of 'invocations (*adhkar*) of the Chishtis and others'. He was requested to write the latter since 'He had written many treatises in the science of *tawhid* concerning the realities, the gnostic sciences, and the intricacies, but a treatise was needed . . . in the science of the wayfaring (*suluk*), the invocations, and the disciplines which take the traveller in the direction of the divine gnostic sciences.'[1] Possibly he is the same as the Chishti Shaykh, 'Abd al-Jalil of Lucknow (d. 1043/1633-4), who, according to Rizvi, showed 'great frankness in expressing his belief in the *Wahdat al-Wujud* and little concern for the strict observance of the *Shar'ia.*' However, Rizvi also refers to 'Abd al-Jalil Ilahabadi, without any elaboration.[2]

'Abd al-Jalil first attracted my attention when I came across a work by him listed as *Su'al wa jawab* in the library of the Institute of Islamic Studies in New Delhi.[3] This short treatise (27 pages of 21 lines each) describes a visionary conversation with Ibn al-'Arabi. During the discussion, Ibn al-'Arabi answers a number of questions connected with difficult passages in his works, mainly *al-Futuhat al-makkiyya*.[4] Most of the questions have in view the long-standing current of criticisms directed against some of the technical terminology and phraseology of Ibn al-'Arabi's *Futuhat*, a current which had been set in motion by figures such as 'Ala' al-Dawla Simnani (d. 737/1336) and was continued by Gisu Daraz (d. 825/1422) and others. The last part of the work alludes briefly to the position of the well-known Naqshbandi Shaykh, Ahmad Sirhindi (d. 1034/1624).

This manuscript provides evidence that the importance of Shaykh Ahmad Sirhindi's criticisms of Ibn al-'Arabi in the history of Sufism has been vastly overrated by modern scholars. After Sirhindi, most of the authorities who supported Ibn al-'Arabi's positions hardly bothered to refer to Sirhindi, since they found his criticism amateurish and self-inflating. In *Su'al wa jawab*, 'Abd al-Jalil alludes to Sirhindi as 'one of the recent Sufis [who] have objected to your persuasion, saying that Oneness is in *shuhud*, not in *wujud*.' Ibn al-'Arabi responds quite rightly by pointing out that he has already said everything such critics have said in the *Futuhat*, where he presents all valid points of view. The problem lies in the critics' inability to see beyond their own limitations. His response nicely sums up the reasons why those familiar with Ibn al-'Arabi's own position never took Sirhindi's criticisms very seriously.

The *Ruh wa nafs* or *'Ubudat al-tazyin*,[5] is similar to the first in both length (22 pages of 21 lines each) and the fact that it is presented as a visionary conversation, the two principles being the spirit (*ruh*) and the soul or self (*nafs*). On the one hand this work discusses many of Ibn al-'Arabi's ideas on existence or being (*wujud*) and its levels, the nature of the things or 'immutable entities' (*al-a'yan al-thabita*), the unknowability of the Divine Essence, and the experience that take place in the afterlife. On the other it provides an interesting example of spiritual psychology, since it analyses the forces at work within the inward dimension of the human microcosm in terms that recall earlier currents of sufi teachings and reflect the developments and debates going on in the subcontinent. It is the psychological theme that I shall discuss.

Given the dismal state of our knowledge of the development of Islamic thought in India, it would be impossible to trace the numerous sufis, theologians, and philosophers whose views may be reflected in the treatise. The best I can do is to point to the roots of some of the ideas in the writings of Ibn al-'Arabi and other relatively early figures. It would be difficult to say to what extent 'Abd al-Jalil is influenced directly by Ibn al-'Arabi in these two treatises, since he may have known Ibn al-'Arabi's work largely through the tradition of criticism and commentary. The one book that he almost certainly had read, though he refers neither to its title nor to its author, is the *Naqd al-nusus fi sharh naqsh al-fusus* by 'Abd al-Rahman Jami (d. 898/1492). In the *Ruh wa nafs*, this work is quoted or paraphrased at least twice, and in one instance where a passage is attributed to 'one of them', it is taken from *al-Fukuk* by Sadr al-Din Qunawi, most likely through the intermediary of *Naqd al-nuṣus*.[6]

Sufi Psychology

Much Sufi theoretical teaching has to do with the invisible dimension of the human being, the ambiguous something that fills the vast 'space' between the body and the essence of God. In referring to this 'something', the earlier texts usually employ various terms derived from the Koran and the *Hadith* soul (*nafs*), spirit (*ruh*), heart (*qalb*), intellect (*'aql*), and mystery (*sirr*)—without much elaboration or explanation. But already by the third/ninth-century sufi authors like al-Hakim al-Tirmidhi[7]—not to mention the early Muslim philosophers—employ such terms to describe a hierarchy of increasingly invisible levels, tendencies, or dimensions reaching as far as the divine realm. In the theoretical discussions provided by al-Tirmidhi, al-Ghazzali (d. 505/1111),[8] 'Izz al-Din Kashani (d. 735/1335),[9] and many others, it is clear that the multiplicity of terms does not imply a multiplicity of independent entities. Instead, the terms represent the various names of a single reality—the 'unseen dimension of the human being—in respect of its different attributes, dimensions, or stages.[10]

Since these aspects of the human being are by definition invisible and difficult to pinpoint, the terminology tends to be fluid. For example, the definitions some authors provide for *nafs* frequently correspond to what others refer to as *ruh*. This is seen most clearly in the discussion, initiated by the philosophical tradition, of the three basic levels in which the inward dimension manifests itself outwardly, i.e. the plant, animal, and human levels. Some texts speak of the plant, animal, and human 'soul' while others prefer the term 'spirit'. Ibn al-Qayyim al-Jawzi's work *Kitab ul-Ruh* devotes a good deal of space to the fact that the early sources do not clearly distinguish among the terms. Nevertheless, many authors do distinguish them, and their descriptions of the differences provide detailed insights into the Muslim understanding of the human reality.

The discussion of the different levels or dimensions of the human being was by no means simply theoretical, particularly for the sufis. Unseen realities were defined so that they could be differentiated and experienced by the traveller on the path to God. Without the theoretical and linguistic 'embodiment' of the tendencies of the soul, it was impossible to come to grips with one's own nature. The descriptions made it possible for the spiritual traveller to picture, localize, and personify his own psychic or spiritual tendencies within the soul.' Once this was accomplished, it was possible to strengthen the tendencies if they needed strengthening, or pass beyond them if they needed to be overcome.

One can recall here the distinctions among the ascending levels of the human reality made by Kubrawi authors, distinctions that have been studied in some detail by Henry Corbin and others. Thus, for example, the founder of the school, Najm al-Din Kubra (d. 618/1220), refers to five basic levels of the self: intellect, heart, spirit, mystery, and the hidden (*khafi*). A later Kubrawi authority, 'Ala' al-Dawla Simnani, refers to body or mould (*qalab*), soul, heart, mystery, spirit, the hidden, and the Real (*haqq*).[11] The Kubrawi authors make especially clear the practical relevance of these classifications for spiritual travellers, since they also discuss the vision of coloured lights, or 'photisms' as Corbin calls them, that signal the experience of the different levels.[12]

Ibn al-'Arabi provides a vast amount of material on the different levels of the self, but the six or seven ascending 'subtle realities' (*lata'if*), so important in the Kubrawi literature and much of the later tradition, are probably not discussed in his works in any systematic manner. In general, he speaks of three basic levels in both the macrocosm and the microcosm: spiritual, imaginary, and corporeal; or spirit, soul, and body. Inasmuch as these three levels are tied to the experiential side of the path to God, the goal of the traveller is to bring them into harmony, and this takes place through the 'heart' (*qalb*), which is the spiritual organ par excellence in Ibn al-'Arabi's teachings.[13] In the writings of Ibn al-'Arabi's followers, especially Sadr al-Din Qunawi and his immediate disciples, emphasis is placed on the heart as the harmonious union of all the attributes of spirit and soul.[14]

Ibn al-'Arabi also discusses the 'mystery' (*sirr*) as a still higher stage of awareness, beyond the level of spirit. In his teachings, the mystery, or more often, the 'divine' mystery (*al-sirr al-ilahi*), is the individual's reality in the knowledge of God and the furthest limit of what the gnostic can come to know, since ultimately no one can know anything but himself, while the Divine Essence remains forever unknowable. In other terms, the mystery is the 'immutable entity', the reality or quiddity of a thing forever fixed with God. It is also called the 'specific face' (*al-wajh al-khass*), i.e. the face of God turned toward one individual rather than any other, thereby defining the reality of that individual.[15] Not only a human being, but everything in existence has a 'specific face', different from God's specific faces turned toward other things, for if God 'looked at' two things in exactly the same way, they would be the same thing. Here we have a corollary of one of Ibn al-'Arabi's most oft-repeated axioms: 'God never discloses Himself in the same manner to two individuals.' Or, 'self-disclosure never repeats itself.'[16]

The Setting

Although 'Abd al-Jalil's treatise deals with two major dimensions of sufi teachings—the psychological and the metaphysical—the development of the narrative emphasizes psychology. The text reaches a climax with an integration of diverse dimensions of the human reality and a vision of the oneness of all things with God. The manner in which this is achieved recalls both the Kubrawi-style hierarchy of levels and the specific teachings of Ibn al-'Arabi and his followers on soul, spirit, heart, and mystery.

The text is presented in the context of the long-standing debates in India over the status of the individual in relationship of God. More specifically, what are the practical results of the spiritual realization of the gnostic? Once the supreme union is achieved, can any distinction be drawn between God and the world? Granted that 'All is He' (*hama ust*)—the slogan which was taken as typifying the position of those who believed in the 'Oneness of Being' (*wahdat al-wujud*)[17]—of what relevance to the gnostic are the commands and prohibitions of the Law?

Shaykh Ahmad Sirhindi's criticisms of Ibn al-'Arabi arose out of this background. Sirhindi was not criticizing Ibn al-'Arabi himself—there is little evidence that he had ever studied his work. Instead, he was attacking the position ascribed to Ibn al-'Arabi by certain groups of Muslims who then used this position to justify their own neglect of the Law or doctrine that Sirhindi considered essential. It is clear that 'Abd al-Jalil had this same background in view, since he goes to great lengths to disprove some of the important arguments of those who maintain the commonly accepted misconceptions concerning Ibn al-'Arabi's position, what one might call 'popularized *wahdat al-wujud*' or the 'religion of All is He'.

The treatise begins as follows. 'Abd al-Jalil is sitting in meditation when two forms appear to him, one luminous and one dark. They greet each other and then introduce themselves. The dark one calls itself the governing power of the whole universe, a power so intermixed with the creatures that they refer to it as their own 'self' or 'soul' (*nafs*). Then the luminous form explains that it is the power through which all things have life; it is called 'spirit' (*ruh*) because within it all creatures find their 'rest' (*rawh*) and 'repose' (*rayhan*).

In the sufi discussion of spirit and soul, the spirit is almost invariably on a higher plane, as is clearly the case here, since light is higher than darkness. The spirit's 'luminous' appearance connects it with the divine name Light and the radiance of the spiritual world populated by angels, who, according to the Prophet, are 'made of light'. The soul is then connected to the opposite pole of manifestation, where light has lost its original intensity and become thoroughly mixed with darkness. 'Abd al-Jalil does not mean to imply here that the soul is absolutely dark, but rather relatively dark, as compared to the spirit. Absolute darkness would be absolutely non-existent and therefore imperceptible, in any mode. Moreover, the soul manifests certain positive dimensions of reality, as becomes obvious later in the text.

The forms then speak about their respective religions. The soul says that it follows the great lover Iblis, who is the locus of manifestation (*mazhar*) for the divine name Misguider (*al-mudill*). The spirit says that it follows him who carried God's Trust (*amana*) and became His vice-regent (*khalifa*), the Prophet Muhammad, who is the locus of manifestation for the names Allah and Guide (*al-hadi*).

With the mention of the term 'locus of manifestation' we are alerted to the fact that the text looks back to Ibn al-'Arabi's specific technical terms and his mode of discussing relationships. The general idea that the divine names are the roots or realities of the phenomena that appear in the macrocosm and the microcosm, while the phenomena are the places where the names manifest their properties and effects, is of course found in a wide range of sufi writings, not only in Ibn al-'Arabi; and it is plainly prefigured in a number of Koranic terms such as the *ayat* (signs) of God that are found in all things. But the term *mazhar* in this meaning is one that Ibn al-'Arabi claims as his own coinage and that typically occurs in discussions of his ideas.[18]

A 'locus of manifestation' for a divine name is a place where the name displays outwardly its properties (*ahkam*), effects (*athar*), or specific characteristics (*khawass*). Each name has innumerable loci of manifestation, and an individual entity may act as the locus of manifestation for many different names. Thus the human being, for example, is 'made upon the form (*sura*) of Allah' or is the locus of manifestation for this particular name. But by the same token, a human being manifests the specific characteristics of every divine name, since Allah is the 'all-comprehensive name' (*al-ism al-jami'*), which embraces within itself the properties of all the names.

All human beings manifest the name Allah—it is this, and this alone, according to Ibn al-'Arabi, which makes them human[19]—but only those who merit the title 'perfect man' (*al-insan al-kamil*) manifest the name Allah in a mode that corresponds to God as He is in Himself. Other human beings—whom Ibn al-'Arabi refers to as 'animal men' (*al-insan al-hayawan*)—fail to actualize the full potential of the human state. Hence they are dominated by characteristics that pertain to one or more of the lesser names embraced by the name Allah. In the case of the 'friends of God' (*awliya' Allah*) and the faithful, these lesser names are names of mercy and gentleness, while in the case of the unbelievers, these names project wrath and severity. In keeping with the *hadith qudsi*, 'My mercy precedes My wrath', mercy is closer than wrath to God's essential reality. As a result, the names of mercy and gentleness demand nearness to God and 'felicity' (*sa'ada*) in the next world, while the names of wrath and severity demand distance from Him and 'wretchedness' (*shaqawa*).

The gentle and merciful divine names bring about the actualization of the full human potential along with harmony and equilibrium among the loci of manifestation. In other words, a human being who is the object of God's mercy in this sense[20] manifests fully and appropriately all the individual divine names (including the wrathful names) embraced by the name Allah. That is why, in this passage, the spirit does not limit itself to saying that Muhammad is the locus of manifestation for the name Allah, since all human beings share in this particular characteristic, though clearly not in the same mode or degree. The spirit adds that the Prophet is also the locus of manifestation for the name Guide, the function of which is to spread God's mercy among the creatures and to open them up to ultimate felicity.

The opposite of the Guide is the Misguider, a divine name that is not usually found in the traditional lists of the ninety-nine names but that is implied by several passages in the Koran, where God is the subject of the verb 'to misguide'. The Koran attributes it specifically to Satan (28:15). That the soul or self is connected to satanic forces is suggested by a number of Koranic verses and made more explicit in the *hadith* literature.[21] In short, every human being has a tendency within himself or herself that is opposed to guidance and rejects the truth, and this is referred to as *nafs*: soul, self, or ego.[22]

The fundamental tendencies of the inner dimension of the human being are summarized in the well-known distinction, based on Koranic terminology, between three types of *nafs*, representing three main stages of human development: the soul 'commanding to evil (*ammara bi'l-su*)', the soul 'blaming' (*lawwama*) itself for its own shortcomings, and the soul 'at peace' (*mutma'inna*) with God. At the first stage, the soul dwells in the darkness of ignorance, forgetfulness, and misguidance, while in the third stage these qualities have been overcome and the soul has itself been transmuted into the light of knowledge, remembrance, and guidance. The middle stage represents a struggle between the opposing forces that are frequently—as in 'Abd al-Jalil's treatise—ascribed to 'spirit' and 'soul': guidance and misguidance, knowledge and ignorance, remembrance and forgetfulness.

In short, 'Abd al-Jalil's description of the spirit and soul reaffirms the well-known opposition between the ascending, luminous, and angelic tendency of the human being, and the descending, dark, and satanic tendency. We are prepared for a replay of the struggle between guidance and misguidance, the prophets and the satans. But we are also dealing here with Ibn al-'Arabi's intellectual universe, a fact that is announced at the beginning by some of the technical terminology and confirmed by many passages in the text itself, where Ibn al-'Arabi's terms are constantly employed and where he himself is quoted twice.

Since Ibn al-'Arabi and the 'Oneness of Being' lie in the background, it is natural that both the Prophet and Satan, the leaders of the two religions represented by spirit and soul, are represented as loci of manifestation for the divine names. The discussion cannot take an exclusively dualistic or oppositional form in the manner of the legalistic polemics of jurisprudence and *Kalam*. Rather, what follows will have to show that opposition among the loci of manifestation for the divine names can be harmonized and made complementary through Unity, or in other words, through the fact that the name Allah is the coincidence of all opposites (*jam' al-addad*).

The point of the debate is not so much that one side should win and the other lose. Rather, the opposition between the two sides prepares the way for a stretching and expansion of comprehension. Opposite positions necessarily have to manifest the same Reality, since God comprehends (*al-jami'*) all things. The task is not to answer yes or no, but to discover the right relationship between two yes's. Then the differing perspectives will be seen to be connected vertically and hierarchically, rather than horizontally and oppositionally. This does not imply that error has no reality, quite the contrary. But error arises not so much from the position as from one's perspective in maintaining the position. It is a mistake to affirm a truth related to one level in the context of another level. Error derives from the mixing of levels.

The Debate

The main part of the text, detailing the contents of the debate between spirit and soul, is interesting both for the topics covered and the intrinsic content of the arguments. At the same time it reflects 'Abd al-Jalil's perception of long-standing controversies over many important doctrinal issues in Sufism. Many of these issues are still relevant on the contemporary scene, where there is a renewed interest in the type of spirituality represented by Ibn al-'Arabi's school, and where one often meets contrary positions similar to those maintained by spirit and soul. But in the 'New

Age', the position represented by the soul seems to have gained the upper hand, while the spirit's perspective appears to be increasingly unpopular, since it reaffirms the necessity of the practice of the Law as the *sine qua non* for the understanding and affirmation of Unity.

The soul is depicted as clever and crafty, skillful in the intricacies of debate and not afraid to change its position when opportune. The spirit is much more stable and somewhat stolid, reflecting the far-seeing prophetic wisdom that it manifests. At the outset the soul mentions Iblis as its guide, so the spirit feels duty-bound to warn it of Iblis's shortcomings. The soul replies by having recourse to the esoteric knowledge of the spiritual path (*tariqa*), which transcends the *Shar'ia* mentioned by the spirit, and by claiming—in the manner of the well-known sufi defenses of Satan[23]—that Iblis was the lover of God par excellence whose secret pact with his Beloved would not allow him to bow to anyone else.

The soul appeals to a privileged, esoteric knowledge in several more passages in the ensuing debate, most of which focuses on the nature of oneness (*wahda*) and that of Being or existence (*wujud*), though the famous expression *wahdat al-wujud* is never mentioned. In brief, the soul wants to claim an absolute Oneness that obliterates distinctions within *wujud* and at the same time to maintain its own privileged identity with *wujud*. Thereby it shows that distinctions among things are sheer illusion. The *Shar'ia* is a veil which misleads the stupid. Those who are truly enlightened follow their own inner light, which is God Himself. The spirit protests that this appeal to absolute Oneness is in fact an appeal to one of *wujud's* many levels, thereby distorting *wujud's* reality. It is contradictory to affirm the absolute Oneness of God's Essence and then deny His many attributes. Both have to be affirmed, and then it will be seen that the divine attributes demand the reality—relative of course—of the cosmos. The necessity of the *Shar'ia* follows from the reality of the cosmos and the real distinctions among the levels.

In the first part of the treatise the soul makes a rather good case for an individualistic type of spirituality shorn from traditional supports. In the second part, where the soul has taken another tack, the arguments mainly attempt to claim the independence of the material world from any first principle. In both cases, the practical result is that the Law and the prophets are useless if not positively harmful.

By the end of the debate, it is not completely clear who has won. Certainly anyone who inclines toward the religious universe of Islam will read the text as giving victory to the spirit, since all the soul's arguments have been neatly answered from within the perspective of the *Shar'ia* in general and Ibn al-'Arabi's school in particular. But much of what the soul has said would be quite convincing to those who incline toward a sufi esotericism cut off from the *Shar'ia* and alien to scholastic philosophizing.

Though 'Abd al-Jalil means to support the spirit's arguments over the soul, he also wants to acknowledge the relative validity of the soul's positions. The soul is a locus of manifestation for a divine name, and that name has its rights. The name Misguider cannot be negated, but must be harmonized with the higher names from which it derives. Though 'God's mercy precedes His wrath', and therefore, by analogy, 'God's guidance precedes His misguidance', both wrath and misguidance are divine attributes and have a positive, if limited, role to play in the total constellation of existence.

The beginning of the process whereby 'Abd al-Jalil will harmonize the positions of soul and spirit is announced at the end of the debate when the spirit realizes that its words have had no discernible effect on the soul. Hence it proposes that they take their dispute to a third person to decide between them.

The Mystery's Judgement

That 'third person' is the 'mystery', the more inward dimension of the human reality that Ibn al-'Arabi identifies with the 'specific face' or immutable entity. In this context, however, 'Abd al-Jalil does not have in mind Ibn al-'Arabi's definition of the mystery, but rather the seven-part hierarchy of the human being which by this period had become a commonplace in sufi writings: body, soul, spirit, heart, mystery, hidden, and most hidden.

The mystery enters the discussion by addressing first the soul and then the spirit. It criticizes the soul for ruining the world of obedience and bringing Adam out from the Garden, but it praises the soul's grasp of the station of oneness and its description of God's self-disclosure (*tajalli*) in all things. Then the mystery says,

> It is clear to me that oneness has become manifest to you in the station of Nature. That is why your love is completely fixed upon the world of form. Your love absorption in sensory passions and immersion in the illusory pleasures that darken the mirror of the heart and bring about punishment and disaster in the next world. If the appropriate love for form were to become established within you, you would undertake good acts and works, since forms in the next world will last forever, while the forms of this plane are obviously perishing and have no

subsistence. You must turn your attention toward the high level in order to reach the [divine] self-disclosure that is beyond the outside and inside worlds. In that self-disclosure, no name or description remains, no expression or allusion.

The mystery then compares the soul to a frog in a puddle of filthy water who thinks that the ocean belongs to it. What the frog needs is for a stream of pure water to pass over the puddle and take it to the ocean. Although the soul's perception of oneness is true enough, no two people perceive the Essence in the same way, and hence there is a hierarchy of levels of perception. In explaining this the mystery refers to the basic degrees of *wujud* through which God reveals Himself, what in another context might be called the 'Five Divine Presences' along with the level of Nonentification (*la ta'ayyun*) that stands beyond them:[24]

O soul, though it is impossible to see the Essence without the veil of the attributes, there is much diversity in the veils. The veil of the World of the Visible is the densest of all veils. Then there is the veil of images (*mithal*). Within both these veils the Beloved wears the clothing of form, which is the most tremendous veil. After this, the veil of subtlety remains in the World of Spirits. Then there is a veil of subtlety in the World of Meanings which is the reality and immutable entity of the traveller and which is called the 'smaller isthmus (*barzakh*)'. All the gnostics see the Real in this veil. Greater than this is the veil of 'the most subtle of the most subtle' in the Presence of the First Entification and the Muhammadan Reality. This is called the 'greater isthmus'. Our Prophet sees the Essence of the Real in this veil, which is the thinnest of veils. Some of the most elect of the friends of God who follow that leader of the prophets observe a flash there by tagging along with him. Finally there is the level of the Disengaged Essence, to which no one has access.

In concluding this address to the soul, the mystery focuses on the soul's particular problem, which is the affirmation of selfhood or 'soulhood' (*nafsaniyya*). The only way to achieve the vision of the inward levels of Oneness is to negate one's selfhood, or to undergo 'annihilation' (*fana'*).

There is no remedy except becoming lost and obliterated:
They buy nothing there but a thing's non-existence and annihilation.

The mystery then turns to the spirit and praises it for its obedience and its attentiveness to the good that can be gained in the next world. But it warns the spirit that it also has not yet freed itself of love for form. The danger remains that it will be so entranced by the rose garden that it will forget the face of the Gardener. The mystery criticizes the spirit for perceiving the station of oneness from the point of view of the rational faculty (*'aql*) and for not abandoning itself in love. The soul's emphasis upon self-identification with the Real is a valid one, and it can only be experienced through love.

'Abd al-Jalil then summarizes the rest of the mystery's advice to the soul and spirit:

The mystery made clear that the entity of the servant has two sides, one the side of non-delimitation (*itlaq*) and the other the side of delimitation (*taqyid*). Servanthood (*'ubudiyya*) and lordship (*rububiyya*) both must be taken into account, since both are established in the entity of the servant. The soul had taken lordship into account and had desired to embrace immediate joy and pleasures, while the spirit had taken servanthood into account and had chosen the ease of obedience in order to grasp endless and everlasting deferred ease. Though both were flying in the world of *tawhid*, out of caprice (*hawa*) the soul-vulture would in the end have stayed with the bones, while the spirit-nightingale would have inclined away from the rose garden of the Beloved's face toward the garden's fruit.

'Abd al-Jalil's assessment of the situation depends upon various teachings of Ibn al-'Arabi's school that have been touched on during the debate and are here harmonized and put into relationship. Since their meaning is far from self-evident, they call for a few words of explanation.

The inner human reality has two basic dimensions, here symbolized by the terms spirit and soul. In one dimension, which stands opposite God's transcendence—or, in Ibn al-'Arabi's language, His incomparability (*tanzih*), independence (*ghina*), and overwhelming power (*qahr*)—human beings are servants overcome by poverty, incapacity, and weakness. They possess nothing with which to affirm their own reality and are totally dependent for their existence and attributes upon the Real (*al-haqq*). This dimension is manifested more clearly in the lower levels of the human being, i.e. in the soul and the body, which display relatively little of the divine light.

In another respect, human beings manifest nothing but God. They are created in God's image or 'upon His form' and are worthy of being His vicegerents. To them 'God has subjected', as the Koran puts it, 'everything in the heavens and the earth' (31: 20, 45:13), so they are 'lords' over all other creatures. This dimension of the human reality corresponds to God's similarity (*tashbih*) and immanence, whereby He discloses Himself in all things and most clearly in His chosen vicegerents. In this respect humans are 'non-delimited', since nothing limits the degree to which they can expand in knowledge and other divine attributes. In this context Ibn al-'Arabi speaks of 'perfect man' as the full outward manifestation of the Real, or the human being who has assumed all the divine names as his own character traits (*al-takhalluq bi asma' Allah*).

Though servanthood and lordship appear at first sight to be contradictory and irreconcilable, in fact nothing but total and absolute servanthood allows a human being to be a rightful lord. Only the perfect servant can be God's vicegerent. Just as God is God because He is both incomparable and similar, non-delimited and delimited, Essence and attributes, so also human beings are human in a full sense only by being both servant and vicegerent, nothing and everything. This is one of the secrets of Muhamamd's titles, *'abduhu wa rasuluhu*, 'His servant and His messenger.'

The soul manifests servitude and weakness, since it is overcome by darkness or distance from God, while the spirit manifests vicegerency, theomorphism, and lordship, since it blazes with the divine light. In other terms, the spirit is connected intimately to nearness, mercy, and guidance, while the soul dwells naturally in the domain of distance, wrath, and misguidance. One might expect that 'Abd al-Jalil would follow these correspondences and connect lordship to the spirit and servanthood to the soul, instead of saying, 'The soul had taken lordship into account . . . while the spirit had taken servanthood into account.' But along with distance and darkness go ignorance and arrogance. The soul looks at itself and does not see its dark nature, but rather the luminosity that allows it to exist and be itself. Ignorant of its own darkness, it lays claim to a light that does not belong to it. In contrast the spirit possesses the luminosity of knowledge and sees itself in its proper relationship with the Real. It is, in Ibn al-'Arabi's terms, 'godfearing' (*muttaqi*), which means that it ascribes light, knowledge, and power to God and darkness, ignorance and weakness to itself. Though it sees its own luminosity, it knows that next to the absolute light of God its own created light is nothing. Hence it acknowledges its servanthood.

At the same time, the soul manifests a positive dimension of the Real even in its claim to lordship, for lordship is a divine attribute. The sin of the soul's prophet, Iblis, is to have said, 'I am better than he' (Koran 38: 76) and to have refused to prostrate himself before Adam. As the spirit says at the beginning of the debate, 'According to the clear meaning of the verse, "I am better than he", the claim of betterness and selfhood—which negate the stage of love—became manifest from Iblis.'[25]

Following Iblis, the soul claims selfhood and betterness for itself. In doing so, it manifests the characteristics of lordship. In other words, by affirming selfhood and I-ness, the soul claims for itself a prerogative of God, since none truly has a right to say "I" except God.[26] Just as 'There is no real but the Real', so also 'There is no I but the [divine] I.'

At the deepest level, the positive nature of the soul's self-affirmation goes back to the fact that it finds *wujud* in itself. *Wujud* as such is the

Divine Essence or Selfhood—the divine 'I-ness'—and it manifests itself even in the darkest realms of the cosmos. And *wujud*, it should be remembered, means not only 'existence' or 'being' but also and primarily 'finding'. God 'finds Himself' through *wujud*, and so also the soul finds itself through *wujud's* light, but it does not notice that the light is not its own. The divine self-affirmation, which is *wujud*, irradiates the darkness of non-existence, and the soul in its darkness clings to the trace of light as its very self and survival. 'Selfhood' and self-affirmation manifest God's Essence.

In short, the spirit represents that dimension of the human reality that is able to see itself and its own limitations objectively and efface itself by self-transcendence, while the soul represents the dimension of the human being that sees itself as central and affirms its own right to existence. The spirit rises beyond itself and affirms the Other, while the soul sinks within itself and affirms its own reality.

At this point in the text 'Abd al-Jalil once again acknowledges the soul's rights to its mode of manifesting the Real, while admitting his limited knowledge of the true situation: 'O friend', he says, 'I do not know which point of view God will take into account tomorrow'. In other words, he does not know if God will treat the human being as a lord or a servant on the Day of Resurrection. However, one should exercise caution in one's dealings with God, and therefore one should observe the instructions of the prophets. The creature should actualize his servanthood here and wait to become a lord in the next world.

> It strikes my mind that on this plane one should act by taking servanthood into account because of the sending of scriptures and angels, so that through their warning one can come out of the well of Nature, remain protected from the disease of ignorance and atheism (*ta'til*), and reach the perfections of knowledge and works. Then, in the manifest abode of the next world, one will seal all this in the mode of lordship, in accordance with 'My mercy precedes My wrath' and 'My mercy embraces all things' (Koran 7: 156). For in that place acts of obedience will be eliminated and all forbidden things will be allowed.

The Birth of the Heart

Having given advice to spirit and soul, the mystery now addresses them both, telling them to become one. And, says 'Abd al-Jalil, who is observing the goings-on,

> From the unification (*ittihad*) of the two a marvellous state and wondrous shape

appeared, called 'the heart', which brings together the two sides and fluctuates between them.

The idea that the heart should be born from the marriage of spirit and soul goes back at least to Shihab al-Din Suhrawardi (d. 632/1234) in *'Awarif-ul-ma'arif.*[27] I have not come across this image in Ibn al-'Arabi's writings, but it is probably present somewhere, since his chief disciple Sadr al-Din Qunawi expands on it in some detail, as does Qunawi's disciple Sa'id al-Din Farghani.[28] The connection between the heart (*qalb*) and fluctuation (*taqallub*) is an important element of Ibn al-'Arabi's teachings, but of course it has a long history in Islamic thought, being referred to in a number of hadiths, including mention of God as 'He who makes hearts fluctuate' (*muqallib al-qulub*).[29]

Next 'Abd al-Jalil says,

> When the mystery found worthiness for the gathering of all meanings in the heart, it pulled the heart to itself and joined it with itself.

Once the heart is born, the mystery sees that the heart has the power to gather within itself all meanings (*ma'ani*). This point, so briefly stated here, is based on a rather complex exposition of the nature of the heart found in Ibn al-'Arabi's works. In short, Ibn al-'Arabi maintains that human beings perceive the Real in two fundamental modes, the incomparability (*tanzih*) and similarity (*tashbih*) referred to above.

Incomparability is the point of view natural to the rational faculty (*'aql*), which innately desires to prove that 'Nothing is like Him' (Koran 42:11). Similarity is the point of view of imagination, which perceives the Real only through His self-disclosure (*tajalli*), i.e. the forms and images that make up the cosmos or 'everything other than God'. Neither point of view is sufficient for a total view of God or things as they are in themselves.

The spirit personifies the rational dimension of human nature that can only understand 'God' as being incomparable, while the soul represents the dimension that can only grasp God in images and symbols, or in the forms of His self-disclosure. That is why the mystery criticised the spirit for putting too much stock on reason, and the soul for perceiving the Real only at the level of its self-disclosure in the forms of Nature.

The heart, in Ibn al-'Arabi's perspective, is limited neither by reason nor imagination, neither by rational thought nor the perception of forms. The heart represents the dimension of the human reality that brings together both kinds of perception in harmony, and since these cannot be maintained simultaneously, it 'fluctuates' from one vision to the next. But the heart never denies the Real, whether in His incomparable and unknowable

Essence or in His self-disclosure to imagination through the sensory forms of the cosmos.

The spirit's self-effacement is connected with reason and incomparability because the spirit grasps that 'Nothing is like Him' and that all positive qualities belong to God; hence it sees that it is nothing in itself. In contrast, the soul's self-affirmation is connected to imagination and the vision of similarity, since it sees God manifesting Himself within itself; hence it grasps that everything it possesses is similar to God and that all the divine attributes belong to it.

In short, by speaking of the heart's worthiness for 'gathering all meanings' 'Abd al-Jalil means to say that the heart had integrated and harmonized the points of view of spirit and soul by combining non-delimitation with delimitation and incomparability with similarity. Hence the mystery saw that the heart was able to perceive all meanings, not simply those which pertain to one side or the other. The mystery understood that the heart was worthy of knowing the level of inwardness and integration represented by itself, so it drew the heart to itself and became united with it.

But this is not the end of the story. Beyond the mystery, in the typical classification of the inward dimensions of the human reality, lie the 'hidden' (*khafi*) and the 'most hidden' (*akhfa*). All differentiation must be eliminated before the vision of absolute Unity.

Final Union

'Abd al-Jalil now provides an explanation for the two terms 'hidden' and 'most hidden'. They represent the innermost dimensions of the human being that can be discerned when the microcosm and macrocosm are viewed as possessing a number of levels. From this point of view, the mystery perceives the Non-delimited Light of the Real manifest both within itself and beyond itself.

> In the beginning, when the light of Non-delimitation had shone upon the mystery, it had found a flash of that light evident in itself; it had seen a kind of hidden (*khafi*) light outside itself, and a kind of most hidden (*akhfa*) light that its understanding and imagination could in no way reach but that it knew to be further away from itself.

At the beginning, in other words, the mystery had perceived the hidden and most hidden lights beyond itself, just as it had perceived a light within itself and the spirit and soul below itself. Hence it would seem that 'mystery' signifies the centre of human consciousness, a point that stands midway between the darkness of the body and the infinite Light of God. As the centre, the mystery is flanked by two dimensions on each side. Once the two lower dimensions, soul and spirit, were joined together and became the heart, the mystery was able to integrate them into itself. Now the mystery can become integrated into the two higher dimensions, the hidden and most hidden. It is able to accomplish this integration because it has been strengthened by the two powers represented by the spirit-dimension and soul-dimension of the heart.

Through joining with the all-comprehensive heart, a strengthening appeared within the mystery.

The spirit- and soul-dimensions of the heart now become the means for a two-fold experience of both the hidden and the most hidden lights. The spirit's attribute is self-effacement before the Other, since it tends toward annihilation (*fana'*) in the Real. But the soul's attribute is self-affirmation, since it tends to see the divine light as its own and to perceive itself as subsisting (*baqa'*) through the divine attributes.

Through the light pertaining to the spirit, the mystery dissolved into the 'hidden' light, and through the strength of the I-ness pertaining to the soul it became identified with that hidden light.

In other words, the luminosity of the heart's spirit-dimension allowed the mystery to become effaced and annihilated in that even greater light called the 'hidden'. But the soul-nature demanded self-affirmation, so in the midst of dissolution the mystery found itself and saw that it was now identical with the hidden light.

Next, 'Abd al-Jalil offers an explanation for the 'words of ecstasy' (*shathiyyat*) of the Sufis. For now the mystery, like Hallaj and Bayazid, speaks from the viewpoint of 'I am the Real':

Here it became a stream joined to the ocean and called out, 'Glory be to me! How tremendous is my rank!'

At the same time, this invisible core of the human reality experiences the 'fluctuation' of the heart, so its gaze shifts from the point of view of the soul to that of the spirit, from that of affirming itself to that of negating itself before the source of its own light.

But when the mystery's gaze fell upon the infinity of the Ocean, it said, 'My God, though I said, "Glory be to me! How tremendous is my rank!" now I repent. I cut off the belt of unbelief and say, "There is no god but God", so that through the blessing of these words I may be obliterated in the most hidden light.'

Once again the mystery experience annihilation, but the selfhood of the soul reasserts itself, and identity with the most hidden is established.

It lifted its head within the world of annihilation and began to say through the strength of the I-ness of the soul, 'I am the most hidden', and it threw up the waves of claiming to be the ocean.

At each level, hidden and most hidden, a dual experience has occurred. Only after self-affirmation within the most hidden light can all trace of duality be erased so that the ultimate union may be experienced. Beyond the most hidden lies the infinite light of the Unseen He-ness (*ghayb-i huwiyyat*). Here 'Abd al-Jalil alludes to what is ostensibly a *hadith qudsi*, whose text I have seen recorded as follows:

Verily within the body of the son of Adam is a lump of flesh, within the lump of flesh a heart, within the heart a spirit, within the spirit a light, and within the light a mystery; and within the mystery am I.[30]
Just as this happened the voice of the He-ness shouted out,
'and within the most hidden am I'.

With this re-assertion of the authority of the Real, the right relationships are established, and all dimensions of the human reality experience a mode of identity with the One. Even the most hidden, the highest dimension of the human reality, finds itself negated in the Real.

Through awe before that sound, the ocean of the most hidden became dry, such that none of the water of existence remained within it. In this state, all of them became one. The most manifest and the most hidden mixed together. All of itself cried out, 'Whose is the kingdom today? God's the One, the Overwhelming!' (Koran 40:16)[31]

In the supreme union, everything in the human being is negated as a self-subsistent reality only to be reaffirmed as God's self-disclosure. As a result of this vision, 'Abd al-Jalil loses consciousness.

Here I had passed away from myself and become selfless. When I became slightly aware, the sound of 'and within the most hidden am I' kept on falling into my ear from my own tongue. Out of the terror of this business I awoke. I said, 'There is no power and no strength except in God, the High, the Tremendous.'

This prophetic formula expresses once again the overriding reality of the servant—his nothingness before God. Then 'Abd al-Jalil offers a final comment that situates the whole episode firmly within the imaginal universe described by Ibn al-'Arabi. He tells us that everything that he had witnessed had been the imaginal embodiment of unseen realities.[32]

I understood that all of this had been I; all of these were the forms of my own knowledge. These discussions had been my own imaginal concepts (*takhayyulat*) that had assumed form.

'Abd al-Jalil's concluding prayer re-establishes his feet firmly on the ground of servanthood, the right attitude to be maintained in the present world.

I ask forgiveness from God for everything that God dislikes and I repent to Him, and I am the first of those who have faith.

In short, this brief treatise demonstrates a sophisticated grasp of the teachings of Ibn al-'Arabi's school and a profound awareness of the complexity of human reality. 'Abd al-Jalil presents none of the simple-minded polemic that often occurs between supporters of *wahdat al-wujud* and *wahdat al-shuhud*, but instead demonstrates that he—like many other Indian Sufis—was completely aware that the only way is to proceed by acknowledging the validity of a wide variety of perspectives and the relativity of each of them, since absolute truth lies in God's Essence alone, and that is inaccessible to human beings.

NOTES

1. Aligarh, Habibganj, 21/365 Farsi.
2. *A History of Sufism in India*, New Delhi: Munshiram Manoharlal, 1978-83, II, pp. 289-90; II, p. 97.
3. Institute of Islamic Studies, Ms. no. 2139.
4. I would have liked to have dealt with this conversation in the present paper, but the manuscript in the Institute of Islamic Studies, a microfilm of which was kindly put at my disposal by the direction, S.A. Ali, has proved exceedingly difficult to decipher.
5. Lucknow, Nadwat al-'Ulama' Maj. 31/2; a second manuscript, of which I do not now have a copy, is found in Aligarh (Subhanullah 297.7/46[4]).
6. Jami quotes the passage twice (cf. *Naqd al-nusus fi sharh naqsh al-fusus*, ed. W.C. Chittick (Tehran: Imperial Iranian Academy of Philosophy, 1977), pp. 28 and 201). One passage of *Ruh wa nafs* seems to be paraphrased from Jami's *Lawa'ih*.
7. *Bayan al-farq bayn al-sadr wa'l-qalb wa'l-fu'ad wa'l-lubb*, ed. N. Heer (Cairo: Dar al-Ihya' al-Kutub al-'Arabiyya, 1958); translated idem, 'A Sufi Psychological Treatise', *Moslem World* 51 (1961), pp. 25-36, 83-91, 163-72, 244-58.
8. See, for example, the section of al-Ghazzali's *Ihya' 'ulum i'd-din* (Book 3, Section 1) on the 'wonders of the heart'. Al-Ghazzali rewrote this passage in

Persian at the beginning of *Kimiya-yi sa'adat*, an extremely influential work in the subcontinent ('Unwan 1, Fasl 1 et seq.; ed. A. Aram [Tehran: Markazi, 1319/1940], pp. 9ff.).

9. *Misbah al-hidaya*, ed. Jalal al-Din Huma'i (Tehran: Majlis, 1325/1946), Bab 3 (pp. 80ff.).
10. For a detailed discussion of the finely nuanced terminology employed in Islamic psychology, see Sachiko Murata, *The Tao of Islam: A Sourcebook on Gender Relationships in Islamic Thought*, Albany: SUNY Press, 1992, Chaps. 8-10.
11. *The Man of Light in Iranian Sufism*, Boulder & London: Shambhala, 1978, pp. 109-10, 124-5. For other relevant Kubrawi texts, cf. H. Landolt, 'Deux opuscules de Semnani sur le moi theophanique', in S.H. Nasr (ed.), *Melanges offerts a Henry Corbin*, Tehran: McGill University Institute of Islamic Studies, 1977, pp. 279-319; Landolt, *Nuruddin Isfarayini: Le Revelateur des Mysteres*, Lagrasse: Verdier, 1986, pp. 54-66 et passim; H. Algar (trans.), *The Path of God's Bondsmen from Origin to Return: A Sufi Compendium by Najm al-Din Razi*, Delmar, N.Y.: Caravan, 1982, pp. 134-5.
12. The idea that a human being is composed of several levels, whether three, four, seven, or some other number, is deeply rooted in sufi thought, and is therefore a commonplace in the texts. A well-known Iranian scholar, Jalal al-Din Huma'i, in a footnote to his edition of Kashani's *Misbah al-hidaya* (p. 82) remarks that the hierarchy 'in general use among the gnostics' is nature (*tab'*), soul, heart, spirit, mystery, the hidden, and the most hidden (*akhfa*). In discussing the general view of the later tradition in the subcontinent, Mir Valiuddin distinguishes self (*nafs*), heart, *sirr*, and spirit as the main levels (*Contemplative Disciplines in Sufism* [London: East-West Publications, 1980]).
13. On various aspects of the heart in Ibn al-'Arabi's thought, cf. Chittick, *The Sufi Path of Knowledge: Ibn al-'Arabi's Metaphysics of Imagination*, Albany: SUNY Press, 1989, index. Also S. al-Hakim, *al-Mu'am al-sufi*, Beirut: Dandara, 1981, pp. 916-20.
14. Cf., for example, al-Qunawi, *Tahrir al-bayan fi taqrir shu'ab al-iman* (Istanbul mss. Carullah 1001/4, 2054/9; Fatih 1394/2, 2630/1; Feyzullah 2163/13; Halet Efendi ilavesi, 66/6; Sehid Ali Pasa 1340/2, 1382/7; Topkapi E.H. 546/3). Detailed elaborations of these teachings can be found in both the Persian and Arabic versions of Sa'id al-Din Farghani's recension of al-Qunawi's lectures on Ibn al-Farid's *Nazm al-suluk: Mashariq al-darari* (ed. S.J. Ashtiyani, Mashhad: Anjuman-i Islami-yi Hikmat wa Falsafa-yi Iran, 1398/1978) and *Muntaha'l-madarik* (Istanbul: 1293/1876).
15. On the specific face, cf. *al-Futuhat al-makkiyya*, I 46.12; II 304.21, 434.17, 647.15; III 32.13, 32.31, 385.17.
16. Cf. Chittick, *Sufi Path of Knowledge*, especially Chapter 6.
17. Quite wrongly if we take this as anything more than a poetic affirmation of an extremely complex situation. Cf. Chittick, 'Rumi and *wahdat al-wujud*', in

The Heritage of Rumi, ed. A. Banani and G. Sabagh, Cambridge: Cambridge University Press, forthcoming.

18. For a detailed explanation of the role of the divine names in Ibn al-'Arabi's teachings, cf. Chittick, *Sufi Path of Knowledge*, Chaps. 2-4. For the term *mazhar*, see ibid., pp. 89-91.
19. Cf. Chittick, *Sufi Path of Knowledge*, p. 276.
20. This is the specific, 'compassionate', mercy (*al-rahmat al-rahimiyya*), not the general 'merciful', mercy (*al-rahmat al-rahmaniyya*). Cf. Chittick, 'The Chapter Headings of the *Fusus*', *Journal of the Muhyiddin Ibn Arabi Society* 2 (1984), pp. 72-4.
21. See P. Awn, *Satan's Tragedy and Redemption: Iblis in Sufi Psychology*, Leiden: E.J. Brill, 1983, pp. 60-9.
22. For a wide selection of texts from the great Sufi Rumi on the *nafs* and its negative qualities, see Chittick, *The Sufi Path of Love: The Spiritual Teachings of Rumi*, Albany: SUNY Press, 1983, pp. 33-5 and index, under 'ego'.
23. Cf. Awn, *Satan's Tragedy*, part III.
24. Cf. Chittick, 'The Five Divine Presences: From al-Qunawi to al-Qaysari', *The Muslim World* 72 (1982), pp. 107-28; also Chittick and P.L. Wilson, *Fakhruddin Iraqi: Divine Flashes*, New York: Paulist Press, 1982, Introduction.
25. On this claim as a characteristic of Iblis in Sufi psychology, cf. Awn, *Satan's Tragedy*, p. 34.
26. Ibn al-'Arabi points out that any 'claim' (*da'wa* or *iddi'a*) contradicts the fundamental ontological poverty of creatures and therefore displays ignorance of the true situation (cf. Chittick, *Sufi Path of Knowledge*, p. 152 and index under 'claim'). See also Awn, *Satan's Tragedy*, pp. 90-6; and Rumi, as quoted in Chittick, *Sufi Path of Love*, pp. 191-3.
27. In Chapter 56, 'Fi ma'rifat al-insan nafsahu wa mukashafat al-sufiyya min dhalik', Beirut: Dar al-Kitab al-Arabi, 1966, p. 450. These passages are amplified on in Persian by 'Izz al-Din Kashani in *Misbah al-hidaya*, pp. 97ff. English translations of both Suhrawardi's and Kashani's discussions are found in Murata, *Tao of Islam*, Chapter 10.
28. Cf. for example *Tahrir al-bayan fi ma'rifat shu'ab al-iman*; Farghani discusses the idea in the introduction to his *Muntaha'l-madarik*. For details, see Murata, *Tao of Islam*, Chapter 10.
29. Cf. Chittick, *Sufi Path of Knowledge*, pp. 106ff.
30. Muhyi al-Din Padishah Qadiri, *Miftah al-haqa'iq fi kashf al-daqa'iq* (Hyderabad [?]: Matba-i Sarkar-i Asafiyya, 1293), p. 57.
31. Ibn al-'Arabi and his followers frequently quote this verse as asserting the point of view of the overwhelming authority of God's Unity, which erases all difference and otherness. Cf. Chittick, *Sufi Path of Knowledge*, p. 314 (note 6).
32. In Ibn al-'Arabi's perspective, human beings perceive only through the veil of imagination, so they never worship any God but the god of their own beliefs,

beliefs that are limited by their own imaginations (cf. Chittick, *Sufi Path of Knowledge*, Chapter 19). It needs to be kept in mind that to say that something pertains to 'imagination' in the context of Islamic thought in general and Ibn al-'Arabi in particular does not necessarily mean that it is 'unreal'. The World of Imagination, where visionary experience takes place, is in fact more real than the physical world of sense perception, since it is closer to the source of existence.

An Untapped Persian Source for the Administrative-cum-Economic History of Gujarat

ZIA UDDIN DESAI

The Aparao Bholanath Collection in the Gujarat Vidya Sabha (formerly, Gujarat Vernacular Society) Library, Ahmedabad, housed in its Post-Graduate Teaching and Research Wing, the Seth Bholabhai Jaisinghbhai Institute of Learning and Research possesses a Persian manuscript, which bears neither the title of the work nor the name of its author, nor the name of the scribe nor the date. As a matter of fact, it has no beginning or end, it is just some details noted down and put together in the form of a book.

The manuscript is thus described in the Descriptive Catalogue of the Arabic and Persian Manuscripts of the Vidya Sabha, totalling 300 (out of 400 manuscripts), of which the Aparao Collection of 130 titles form a part:

> It is a very important work. It is of great historical value. In the beginning, there is an account of the city of Ahmedabad; then, there are details of the edifices therein. There is also the record of the revenue of different districts and of their sub-divisions, the total expenditure incurred annually during the later Mughal period. In short, it contains the statistical and geographical details of Gujarat.[1]

The above description is, at best, an understatement. It does scant justice to the importance of the manuscript, the contents of which provide ample administrative (in its vast sense), geographical and statistical information on Gujarat province in the sixteenth to eighteenth centuries.

No mention of the author or compiler of this compendium of invaluable statistical information under different heads is available—it does not conform to the usual pattern of Persian treatise commencing with *Basmala*, praise of the Holy Prophet, the reigning king, etc. Yet from the fact that a substantial portion of the text has been found reproduced *verbatim* in the Supplement of the late eighteenth-century history of Gujarat, the *Mirat-i-Ahmadi* of Ali Muhammad Khan, the last Diwan of Gujarat under the Mughals and the Marathas. This and the several dated references in the work make it almost certain that our manuscript comprises the notes from which Ali Muhammad Khan compiled his famous statistical account of Gujarat considered not only the only work of its kind after the celebrated *Ain-i-Akbari* of Abul Fazl, but in a way more informative than the latter. It may be recalled that the author of this important work says that he was assisted in the task of collecting information about all major and minor affairs and particulars of the towns, parganas, sarkars, etc., with their area, revenue, and tribute by Mitha Lal Kayasth, who belonged to a family of employees in the *subanawisi*—assistant—in the provincial secretariat of civil affairs and was associated with the financial affairs of the province. Mitha Lal collected detailed information from the official records at his disposal, but died about a year and a half before the actual composition of the *Mirat*; the author, Ali Muhammad Khan, utilized his notes in a Supplement to his history of Gujarat the *Mirat-i-Ahmadi*.[2]

The manuscript under consideration in my opinion, constitutes these notes of Mitha Lal and based as they are on state records at his disposal, their authenticity can safely be vouchsafed. No doubt the author of the *Mirat-i-Ahmadi* did make extensive use of these notes, but he had naturally to be selective; a substantial part of them containing important details on various topics, could not find place in the *Mirat's* even otherwise very valuable Supplement.

A cursory glance at the contents of the manuscript shows that these notes contain detailed information on practically every aspect of governmental machinery relating to economic, commercial, agricultural, industrial and other aspects of the province and less known departments of state relating to welfare, government grants for religious and like purposes, dispensaries, and so on. For example, while the printed edition of the *Mirat's* Supplement refers to the Wardrobe Department—tailoring, stitching, etc., of royal garments and clothing and state requirements—called the Karqiraq Khana, it omits to give its location, which according to the notes was in the Chakla Ulugh Khan Gujarati (a locality which does not find mention in the list of localities given in the Supplement), situated next to the Diwani office in Jhaveriwada, a well-known locality of the walled city of Ahmedabad even today. Likewise, while mentioning the Arsenal Department and Artillery, the printed Supplement omits details as to the number of guns kept at various stations—towers, gates—in the city of Ahmedabad, their names, measurements, maintenance, gun-powder and other material required for them, and their raw materials and manufacture.

Other matters include the area (length and width) of the province (which at one time included Jalore, Jodhpur and Nagaur in the north and Baglana and Talkokan in the south) their revenue from different heads, including tribute from the Deccan rulers and vassal chiefs like Raj Singh, the Zamindar of Rajpipla (erstwhile princely state, now in Bharuch district), or Rao Bhara and Khengar of Kachchh, Duda and Kanji Koli of Chunwal (a region comprising parts of Ahmedabad and Mehsana districts of Gujarat), Kanji, the Zamindar of Bhakora, Askaran the Zamindar of Dekawada (in Viramgam taluka of Ahmedabad district), and Nanhaji of Kholwad (in south Gujarat), the amount to be paid by the Desais like Mitha, Musa, Prag Das, brother of Udai and Askaran, and the number of soldiers to be maintained by them. It also gives a list of officials of the various state administrative departments: Mutasaddis of the Diwan, Sadr, Amin, Darogha, Karori, news-writers, preachers (*Khatib*), agents (*Amil*), physicians of Unani and Ayurvedic dispensaries run by the government; agents, assistants, Faujdars, Mir shikars, suba-nawis, etc. At times the names of the incumbents is given. There are some particulars of the province under Aurangzeb's rule (1658-1707). The text defines the area under different sarkars like Islamabad (Halar), Muhammad Nagar (Halwad), Sorath, etc., in Saurashtra and the jagirs of different amirs like Sayyid Miran, Changiz Khan, Kamilul-Mulk, Nasirul-Mulk, Bohorji (of Baglana), Ghazni Khan Jalori and others in about AH 984 (AD 1576).

The manuscript also contains additional information on the topography and localities of Ahmedabad, a close study of which might help in the identification of some hitherto unidentified places like Ahmadpur, and Nurganj, mentioned in historical works. We know, perhaps for the first time, that a fine *mogra* garden was laid out by Mirza Abid, a deposed governor of Baroda and that Haidar Quli Khan, the Mughal governor under Emperor Farrukh Siyar (1712-19), had laid out a garden outside the city wall. There is additional information on their water system, the bullocks kept for drawing water, the expenditure incurred on them, the personnel engaged for their supervision with a head supervisor, and their stipends. The notes also furnish the information that the Bhadra Gate of the citadel of Ahmedabad was constructed by Azam Khan, Governor of Gujarat under Shah Jahan (1628-58) and that there were shops owned by Bohras under it. The large Bhadra citadel, of which now only the front part remains intact, had two gates and four wickets, with official residences, a hammam (bath), the court of justice, watch-posts, state factories or workshops (*karkhanas*), and *kachehri*. The diwan-khanas (Public Audience Halls) were built by various governors and high officials; the European *haveli* was in the central Manek Chowk area of the walled city; a number of serais are mentioned, with the names of their builders and their locations.

These notes are the only source on the construction of the city wall by the noblemen of Sultan Mahmud Begda (1458-1511) and under his orders. While the Supplement does give the names of chaklas, and streets, the Notes refer to different professions: sellers of intoxicants like opium, bhang, etc.; *tantigàr* (weavers); vegetable-sellers; beef (buffalo-meat) and meat (goat meat) sellers; oil-sellers; ghee-sellers; *karaliyas*; *tarkash* (wire-drawers), weapon (*jamdhar*) makers, etc. The Gujri Bazar—held even today—was held everyday at the main ground in the city and on Fridays in the suburbs; it is now held on the banks of the Sabarmati just outside the city wall and the Raikhad Gate. We find more and at times new details about the buildings of the city of Ahmedabad, with the cost of building material, wages of artisans, and other data.

The Notes give details about various state departments and their manuals or work codes (*Dastur-ul-Amal*), mentioning the items used or produced therein. The Supplement does not mention all of these nor in detail. For example, the Notes supply the new information that the *cheetahs* of Jamnagar and Palanpur (the headquarters of Banaskantha district) were famous. It also refers to an ordinance, not mentioned in the Supplement, that *cheetahs* could not be trapped or caught (except by the men of the Chitahkhana) to be sent to the court as gifts.

About the Department of Ports—Gujarat had a large number of ports along its coast—while the Supplement gives a list, it omits details contained in the Notes, about the working of ships, their crews (Tandel, Mallah, Muallim/Malam) and their duties, the requirements of war-ships in respect of provisions (food and other items), gun-powder and like material, repairs of ships, materials kept on hand in ships for urgent minor repairs, etc. That the great merchant—Prince of Merchants (Malik-ut-Tujjar) Mulla Muhammad Ali had started construction of a shipyard on Piram island in the Gulf of Cambay off Bhavnagar is known only from this manuscript.

Another such department which the Supplement omits to mention is the office of the Sadr or the Ecclesiastical Department, which was in charge of proposing or sanctioning the grants-in-aid to religious establishments, state-run alm-houses (*langar*), schools and their teachers and students, personnel of religious places like mosques (the leader of prayers (Imam), the sermon-giver (*khatib*) of Id and Friday prayers, the mukabbir (reciter of *takbir* for obligatory prayers), sweeper-attendants (*farrash*), managers and trustees (*mutawallis*) and the *langar* and other public endowments. The chief office-bearers in this department were the Sadr, Qadi and Muhtasib. As in other cases, persons holding these posts at the time of writing, and then daily stipends or allowances are also recorded. Among this, we come across the name of one such official which is not without interest. He is Maulana Muhammad Riza, son of Maulana Ghulam Muhammad, and grandson of a famous teacher-scholar-author of great reputation, Maulana Ahmad whose father again (Maulana Sulaiman Kurd Lahori Ahmadabadi) was a great scholar and a disciple of Shaikh Abdul-Haq Muhaddith of Delhi.[3] A fairly good number of Arabic and Persian manuscripts from the personal library of Maulana Muhammad Rida bearing marginal glosses, brief accounts of authors taken from well-known biographical works and endorsements with his seals are found in the library of Dargah Hadrat Pir Muhammad Shah Trust, at Ahmedabad. Another important, thought not as well-known person, a calligrapher of note, Khush-Raqam Khan, also finds mention as the manager of the state-run *langar*.[4] Lists of students receiving stipends under Aurangzeb, Muhammad Shah (1719-48), and later rulers is also contained in the Notes. Subsistence grants to the poor were paid from the rents of certain shops endowed specifically for the purpose. Similar details are given in respect of outlying sub-divisions (sarkars) like Ahmadnagar (modern Himmatnagar, Idar (Sabarkantha district), Bahiyal, Dhandhuka, Viramgam (Ahmedabad district) and Umreth (Kheda district).

The Notes also provides information on internal and external trade. Sea trade was carried by ships sailing to and from Surat and ports under the sarkars of Mangrol and Junagadh. The manuscript also furnishes some details on markets—retail (bazar) as well as wholesale (*ganj*)—and gives the names of merchants trading in the second half of the eighteenth century: Mangal Seth, Mulji Seth, Sanwal Seth, Gang Das and the like. Such sections detail the merchandise and its qualities, as for example and various kinds of iron, saffron, perfumes, sandalwood and other odiferous herbs. The indigo market also finds mention. The Notes quote the prices of commodities sold in the *kotha-parcha*: opium, pomegranate seeds, ispgol, parsley, figs, walnuts, etc.

The city or town octroi posts (mandavi and naka) regulating trade and collecting levies on different items also figure in the Notes. It appears that different provincial governors used to impose levies on different items. Sometimes it was seasame seeds, tobacco, tur and jhalar dal, mustard, ghee brought in carts (but not head-loads), castor seeds, rice and salt. The procedure of levy-collection is also given.

About coinage too, the Notes furnish interesting details. Apart from the weights of coins of different metals, the working of the mints is described. The manuscript also gives the standard weights and measures used by different artisans and professionals.

The Notes also contain interesting information about the orders issued by Aurangzeb and by governors like Azam Khan under Shah Jahan. The amount of brokerage on oil (evidently that which was still in vogue in the time of the compiler of the Notes) was fixed as per an edict of Azam Khan issued a century earlier. This same official of Shah Jahan had abolished the cess levied on the Qanungos of chaklas. Another official, Rahmat Khan, a Diwan under Aurangzeb, had remitted the *ijara* (contract)—cess on intoxicants. Mention is also found of the remission of imposts and levies fixed in contravention of the *Sharia*.

The Notes contain information on the military and security arrangements of forts and ports. The protocol of public audience, lists of men and women in different walks of life at a particular period, etc.

While the above overview of the Notes is sufficient to give an idea of the rich material contained therein, the list of contents, given below, will, it is hoped, be of added interest to scholars and students of non-political aspects of history.

Foundation of Ahmedabad: Note dated AH 1161 (AD 1748)

The length and width of the citadel named Bhadra and its bazar up to Manek Chowk; names of offices situated therein—Jilau Khana from the gate (of Bhadra) up to Tripolia (Three Gates) towards east; House of Kariz (modern Karanj) Charity; Legal Department; Kachehri of Dagh-wa-Tashih (Branding and Verification); Kotwal's Chabutara, Nakhas-pith (cattle-market); Alif Masjid near Kariz (modern Karanj), Salah-Furush Gate (now no more), Lal Darwaza, Kharu Darwaza, Farhatul-Mulk's mosque (a lofty stone edifice, intact) near Kharu Darwaza, etc.

Account of the Jami Mosque

The city wall, its history and measurements including those of the foundation.

Revenue under the last Sultan of Gujarat (1581) under different heads. Ports including those under Portuguese control, parganas, jagirs (with names of holders), etc. Peshkash of chiefs and rajas of Deccan.

Area of Gujarat province territory

Dispensaries, alms-houses and the personnel for their maintenance.

King's Personal Estate and Expenditure

Sarkars, parganas and villages with their area as in AD 1576.

Text of a *Parwana* of Jumdatul-Mulk Asad Khan, dated 25 Rabi I, 25 Regnal Year (AD 1683).

Suburbs of Ahmedabad

Buildings and markets: imperial sarai, *madrasa* and hammam (bath); mint, *kotha-parcha* bazar; jawahir bazar, minhar bazar.

Mansions of Shah Jahan in Shapur (non-extant); sarai and hammam of Saif Khan (Gujarat's governor under Jahangir and Shah Jahan (non-extant); sarai of Azam Khan (intact and in a fairly good state of preservation, used as the printing and stationary office of the Gujarat government and for courts); sarai of kotha in Raikhad (non-extant). Mansion of Abul-Qasim, son of Saif Khan and of Imam Quli *alias* Shahryar and his son Shah Wardi Khan (the last mentioned, an official and governor of Sorath under Aurangzeb, is known from his inscriptions in Junagadh and Mangrol; sarai of Muazzam Khan Khan Khanan (Aurangzeb's time).

Horoscope for the Foundation of Ahmedabad

Subsistence grants to poor and needy people from rent of (state-owned) shops.

Description of citadel with mention of buildings therein (sarai, hammam, shops of Bohras, court of justice, police-post, royal workshops or factories, ghuslkhana, garden and mansion of Muizzul-Mulk Haidar Quli Khan outside the citadel, diwan-khanas of various governors like Maharaja Abhe Singh and Ibrahim Quli Khan. (A mosque called after the latter and renovated about five or six years ago, still exists in the citadel area.) Extension of citadel area towards the north was made by Sripant Raoji, a deputy of Raghu Nath Rao 'at this time'.

Jami Mosque of the citadel (intact), adjacent to the Raikhad wicket which opens into Kotla of Saif Khan (non-extant); plaza in front of the citadel and its area; mansions of firangis (Europeans) between Three Gates and Manek Chowk; city (main) road, not more than 20 yards and less than 7 yards wide; public water-store; Sarai Azam Khan; state treasury; *kachehri* of Jawahir Bazar (jeweller's Market); Minhari Bazar; kotha (store) of goods (*amwal*). Kotha of Baitul-Mal; 150 rupees set apart in the sarai's horse-stable for *kotha-parcha* department; *pan* market; hammam (then in the possession of Khizr Yar Khan); Nakhas platform, public charitable dispensary adjoining to the right hand side of Saif Khan's sarai; Kariz Bazar with government offices on its four sides; legal (*Sharia*) department office opposite the (Bhadra) citadel gate; office of branding and verification (Dagh-wa-Tashiha) opposite Kharu Gate; city wall with gates and bastions and their sizes; names of noblemen who constructed the city wall in parts, with portions built by them specified; mansions of Rustam Ali Khan, Muhammad Baig Khan, Qazi Mustaid Khan and other mansabdars overlooking the river to the right of the passage of Maratha invaders; account of the city wall (its foundation, depth being no less than two heights of a man except on the river-front); additions, alterations, etc., during the war with the Marathas or among imperial mansabdars; strength of the wall ('daily there would be 100 gunshots fired at it, but it does not shake'); material for plaster; wages of masons.

Personnel of Kotwal's chabutara, their duties and salaries. Names of chaklas under the Kotwal, traders: opium-sellers; boragar (?); *tantigar*, bhang-sellers, green-vegetable sellers, butchers (buffalo, goat meat); cap manufacturers; dolagars (who transport dead animals); sweepers; torch-bearers; oil-sellers; oil-brokerage fixed in Azam Khan's time; Gudhri market held everyday in the city and on Fridays in four suburbs (until a couple of decades back, it used to be held in the plaza between the Bhadra Gate and Three Gates, but now it is held on Sundays on the river outside Raikhad Gate); oxen and camel carts; procedure of octroi duties (fixed by Izzat Khan) for goods carried in these carts from Agra towards the ports of Surat and Cambay to be paid in Shadmanpur and Firuzpur (unidentified suburbs of Ahmedabad) as per Kotwal's tariff; monthly cess paid by qanungos of chaklas remitted by Azam Khan; abattoir (slaughter-house) outside the city in Firuzpur and Asawal; system of contract for intoxicants like gutti and bhang which was given for the whole year discontinued by Rahmat Khan the Diwan.

Craftsmen: Motiya (?)-makers; *tarkash* (wire-drawers); karaliyas (makers of earthen vessels—their descendants now following different professions call themselves even now as Kuza-furush (earthen jug-sellers); tent-makers; thread-makers; jamdhar-makers (a kind of dagger).

Chitakhanas; ramnas (animal parks) at Hansol (now near Ahmedabad airport), Thaltej, Fateh Bagh, Hathijan, Odhav, Nahrwala (Naroda) under Qarawal-Begis; Palanpuri Chitas (Aurangzeb's Governor Shujaat Khan's orders not to catch them).

Gharyal Khana (watch-house) and its officials—Darogha, Mushrif and Tahsildar.

Manual for the department of state buildings under the Mir Saman in Ahmedabad and mofussil areas; its officials—Amin, Darogha, Mushrif, Tahwildar, Mason, Carpenter; Expenditure on material for buildings; brick-work; rekhta-work; clay work; plaster-work.

Manual of rates for wood-work: ordinary, plain Baghdadi style (?); pillar with carving work; 12-sided pillar-work; method of calculation of cost of wood.

Regulation about tankas (underground water-tanks) and reservoirs.

Alms-houses (*langar*) and amount spent thereon.

Rent from state-owned shops endowed for subsistence of faqirs and poor men (a list of such men from different walks of life is also given) and the staff involved—Darogha, Amin, Payadas (foot-couriers) of Tahvildars (whose names are given as on 1st Rajab AH 1126/13 July 1714).

Expenditure incurred by the state on such and such a mosque including stipends of leaders of prayers (names of quite a few mosques of Ahmedabad are given).

Royal workshops like Karkiraq Khana, Chira-baf-Khana, etc., situated in chakla of Ulugh) Khan Gujarati adjoining the kachehri of the Diwan in Jawhariwada (modern Jhaveriwada); manual of Chira-baf-Khana—varieties of cloth: qutbi, velvet, kamkhwab, atlas, tash, patola; time of purchase (as in Hamid Khan's regime); wages of Safaigar.

Artillery material under Khan Saman; personnel; Darogha, Mushrif, Tahvildar, Payadas; Golandaz (Gunner); Khalasis; cart-drivers; rocketeers; iron-smiths; beldars; kahars (porters); carpenters of *dhak* (wood); gun-powder makers with assistants; firemen, wood-makers, water-carriers, kalal. Names and shapes of guns; number of guns then in the province; places where mounted (city-gates, walls); gun-powder ingredients and other details on their maintenance.

State treasuries: imperial treasury, treasury of outstanding dues, treasury of charity, situated in the Sarai of Azam Khan and their managerial staff.

Revenue heads and expenditure heads.

Weights of ashrafis, rupees, alamgiri fulus (paisa).

Kathra Parcha of the city: octroi posts and nakas; imperial officers-in-charge of these (Amin, Darogha, Karori, Mushrif, Tahwildar).

News-reporters (waqia-nigar and sawanih-nigar) of the provinces and functionaries of his office.

Price-list of items of Kathra Parcha—perfumes, dry fruits, etc. This is a long list occupying four folios.

Island near the sea-coast with officials posted there (e.g. Piram between

Gogha and Surat in the Gulf of Cambay, in which the chief of merchants Mulla Muhammad Ali had built a shipyard for his ships); personnel and functionaries employed there (Bandardar or port-master, Qanungo of the harbour; Mir Bahr, Mushrif, Tahvildar).

Functionaries of ships, their jobs and position in ships (Nakhuda, Muallim, Tandel, Mallah, with their assistants). Material for new ships—provisions of grains, oil, gun-powder, lead, material for ready repairs of ships; material for protection against rain (ghata-top, chadra, momjama, etc.), buckets, etc.

Ships from ports like Surat, for example sailing for foreign ports; large and small ports.

Military cantonments and security arrangements at forts, river-fords, different strategic stations.

Dispensation of justice (Wednesdays set apart for special cases).

Faujdar and Thanedar offices in Ahmedabad and names of puras (suburbs).

Places in and around earmarked for the encampment of rajas visiting Ahmedabad to pay obeisance (Asarwa for the Raja of Dungarpur, vicinity of Kankariya, near the Garden of the Firangis (Dutch) for Jam Ranmal of Islamnagar (Jamnagar).

Personnel of Diwan's department; Taqavi (Assistance to Farmers); Gras (petty land-holdings); Madad-i-Maash (land in subsistence-grant).

Personnel of the Finance Department of the province.

Office of the Qadi and his staff (with a Mushrif in charge of stipends for neo-Muslims).

Mints (at Ahmedabad, Cambay, Jamnagar, Junagadh and Surat) with their personnel (Amin, Darogha, Mushrif, Tahwildar, Karori, Weigher, Assayer).

Royal gardens of fruits, their products with personnel looking after them with their salaries (name of one gardener, Manohar, also given).

Karqiraq khana (Wardrobe); dispensaries, their personnel and salaries (Hakim, Darogha, Mushrif, Tahwildar, Physician, Surgeon).

Places of free distribution of blankets and gowns.

Expenditure on the mausoleum of Sultan Ahmad I, founder of Ahmedabad (for *langar*, cash as well as cooked food), neo-Muslims, needy persons, etc.

Mosques and endowments with details of expenditure on their maintenance.

Postal services and dak-chowkis.

Personnel and names of Qadis, Muftis, Sadrs, Muhtasib (including teachers and pupils), etc., and their stipends.

Mutawallis of the Tomb of Sultan Ahmad I, *langar* of Ahmedabad city (and its then manager Khush-raqam Khan).

Muhtasib (religious Censor) and his jurisdiction: (1) some levies which were against the provisions of *Sharia* were remitted, as for example, levy on bathing at the sacred rivers Gomti at Dwarka, Saraswati at Siddhpur, Sabarmati at Vautha (in Dholka Taluka of Ahmedabad), Narbada at Surpan (in Broach district), Parikrama (tawaf) at Ambaji in Danta (Banaskantha district), Untkeshwar Mahadeva at Bhagipur under Punadara (Kheda district), Dakor (Kheda district), Bahucharaji (Banaskantha district), bathing and Parikrama at Somnath, etc. (2) On banning intoxicants, drinks and inflicting punishments on drunkards and dealers or manufacturers of these: toddy-sellers, bhang-sellers, and liquor-distillers and enforcing closure of wine-houses. (3) Ensuring accuracy of weights and measures; details of stone-weights for corn, weights of goldsmiths (these were stamped with the seal of authority in mints), tanks of jewellers and shroffs, weights of oil and ghee-sellers and fuel-sellers. (4) other items falling within his jurisdiction.

List of items to be stamped with the seal of Ali Muhammad Khan Bahadur, asylum of Vazirate (i.e. minister, the famous author of the *Mirat-i-Ahmadi*) containing much important information.

Sarkars on the borders of the province, mahals and villages of rajas, jagirdars and zamindars (names given) paying tribute—from Banswala in the north on Rajasthan border to Surat in the south, revenue in rupees or Mahmudis.

Names of varieties of iron used for building purposes, jalis, implements and tools like *kudal* (spade), mortar and pestle, nails, sickles (*daranti*), etc.

Names of perfumes and grocery items.

Manual of taxes or levies on goods exported (cotton, silk) imported. Names of trading centres and places in India (as far as Hooghly in Bengal, Thatta in Sindh, Bijapur in south).

Manual of *kharaj* levied on Hindus and *zakat* on Muslims as fixed in Aurangzeb's time for the city of Ahmedabad.

Road tax.

Eatables taxed during the governorship of Jawanmard Khan Babi, revenue and expenditure under Sarbuland Khan (AD 1750).

Different market and trade guilds like the Seths of the suburbs (with their names: Mangal Seth, Mulji Seth, Sanwal Seth, Gang Das).

Octroi posts and points and their regulations. Kotha of Minhari Bazar cattle-market—horses and other animals.

Revenue from grain, pulses, etc., during the time of Raghu Nath Rao as per regulation of Aurangzeb, AD 1752.

Aurangzeb's *farman* dated 1660 remitting certain taxes and levies.

Aurangzeb's *farman* promulgated in his fourth regnal year and its directives in force.

Mints of Ahmedabad, Sorath and Islamnagar sarkars, expenses on minters.

Particulars of sarkars and *zat* and *sawars* maintained under each, agricultural produce (bajra, jowar, mandawa, moth, etc.).

Manual of the Admiralty: sea-trade, ships, cargo, ships carrying exclusively one commodity (*pan* or betel-leaf, or fuel, plantains or gum, silk, etc.).

Royal buildings and mansions in the Bhadra citadel, gardens in and around Ahmedabad with wells, summer-houses, watering arrangements, trees, fruits. Garden, exclusively of *mogra* laid out on behalf of Mirza Abid, the deposed Governor of Baroda, garden of *halila* (Myrobalan), garden of *tut* (mulberry), gardens of flowers, fruits and trees (about one dozen gardens mentioned).

Manual of indigo market-store (Kotha-i-Nil).

Lists of mosques receiving grants, furnishing valuable information for identification of certain localities and mosques; for example, a mosque in Bara-Nainpur suburb, which architecturally resembles at least two built by queens of the Sultans, has been mentioned as the mosque of Rani Jamuna.

River ghats, thanas.

Peshkash of Desais.

Manual of flowers, fruits and its like ginger, lemon and karwandi.

Sale of wood of dried up or fallen trees—half of the proceeds to owner of the land and half to the state; if there was no owner, then the entire amount to the state, subject to the exemption in case of trees in graveyards, or trees of *Bairagis* and soldiers. Levy on the contracts of forest wood.

Toll-tax at river-fords.

Grazing tax.

Statistical details about the Haveli pargana (Ahmedabad rural district)—names of villages, with area, distances between them, agricultural and other type of land, fallow or otherwise, their ownership, ponds, wells, water-tanks, etc., running into about seventeen folios.

This manuscript, according to its owner's endorsement, belonged to

Bholanath Sarabhai, the father of the person to whose library it belonged before its transfer to the Gujarat Vidya Sabha's Seth Bholabhai Jaisinghbhai Institute of Learning and Research. Bholanath apparently inherited it along with all the other manuscripts from his father Sarabhai Mehta, a great scholar of Persian and an author of books in that language including a history of the Gaikwads of Baroda, who served as Daftardar at Baroda under the British in half of the nineteenth century.[5]

NOTES

1. Dr. C.R. Naik, *Descriptive Catalogue of Arabic and Persian Manuscripts*, Gujarat Vidya Sabha Collection, Part II, Ahmadabad, 1964, p. 560, S.N. 300.
2. Ali Muhammad Khan, *Mirat-i-Ahmadi*, ed. Syed Nawab Ali, Part I, Baroda, 1928, p. 9. The author also says that he incorporated in his account of the details of sarkars and peshkash of vassals, petty chiefs, etc., from the records maintained by Mul Chand, the Record-keeper (Sar-rishtadar) in the office of the provincial governor (ibid., p. 24).
3. For an account of Maulana Sulaiman, author of about twenty works in Arabic and Persian, see Dr. Z.A. Desai, 'A 17th Century Persian Litterateur of Gujarat', *Studies in Gujarat Persian Literature*, Baroda, 1985.
4. He seems to have been a calligrapher of great skill. A specimen of his excellent *naskh* penmanship can be seen in his short biographical notice of the famous pioneer of Islamic calligraphy, Ibn Bawwab, on a copy of the Koran in the Chester Beatty Library, Dublin. See D.S. Rice, *The Unique Ibn al-Bawwab Manuscript in the Chester Beatty Library*, Dublin, 1955, margins of the last page. The biographical note is signed by Khush Raqam Khan Gujarati in AH 1155 (AD 1742).
5. *Haqiqat* (*Haqaiq, Ahwal*) *i sarkar i Gaykwar*, India Office Library, No. 4525, 4526, quoted in C. Storey, *Persian Literature, A Bio-Bibliographical Survey*, Section II, London, 1936, p. 732, No. 987 (1); Naik, op. cit., p. 458, No. 244.

   The Bhola Nath Sarabhai family perhaps enjoys the unique distinction in Gujarat of having produced generations of high government officials, statesmen, scholars and authors, right from the time of the Gujarat Sultanate to date (now known by the surname Divetia, adopted first in all probability by Bhola Nath's son Narsimh Rao, a household name in Gujarati literature in the early part of the present century). Among other Persian works of Sarabhai, a collection of letters addressed to his son Bhola Nath in about 1844, and a brief history of Gujarat entitled *Mukhtasar Tarikh-i-Gujarat* are also to be found in the Aparao Bhola Nath Collection mentioned above (Naik, op. cit., Part I, Ahmadabad, 1964, p. 232, No. 147; ibid., Part II, p. 474, No. 254.

Literary Works of Qa'iam Chandpuri: A Source for Socio-Economic History of Rohilkhand during the Later Half of the Eighteenth Century

IQTIDAR HUSAIN SIDDIQUI

The decline of the Mughal Empire in the eighteenth century encouraged the *subedars* (governors of the Provinces) and the vassal chiefs to become practically independent of the centre. They still acknowledged the over-lordship of the Emperor but ceased to pay the surplus revenue or the annual tribute to the central exchequer. They rather set to develop their territories and enhance their limited resources. New towns and cities were founded with *gunjs* (shopping centres), *madrasas* and serais. In every province and principality, the standards set by the powerful Emperors were followed by the rulers in literature, arts, architecture, dress and social etiquette. All this led to the flowering of that intellectual and material culture that had emerged under the patronage of the Emperors in Delhi and Agra during the preceding centuries.

The new regional rulers seem to have vied with one another to found new villages, towns and cities. Their administrative headquarters were developed into centres of culture, learning and trade. Scholars and poets were extended liberal patronage. Traders and craftsmen were also encouraged to settle down in the new towns and cities. Consequently, the later eighteenth century in northern India is not only marked by socio-economic growth but also by intense intellectual activity.

Strangely enough, the Rohila (Pathan) chiefs who came from the tribal Afghan region in the north-west of the Panjab, with no pretensions to a cultural or literary background, carved out principalities in the upper Doab and emulated Mughal culture and politics. They extended patronage to men of learning, arts and crafts. Attracted by their munificence, many scholars, poets and artists who had been left without sources of livelihood in Delhi flocked to the courts of the Rohila chiefs. The literature produced under their patronage is rich in quality as well as in variety. Besides historical works, *diwans* and *kulliyats* (collection of poems) and *tazkiras* form an important part of the sources of information about socio-economic conditions in different regions.

Attention may be drawn to the fact that the Urdu poets of the eighteenth century, being sensitive people, witnessed in anguish the dismemberment of the Mughal Empire. The decline seemed to destroy all that they had been cherishing for generations. From the early Urdu poets, Jaffar Zatalli up to Nazir Akbarabadi (d. 1830) every one of them wrote a *Shahr-i-Ashob* (long poem) lamenting the loss of life and property in the city of a particular region.[1]

Odd fragments culled from literary works not only help us analyse the elements of change and continuity in the history of the region but also shift our focus from our pre-occupation with battles, factionalism and court intrigues of the period. Furthermore, these works provide us with insights into social relations between different religious communities in our pluralist society. The aim of this paper is to introduce the *Makhzan-i-Nikat* (a Persian *tazkira* of Urdu poets) and the *Kulliyat* written by Qa'iam Chandpuri (an eighteenth-century Urdu poet) as sources of information.

First, we may briefly discuss the life and career of Qa'iam Chandpuri. The name of the poet as mentioned by him in his *Tazkira* is Muhammad Qiyam-u'ddin. But he is known by his nom-de-plume, Qa'iam Chandpuri.[2] He was born to a Shaikhzada family in the town of Chandpur (district Bijnore), in the reign of Muhammad Shah (1719-48). Having completed his early education in his hometown, he left for Delhi where his elder brother. Mun'im had been residing, most probably as a royal employee.[3] The latter is said to have been a talented Persian poet. The leading Urdu and Persian poets used to visit Mun'im to discuss literary problems. In their company, Qa'iam was seized with a passion for Urdu poetry. His employment as Darogha (superintendent) of the royal artillery also helped him in associating with the leading poets of Delhi such as Siraj-ud-Din Ali Khan Arzu, Muhammad Shakir Naji, Khwaja Mir Dard, Mirza Muhammad Rafi Sauda and Mir Taqi Mir.[4]

The exact date of Qa'iam Chandpuri's return from Delhi to Chandpur is not known. The chronogram composed by Khwaja Akram for the *Makhzan-i-Nikat* would suggest 1754 as the year of the completion of the *Tazkira* as well as the year of his departure from Delhi to Chandpur,[5] for the poet states that when the vicissitudes of time forced men of talent to disperse and seek jobs outside Delhi, he decided to compile his work, so that it might keep their memory intact for future generations. But the internal evidence available in the *Tazkira* tends to suggest that he stayed in Delhi until 1758 and then returned home. Moreover, he seems to have made new entries on Urdu poets who flourished in the service of the Rohila chiefs in his *Tazkira* even after 1758.[6]

The *Makhzan-i-Nikat* is divided into three parts, each containing biographical details of poets and with specimen verses in a chronological order. The first part, though brief, is interesting as it emphasizes the contribution of Deccani and Gujarati poets in making Urdu poetry popular in Delhi in the seventeenth century. The second and third parts are on eighteenth-century Urdu poets, most of whom our author knew personally. The details about Hindu poets who happened to be the scholars of Persian but wrote in Urdu not only casts light on social relationships among the Hindu and Muslim elite in towns and cities, but also reveals how powerful a vehicle of thought and expression the Urdu language had become in the north. Further, this *Tazkira* furnishes information in some detail about the Urdu poets born to families of the Shaikhzadas and Sayyids who generally held *madad-i-ma'ash* grants in the upper Doab. The leading poets mentioned are Mir Sa'adat Ali Sa'adat of Amroha (district Moradabad), Shihab-ud-Din Saqib of Seohara (district Bijnore), Muhammad Ali Hashmat Kashmiri who had settled in Moradabad, Mir Abdul Rasul of Amroha, Lala Khushvat Rai Shadab of Chandpur, and Lala Newal Rai Wafa.[7] We find interesting information about Rohila liberality to their Hindu officers. The diwan and the revenue collectors of the Rohila dominions were generally Hindus. For instance, Qa'iam makes mention of Gulab Rai and his nephew, Lala Newal Rai Wafa. The former was the diwan of Najib-ud-Daula, while the latter held charge of a few *parganahs* beyond the river Ganga in Saharanpur region.[8] Likewise, Raja Hilas Rai Rangin of Bareilly served as diwan under Hafiz Rahmat Khan. The *Tazkira* also contains references to old and new terms of political and economic importance. The reference to the *zila*[9] (district) suggests that the vast *sarkars* had become divided and re-organized into smaller units for administrative convenience and economic development. Moreover, a large number of the officers in the regional kingdoms and principalities could also be entrusted with the charge of *zila* administration independent of each other. Thus the *zila* or district of north India was emphatically not the creation of the British administration.

Like the *Tazkira,* the poems contained in the *Kulliyat* of Qa'iam Chandpuri[10] also yield interesting data on the society of Rohilkhand region during the later half of the eighteenth century. There are *qasidas* (panegyrics), *rubais* (quatrains), *qitas* (short poems) and *mathinavis* (long poems). The Rohila nobles and zamindars, Hindu and Muslim, financially helped the men of learning who were facing hardship after the decline of the Mughal power. Several *rubais* composed either in their praise or to condemn government officers, tell us about both generosity as well as corruption.[11] The *qadi* of Sambhal is condemned as a corrupt man notorious for taking bribes.[12]

In the *qitas* we find small bits of information about the celebration of important festivals. Holi, Id and Nauroz were celebrated. The Muslim aristocrats arranged banquets on a grandiose scale in connection with the celebration of Id-ul-Fitr at the end of the month of Ramdan. One of the patrons of Qa'iam Chandpuri spent a huge amount of money in charity as well as on hosting a banquet on this occasion. The Nauroz (spring) festival was also celebrated by him in the same way.[13] Hindu zamindars and nobles spent lavishly on Holi. The *mathnavi* composed for that occasion describes the festivities arranged by the rich. Muslims visited Hindu friends and celebrated Holi with them. The rich people sprinkled colour all around; the poor used all sorts of things, including mud and filthy water in sport.

The poet glows with pride when he praises a certain Kunwar (a Hindu zamindar), his friend in Chandpur, who used to invite others on this occasion.[14]

Certain poems shed light on the means of recreation available in the cities and towns. The aristocracy patronized musicians and dancers. Some of the members of ruling elite appear to have spent enough money on the training of dancing girls. The girls were trained in different classical dances, particularly *akhara*, that held great fascination.[15] Children and even young men were fond of kite flying in every town and city.[16] Likewise, people enjoyed fireworks on certain occasions.[17] The weddings of the rich were expensive affairs. Besides the distribution of money and other gifts among the servants, money was thrown from above the palanquin of the bride at the time of her arrival at her father-in-law's residence.[18] Shows staged by magicians, mimics, buffoons, called *nats* and *naqals* were enjoyed by rich and poor both. The long *masnavi* (no. 2) about the art of a certain *nat* and his wife shows that some of them could hypnotize their spectators. Such artists were richly rewarded by the rajas and nawabs.[19]

The Indo-Persian chronicles and the accounts of European travellers provide insights into the process of urbanization in the principalities and regional kingdoms during that century. Everywhere new towns and grain markets were founded. Foster gives a graphic description of Najibabad, founded by Najib-ud-Daula, in his principality. According to him,

> Najab-ud-Daula, who built this town, saw that its situation would facilitate the commerce of Kashmir, which having been diverted from its former channel of

Lahore and Delhi, by the inroads of Sicques (Sikhs) Marathas, and Afghans, took a course through the mountains at the head of the Punjab, and was introduced into the Rohilla country through the Lall Dong pass. This inducement with the desire of establishing a mart for the Hindus of the adjacent mountains, probably influenced the choice of this spot; which otherwise is not favourable for the site of a capital town, being low, and surrounded by swampy grounds.[20]

Further, Foster tells us that the merchant caravans travelled from Rohilkhand to Kashmir, Kabul and Central Asia for overland trade. In other districts too towns were founded, along with strong forts. The famous fort of Pathargarh was built about a mile away from Najibabad. The town of Ghausgarh was founded 35 miles south-east of Saharanpur and Shukrtal, near an area of ravines and ridges east of Muzaffarnagar. The fortifications erected around these towns served military purposes but also attracted traders to settle down there. Serais were built around Najibabad.[21]

The references contained in the verses to the buildings and the towns supplement the information available in contemporary historical works. The members of ruling elite vied with one an other to build beautiful palaces and the poets attached to their establishments composed chronograms about the date of their completion and in praise of their grandeur and beauty. The *Kulliyat* of our poet contains a few chronograms about the buildings in the towns of Rohilkhand. For instance, the Raja Ram Prasad of Chandpur had a beautiful and lofty palace built in the midst of a garden in 1758. The tank and the flower-beds in the garden made the *diwan khana* (reception hall) so fascinating that it wore the look of a paradise.[22] Another chronogram described the completion of the Khilwatkhana (a building used for retreat) of Nawab Ghulam Ahmad Khan, son of Nawab Faizullah Khan of Rampur in 1781.[23] Similarly, the *mathnavi* composed about hardships caused by water logging to the residents in Bisauli[24] during the rains gives insights into how Bisauli developed from an ordinary village into an important township under the fostering care of Nawab Dunde Khan (d. 1771). The Nawab made it the headquarters of his *jagir* and then officers and scholars associated with him took up their abode on a permanent basis. Soon the construction of buildings started. The artisans, craftsmen and masons settled down there in a large number. But the construction of roads and streets was not taken into consideration, with the result that all of it was inundated in the monsoon season. The officers and courtiers of the Nawab who went to attend the darbar either on the horseback or in their palanquins got their clothes spoilt. In the same poem there are references to the *rath* (chariot), bullock-carts, horses, elephants and palanquins that were used as means of transportation.[25]

Of the weapons mentioned in the verses, the poet attaches great importance to the European gun (*bandooq*). He tells us that the gun imported from Europe was a coveted possession. The traditional weapons used and manufactured in India had become obsolete.[26]

Likewise, the poem composed on the severity of winter provides us with information about the conditions of people belonging to different strata in the towns and cities. The wealthy people heated the rooms in their houses with *kangri* (a fire pot made of earth) and covered the windows and doors with heavy curtains made of costly cloth whereas the artisans and daily wage-earners suffered from the want of sufficient clothing. Generally they stayed indoors during the extremely cold days and could not earn their daily wages. Even craftsmen could not afford sufficient clothing.[27]

The most important poem from our point of view is the *Shahr-i-Ashob*, treating the destruction of life and property in the towns and cities of Rohilkhand in 1772 as a result of war between Shah Alam and Zabita Khan, the successor of Najib-ud-Daula.[28] According to it the return of Shah Alam from Allahabad to Delhi (1772) filled Hindus and Muslims with hopes for a more peaceful and better future. But soon people got disillusioned on account of the misery that his invasion of Rohilkhand caused all around. Since the poet belonged to the region of Rohilkhand and was associated with the Rohila chiefs, he laments the loss of life and property and condemns in severe terms both Shah Alam and his allies, the Marathas. He calls Shah Alam a tyrant unworthy of kingship.

> He (the King) is a scoundrel moving at the head of an army of plunderers. Nobody's honour is safe because he is the shadow of devil and not that of God. People cry everywhere in agony owing to his tyranny.

Likewise, the Marathas are condemned as free booters. Shah Alam's grandfather and father, Jahandar Shah and Alamgir Thani (1754-60) are mentioned as fools and the poet would have us believe that their descendants were known for their stupidity. Illustrating his point he states that Shah Alam brought Marathas into Rohilkhand for the destruction of the Pathan race but could not achieve his end. The Pathans fled to safer places, but innocent people were killed and pillaged everywhere. The whole region was laid waste. Left without food, people faced starvation in every town and city. Those rich people who thought it derogatory to wear fine cotton clothes, could not afford to have even coarse cloth for their turbans. Those who maintained large kitchens and fed others had no food for themselves. The stables become empty of horses and fodder. The beautiful cities that could be compared with Cairo had been denuded of everything worth mentioning. Markets were left without goods; even medicines could not be found there. Moneylenders disappeared from the cities and towns. The lanes were full of corpses. Beautiful buildings were razed to the ground and noblemen like Raja Gulab Rai (the *hakim* of a *zilla* [district] who maintained more than a thousand servants) became penniless.[29] The Kaisths, the *ulama*, comprising *qazis* and *muftis* (judges and jurists) all began to face starvation. Revenue collectors were also ruined. Those who survived the carnage found it difficult to keep their soul and body together. On the withdrawal of Shah Alam and his Maratha allies from Rohilkhand (in May 1772), people suffered from chaos and anarchy that lasted till the Rohila chiefs could restore law and order. The Pathan soldiers who had returned from their hideouts deprived people of whatever was left with them.[30]

The *qasidas* (panegyries) in the *Kulliyat* also give vital insights into cultural life and the patronage extended by the nobles to the men of learning and talents. Even minor nobles and chiefs associated with the Rampur court, after the fall of Rohila power in 1774, went out of their way to support financially poets and scholars.[31]

Last, we may make brief allusion to a long *mathnavi* relating to platonic love between a recluse, Shah Ladha, and a newly-married girl of the Panjab. Apparently the poet has successfully versified in Urdu a sixteenth-century romance; this is important as it helps us measure the depth to which popular sufism had sunk. It also shows that in consequence of the mystical philosophy of *Wahadat-ul-Wujud* (unity in essence of the Creator and the created), platonic love had become popular among the sufis. No doubt the educated sufis among the followers of Ibn Arabi continued to adhere to orthodox Islam and tried to gain spiritual excellence through self-purification; but they also considered *Ishq-i-Majazi* (platonic love) a means to spiritual progress, at least since the fifteenth century.[32] As a result, the less educated or unlettered sufis became negligent of the *sharia*. They did not attach importance to daily ritual and lived in isolation from people. If by chance they cast their eye on a beautiful girl or boy and fell in love with him or her at the very first sight, the departure of the beloved would cause severe grief. Ultimately the lover dies and is followed by the beloved to the grave. Their union was possible only in death. Qa'iam being a sufi also believed in the *Ishq-i-Majazi* as a means to the path of real love and gnosis.[33]

In conclusion it may be stated that the *tazkiras* and the *kulliyats* of the eighteenth-century Urdu poets form an important part of historical sources. In them we find information of supplementary as well as of corroborative nature. The verses provide us valuable insights into economic and cultural life in different regions of the country. In particular, the *Shahr-i-Ashob* poems not only depict the sufferings caused by the rise of disruptive forces but also the concern felt by the Indo-Muslim intelligentsia over the political instability that threatened the social institutions. They appear to have developed predilection for cultural values, cherished by the elite for generations. Though the explosion of the values and norms was temporary, no educated man seems to have entertained any hope of their survival, owing to the depredations carried out by the Marathas, Sikhs, Jats and the Pathans. In short, the bits pieced together from Urdu poetry help us to reconstruct the portrait of life and culture in different regions of north India in different hues during the later eighteenth century.

NOTES

1. Mir Jaffar Zatalli executed by the order of Farrukh Siyar some time in the beginning of his reign, was a popular humorist and satirist. He composed poems in Urdu in condemnation of the corrupt princes and nobles or the vicissitudes of time after the death of Aurangzeb in 1707. Although most of his poetry is characterized by obscenity, it helps us analyse the complex social phenomena then prevailing in India. The poet is full of praise for Aurangzeb because the latter successfully fought disruptive and anti-social forces in his old age. But his sons and successors became negligent. They fought for the throne and one another's blood, weakening the military power of the empire. Their over-indulgence led to lexity in public morality; the poet witnesses in anguish the old values going down the drain but his complaint about the rise of upstart rogues in the official hierarchy in lieu of the members of old aristocratic families indirectly sheds light on social mobility during the empire under the successors of Aurangzeb. In short, the *Kulliyat* of Mir Jaffar Zatalli is a mine of historical information about the life and conditions in the later Mughal Empire. *Cf. Kulliyat-i-Jaffar Zatalli*, ed. Naim Ahmad, Adabi Academy (Shamshad Market), Aligarh, 1979.
2. Qa'iam Chandpuri, *Makhzan-i-Nikat*, ed. Maulavi Abdul Haque, Aurangabad, n.d., pp. 1, 77.
3. Ibid., p. 17.
4. Ibid., pp. 24, 77.
5. Ibid., p. 67.
6. The account of Lala Newal Kishore Wafa, the nephew of Najib-ud-Daula's Hindu diwan, Gulab Rai, must have been included in the *tazkira* after 1754, for Najib-ud-Daula entered the Mughal service in 1753 and in return for his services to the Emperor against Safdar Jang got the jagir comprising the large area now included in the districts of Saharanpur, Muzaffarnagar and Bijnore. Gulab Rai was appointed by Najib-ud-Daula as his diwan afterwards. His nephew must have got the *jagir* a few years later. Cf. *Makhzan-i-Nikat*, p. 72.

7. *Makhzan-i-Nikat*, pp. 18, 24, 26, 27, 66, 72, etc.
8. Ibid., p. 72.
9. Ibid., pp. 49, 71.
10. Qa'iam Chandpuri, *Kulliyat-i-Qa'iam Chandpuri*, vol. II, ed. Iqtida Hasạn, Lahore, 1965, hereafter cited as *Kulliyat*.
11. *Kulliyat*, ii/14, 16, 78.
12. Ibid., pp. 14-16.
13. Ibid., ii/32-34.
14. *Kulliyat*, ii/197, 202, *mathnavi*, no. 10.
15. In the *akhara* a group of dancing girls turned up, decked with jewels, embroidered silk clothes and quickened their movements with lighted earthen lamps on their palms. The *qasida* no. 11 shows that Nawab Muhammad Yar Khan the nephew of Nawab Faiz Ullah Khan of Rampur maintained such a group. It was very popular in medieval times.
16. *Kulliyat*, ii/158-64, short *mathnavi*, no. 2.
17. Ibid., ii/255-7.
18. Ibid., ii/316.
19. Ibid., ii/255-7.
20. Cf. G. Foster, *Foster Travels*, London, 1798, p. 190.
21. Ibid., p. 191.
22. *Kulliyat*, ii/43-4.
23. Ibid., ii/112.
24. Bisauli is a tahsil town in the district of Badaun.
25. *Kulliyat*, ii/181-4.
26. Ibid., ii/168, line 8.
27. Ibid., ii/188-9, *mathnavi*, no. 7.
28. The invasion of Rohilkhand by Shah Alam and his Maratha allies took place because Zabita Khan was not willing to pay the arrears of revenue dues, collected in the Khalsa *parganas* during Najib-ud-Daula's times. The Marathas having defeated the Afghans plundered all the important towns and cities in the Doab under the Rohila chiefs.
29. Raja Gulab Rai, the diwan seems to have been appointed by Zabita Khan the *hakim* of some *zila* in the latter's jagir after the death of Najib-ud-Daula. In 1771 some other person might have been entrusted with the post of diwan instead.
30. *Kulliyat*, ii/57-64.
31. Ibid., ii/119, 130, 131, *qasida*, nos. 10, 12, 13, etc.
32. Sayyid Muhammad Akbar Husaini, *Jawami-ul-Kilem*, Kanpur, 1356 H, pp. 13-14.
33. I.H. Siddiqui, 'Sufis and Sufism in the Territorial Unit of Kalpi, 15th and 16th Centuries', *Pakistan Journal of History and Culture*, vol. V, 1, Islamabad, Jan.-June 1984, p. 68.

Contributors

William C. Chittick, Professor, Department of Religious Studies, The State University of New York, Stony Brook, U.S.A.

Ziya Uddin Desai, Director of Epigraphical Survey of India (retd.), 14 Khurshid Park, Juhapur, Ahmedabad (Gujarat).

Peter Hardy, Professor (retd.), 13 Damesh Mead Close, York, YO1O 404, England.

Late S.A. Athar Abbas Rizvi, was Reader, Department of History, National University; Canberra Australia.

Afzal Husain, Reader, Centre of Advanced Study in History, The Aligarh Muslim University, Aligarh.

Iqtidar Husain Siddiqui, Professor (retd.), 61, Ahmad Nagar, Civil Lines, Aligarh.

Ishtiyaq Ahmad Zilli, Professor, Centre of Advanced Study in History, The Aligarh Muslim University, Aligarh.

Index